Wok and Stir Fry

Practical Cooking

Wok and Stir Fry

p

This is a Parragon Book
This edition published in 2002

Parragon
Queen Street House
4 Queen Street
Bath BA1 1HE, UK

ISBN: 0-75258-315-8 (Hardback)
ISBN: 0-75258-321-2 (Paperback)

Printed in China

NOTE

Cup measurements in this book are for American cups.
Tablespoons are assumed tobe 15ml. Unless otherwise stated,
milk is assumed to be full fat, eggs are medium
and pepper is freshly ground black pepper.

Recipes using uncooked eggs should be
avoided by infants, the elderly, pregnant women and anyone
suffering from an illness.

Contents

Introduction   8   Regional Cooking 10–13
Cooking Techniques 14–15   How to Use This Book 17

Soups & Starters

Hot & Sour Mushroom Soup 20
Crab & Sweetcorn Soup 21
Spicy Prawn Soup .22
Coconut & Crab Soup 23
Chilli Fish Soup 24
Fish Soup with Wontons 25
Fish & Vegetable Soup 26
Prawn Soup 27
Spicy Chicken Noodle Soup 28
Chicken Noodle Soup 29
Spicy Sweetcorn Fritters 30
Vegetable Spring Rolls 31
Seven-Spice Aubergines 32
Fried Tofu with Peanut Sauce 33
Chicken Balls with Sauce 34
Crispy Pork & Peanut Baskets 35
Crispy Seaweed 36

Thai-Stuffed Omelette 37
Thai-Style Fish Cakes 38
Chilli & Peanut Prawns 39
Prawn Parcels 40
Chinese Prawn Salad 41
Prawn Omelette 42
Salt & Pepper Prawns 43
Sesame Prawn Toasts 44
Sweet & Sour Prawns 45
Rice Paper Parcels 46
Crispy Crab Wontons 47
Crab Ravioli 48
Spicy Chicken Livers 49
Honeyed Chicken Wings 50
Steamed Duck Buns 51
Spring Rolls 52
Pancake Rolls 53

Poultry & Meat

Stir-Fried Ginger Chicken 56
Coconut Chicken Curry 57
Cashew Chicken 58
Lemon Chicken 59
Sweet Mango Chicken 60
Chicken with Cashew Nuts 61
Chicken Chop Suey 62
Chicken with Chilli & Basil 63
Crispy Chicken 64
Spicy Peanut Chicken 65
Chinese Chicken Salad 66
Speedy Peanut Pan-Fry 67
Chicken & Corn Sauté 68
Spicy Chicken Tortillas 69
Chicken & Mango Stir-Fry 70
Thai Stir-Fried Chicken 71
Chicken with Black Bean Sauce 72
Chilli Coconut Chicken 73
Turkey with Cranberry Glaze 74
Duck in Spicy Sauce 75
Duck with Mangoes 76
Duck with Broccoli & Peppers 77
Duck with Leek & Cabbage 78
Fruity Duck Stir-Fry 79
Pork Satay Stir-Fry 80

Spicy Pork & Rice 81
Spicy Pork Balls 82
Sweet & Sour Pork 83
Twice-Cooked Pork 84
Pork with Mooli 85
Pork Fry with Vegetables 86
Sweet & Sour Pork 87
Pork with Plums 88
Deep-Fried Pork Fritters 89
Spicy Fried Minced Pork 90
Stir-Fried Pork & Corn 91
Lamb with Satay Sauce 92
Lamb with Black Bean Sauce 93
Oyster Sauce Lamb 94
Garlic Lamb with Soy Sauce 95
Lamb with Lime Leaves 96
Stir-Fried Lamb with Orange 97
Lamb's Liver with Peppers 98
Lamb Meatballs 99
Lamb with Mushroom Sauce 100
Red Lamb Curry .101
Lamb with Garlic Sauce 102
Hot Lamb 103
Sesame Lamb Stir-Fry 104
Beef with Lemon Grass 105

Savoury Meals (continued)

Stir-Fried Beef & Vegetables 106
Chilli Beef Stir-Fry Salad 107
Beef with Bamboo Shoots 108
Caramelised Beef 109
Beef & Black Bean Sauce 110
Soy & Sesame Beef 111

Beef & Broccoli Stir-Fry 112
Oyster Sauce Beef 113
Spicy Beef 114
Beef & Beans 115
Beef & Peanut Salad 116
Beef with Beansprouts 117

Fish & Seafood

Stir-Fried Cod with Mango 120
Braised Fish Fillets 121
Fish with Coconut & Basil 122
Szechuan White Fish 123
Crispy Fish 124
Gingered Monkfish 125
Trout with Pineapple 126
Stir-Fried Salmon with Leeks 127
Salmon with Pineapple 128
Five-Spice Salmon 129
Spicy Thai Seafood Stew 130
Tuna & Vegetable Stir-Fry 131
Coconut Prawns 132
Szechuan Prawns 133
Prawn Omelette 134
Prawns with Tomatoes 135
Prawns with Ginger 136

Prawns with Vegetables 137
Fried Prawns with Cashews 138
Shrimp Fu Yong 139
Cantonese Prawns 140
Scallop Pancakes 141
Seared Scallops 142
Scallops in Ginger Sauce 143
Mussels with Lettuce 144
Mussels in Black Bean Sauce 145
Oysters with Tofu 146
Crab Claws with Chilli 147
Crab with Chinese Leaves 148
Crab in Ginger Sauce 149
Crispy Fried Squid 150
Squid with Black Bean Sauce 151
Squid with Oyster Sauce 152
Seafood Stir-Fry 153

Vegetables

Honey-Fried Chinese Leaves 156
Green Stir-Fry 157
Crisp Cabbage & Almonds 158
Creamy Green Vegetables 159
Stir-Fried Chilli Cucumber 160
Garlic Spinach 161
Green Bean Stir-Fry 162
Gingered Broccoli 163
Green Lentil Pan-Fry 164
Bamboo with Peppers 165
Bamboo with Spinach 166
Oriental Vegetables 167

Vegetable Dim Sum 168
Chinese Fried Vegetables 169
Spicy Mushrooms 170
Fried Tofu & Vegetables 171

Vegetarian & Vegan

Spiced Aubergine 174
Spicy Aubergines 175
Carrot & Orange Stir-Fry 176
Deep-Fried Chilli Corn Balls 177
Butternut Squash Stir-Fry 178
Leeks with Yellow Bean Sauce 179
Pak Choi with Cashew Nuts 180
Green & Black Bean Stir-Fry 181
Deep-fried Courgettes 182
Asparagus Parcels 183
Honey-Fried Spinach 184
Sweet & Sour Cauliflower 185
Broccoli & Black Bean Sauce 186
Cabbage & Walnut Stir-Fry 187
Stir-Fried Japanese Noodles 188
Tofu with Peppers 189

Quorn & Vegetable Stir-Fry 190
Tofu Casserole 191
Sweet & Sour Tofu 192
Tofu with Mushrooms & Peas 193
Sherry & Soy Vegetables 194
Chinese Vegetable Rice 195
Vegetables with Hoisin 196
Vegetable Stir-Fry 197
Peppers with Chestnuts 198
Vegetable Stir-Fry with Eggs 199
Vegetable Chop Suey 200
Vegetable Sesame Stir-Fry 201
Eight Jewel Vegetables 202
Spicy Fried Tofu Triangles 203
Chinese Vegetable Casserole 204
Cantonese Garden Vegetables 205

Rice & Noodles

Fried Rice with Spicy Beans 208
Fragrant Coconut Rice 209
Egg Fried Rice 210
Stir-Fried Rice with Egg 211
Vegetable Fried Rice 212
Green Fried Rice 213
Special Fried Rice 214
Crab Congee 215
Crab Fried Rice 216
Rice with Seafood 217
Rice with Five-Spice Chicken 218
Chinese Chicken Rice 219
Chicken & Rice Casserole 220
Chicken Chow Mein 221
Sweet Chilli Pork Fried Rice 222
Fried Rice with Pork 223
Rice with Seven-Spice Beef 224
Stir-Fried Rice with Sausage 225
Chinese Risotto 226
Crispy Rice Noodles 227
Spicy Japanese Noodles 228
Rice Noodles with Beans 229
Hot & Sour Noodles 230

Fried Vegetable Noodles 231
Noodle & Mango Salad 232
Yellow Bean Noodles 233
Noodles with Cod & Mango 234
Sweet & Sour Noodles 235
Chilli Prawn Noodles 236
Special Noodles 237
Curried Prawn Noodles 238
Noodles with Prawns 239
Cellophane Noodles & Prawns 240
Sesame Noodles with Prawns 241
Oyster Sauce Noodles 242
Chicken Noodles 243
Singapore Noodles 244
Chicken on Crispy Noodles 245
Chilli Pork Noodles 246
Pad Thai Noodles 247
Mushroom & Pork Noodles 248
Twice-Cooked Lamb 249
Lamb with Noodles 250
Beef with Crispy Noodles 251
Beef Chow Mein 252
Cantonese Fried Noodles 253

Introduction

One of the quickest, easiest and most versatile methods of cooking is to stir-fry in a wok. It takes only a few minutes to assemble the ingredients – a selection of vegetables, to which may be added meat, fish, seafood, tofu, nuts, rice or noodles. The possibilities are endless for ringing the changes with different oils, seasonings and sauces, and the result is a colourful, delicious, healthy meal that is as pleasing to the eye as it is to the tastebuds.

A wok is a metal cooking implement in the shape of a shallow, curved bowl, with either one long wooden handle or two looped handles. The wok comes in a variety of sizes – one approximately 30–35cm/12–14 inches in diameter is suitable for the average family – and, as with most kitchen equipment, it is worth investing in the best you can. Woks are made from stainless steel, copper or cast iron, and the latter is ideal as it retains heat more efficiently, especially once it has become well-seasoned.

Although it is possible to stir-fry in a frying pan, there are several good reasons to use a wok. The key to successful stir-frying is to move and toss the ingredients constantly as they cook, and this is much easier to achieve in the convex shape of a wok. The curved sides allow the heat to rise, so that the whole wok becomes hot, speeding up the cooking process; and as the food cannot become lodged in corners or edges, it is extremely easy to clean the wok after use.

A useful addition in the Western kitchen is a metal collar, shaped like a crown, with angled sides and a hollow in which to sit the wok. The collar aids heat convection from the hob or oven ring, and the wok heats up more evenly than if it were placed directly on the heat source.

A spatula with a long wooden handle is ideal for stir-frying and removing foods, as the curved edge follows the curve of the wok.

By adding a frying strainer or shallow wire-meshed basket, the wok may be used for deep-frying, while a steaming trivet and a domed, tight-fitting lid will convert the wok to a very efficient steamer. These extra items are often supplied with the wok when it is first purchased.

Before using the wok, it is essential to season it properly. Use oiled kitchen paper to wipe the wok both inside and out, then heat it to a high temperature in the oven or on the hob. Remove the wok from the heat, allow it to cool, then repeat the process several times to create a good, non-stick coating. After the initial seasoning, the wok can simply be wiped clean, or washed in soapy water – but if the wok is made of cast iron, it is essential to dry it thoroughly immediately after washing, to prevent rusting.

Regional cookery

Although its popularity is now far more wide-ranging, wok cookery originated in Asia and the Far East, where variations of this useful implement are commonly used in the preparation of many dishes. In India, the curry derives its name from *karahi*, a large pan that sits over a hole in a brick or earth oven and is used for braising and frying, while in Mongolia the convex

iron griddle used for barbecueing meat, especially lamb, is very similar in shape to a wok.

It was the Chinese, however, who devised stir-frying in a wok. There are regional variations in ingredients throughout this vast country, but fresh vegetables play a very important role in all Chinese cookery. This rapid and efficient method of cooking the vegetables ensures that

they retain their individual flavours, their vibrant colours and their crisp texture, as well as preserving their vitamin content. Poultry, lamb, beef and pork are also cooked in the wok – either stir-fried or steamed – and are combined with sauces and seasonings. Long- or short-grain rice is often added or served as an accompaniment, and noodles made from wheat, buckwheat or rice flours are also widely used.

Chinese influence has spread to its neighbouring countries.

Throughout Indonesia, Japan, Thailand, Singapore and Malaysia the wok is used over wood or charcoal for curries and rice dishes as well as stir-fries, with variations in the addition of different meat, fish, spices and sauces.

Regional cookery

A style of cuisine that has enjoyed a huge rise in popularity in recent years is Thai. For the people of Thailand, the preparation and eating of good food, beautifully served, is taken very seriously. The ingredients, locally grown and very fresh, are carefully chosen and skilfully balanced for texture and flavour, combining bitter, salt, sour, hot and sweet tastes.

The monsoon climate and abundant rainfall in Thailand produce ideal conditions for growing rice, so it's not surprising that Thai cuisine is centred around this, the country's most important staple. Thai fragrant rice is a long-grain, fluffy white rice, delicately scented, while glutinous rice is short-grain with a high starch content, which makes it sticky when cooked. Rice flour is also used to make noodles, usually in the shape of flat ribbons or thin vermicelli.

The warm Gulf seas around Thailand, and the inland waterways, produce a wide variety of fish in abundance, and in all the coastal towns fresh seafood is sold from thatch-roofed beach kiosks –

barbecued or sautéed fish with ginger, prawns with coconut milk and coriander, or steamed crab. Meat is often combined with seafood such as prawns or crab meat.

Other essentials in Thai cookery are coconut (almost as important as rice), lime, chilli, garlic, lemon grass, ginger root and coriander, as well as seasonings such as soy sauce, rice vinegar and Thai fish sauce. All of these ingredients are now readily available in your local supermarket.

Cooking techniques

Although the wok can be used for steaming and deep-frying, its main use is for stir-frying. In China, where this is the most widely used method of cooking, it is called Ch'au, a term that describes cooking a number of ingredients, thinly sliced, in oil. As it cooks, the food is tossed and turned with long bamboo chopsticks.

There are two basic types of stir-frying, known as Pao and Liu. Pao, or 'explosion', is a method where the food is stirred rapidly in a dry wok over the highest heat for about one minute. Foods cooked in this way are often marinated beforehand for flavor and tenderness. Liu is wet frying, where the foods are constantly turned until cooked. Peanut or corn oil are usually used for stir-frying. Sesame oil burns easily, but can be drizzled over the finished dish as a seasoning.

Some foods need a slightly longer cooking time than others and, for this reason, stir-frying is often done in stages. This also allows the individual ingredients to retain their distinct flavours. As they cook, the foods are removed from the wok, but they are always combined once everything is cooked, and served as a whole dish. In Liu, a mixture of cornflour and stock is added to the wok at the end of cooking, together with sugar, vinegar and soy sauce, to make a delicious, almost sticky coating sauce.

There is plenty of scope for creativity when choosing ingredients, even for the simplest stir-fry. A combination of onions, carrots, peppers (green, red, yellow and orange), broccoli and mangetout peas will provide the basis for a colourful dish. Add beansprouts at the end of cooking and toss quickly for texture, or some canned water chestnuts, which add a delicious crunch. A few cashew nuts or almonds, some cubed tofu or chicken breast, or a handful of prawns provide protein, while adding some pre-cooked rice or noodles makes a gutsy stir-fry. A ready-made sauce – perhaps oyster, or yellow bean – will finish off the dish.

Ginger, garlic and chillies are wonderful for flavouring stir-fries. Chillies come in a wide variety, ranging in heat from very mild to fiery hot. Red chillies are slightly sweeter and milder than green, and larger chillies also tend to be milder. Crushed dried chillies are useful for seasoning. The Thais favour the small red or green 'bird-eye' chillies, which are very fiery, and their curries are flavoured with ferociously hot chilli pastes.

Some of the 'kick' can be taken out of a hot chilli by removing the seeds, but this must be done very carefully as they can cause a nasty reaction. Cut fresh chillies in half, and scrape out the seeds with the point of a knife, and with dried chillies, simply cut off the end and shake out the seeds. Always remember to wash your hands!

How to Use This Book

Each recipe contains a wealth of useful information, including a breakdown of nutritional quantities, preparation and cooking times, and level of difficulty. All of this information is explained in detail below.

The nutritional information provided for each recipe is per serving or per portion. Optional ingredients, variations or serving suggestions have not been included in the calculations.

The number of chef's hats represents the difficulty of each recipe, ranging from easy (1 chef's hat) to difficult (5 chef's hats).

This amount of time represents the preparation of ingredients, including cooling, chilling and soaking times.

This represents the cooking time.

The ingredients for each recipe are listed in the order that they are used.

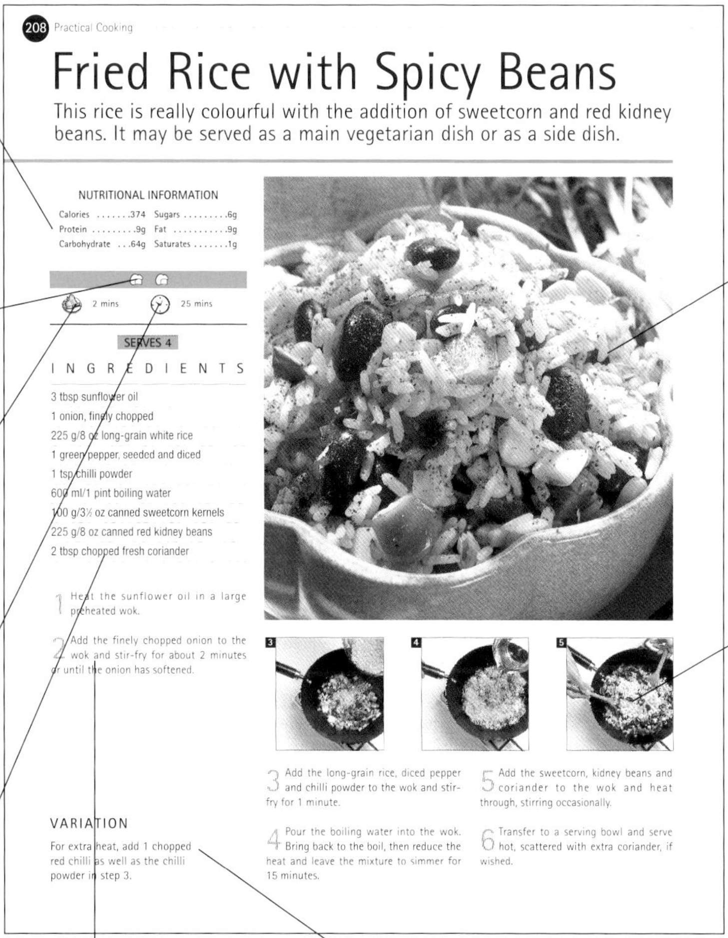

208 Practical Cooking

Fried Rice with Spicy Beans

This rice is really colourful with the addition of sweetcorn and red kidney beans. It may be served as a main vegetarian dish or as a side dish.

NUTRITIONAL INFORMATION

Calories	374	Sugars	6g
Protein	9g	Fat	9g
Carbohydrate	64g	Saturates	1g

2 mins 25 mins

SERVES 4

INGREDIENTS

3 tbsp sunflower oil
1 onion, finely chopped
225 g/8 oz long-grain white rice
1 green pepper, seeded and diced
1 tsp chilli powder
600 ml/1 pint boiling water
100 g/3½ oz canned sweetcorn kernels
225 g/8 oz canned red kidney beans
2 tbsp chopped fresh coriander

1 Heat the sunflower oil in a large preheated wok.

2 Add the finely chopped onion to the wok and stir-fry for about 2 minutes or until the onion has softened.

3 Add the long-grain rice, diced pepper and chilli powder to the wok and stir-fry for 1 minute.

4 Pour the boiling water into the wok. Bring back to the boil, then reduce the heat and leave the mixture to simmer for 15 minutes.

5 Add the sweetcorn, kidney beans and coriander to the wok and heat through, stirring occasionally.

6 Transfer to a serving bowl and serve hot, scattered with extra coriander, if wished.

VARIATION

For extra heat, add 1 chopped red chilli as well as the chilli powder in step 3.

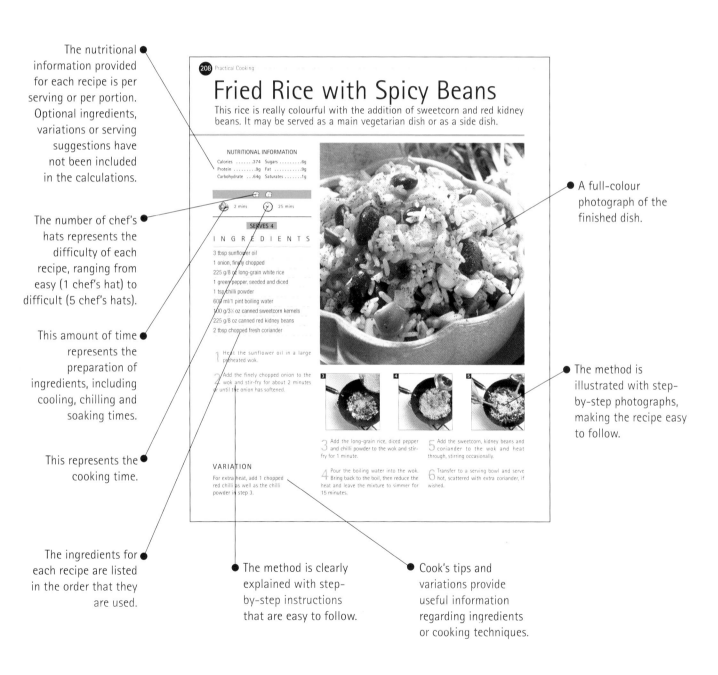

A full-colour photograph of the finished dish.

The method is illustrated with step-by-step photographs, making the recipe easy to follow.

The method is clearly explained with step-by-step instructions that are easy to follow.

Cook's tips and variations provide useful information regarding ingredients or cooking techniques.

Soups & Starters

Soup is indispensable at Asian tables, especially in China, Japan, Korea and South East Asia. It is generally eaten part way through a main meal to clear the palate for further dishes. There are many different types of delicious soups,

both thick and thin and, of course, the clear soups which are often served with wontons or dumplings in them.

Starters or snacks are drier foods in general; the spring roll is a well-known Chinese snack and these come in many variations and shapes across the Far East. Other delights are wrapped in pastry, bread and rice paper or are skewered for ease of eating; vegetables, fish and meat are also deep-fried for a crispy coating.

These dishes are served as starters in Westernized restaurants to animate the tastebuds for the main course.

Hot & Sour Mushroom Soup

Hot and sour soups are found across South East Asia in different forms. Reduce the number of chillies added if you prefer a milder dish.

NUTRITIONAL INFORMATION

Calories . . . . .87 Sugars 7g
Protein . . . . .4g Fat 5g
Carbohydrate . . . .8g Saturates 1g

10 mins   20 mins

SERVES 4

I N G R E D I E N T S

2 tbsp tamarind paste

4 red chillies, very finely chopped

2 cloves garlic, crushed

2 tsp finely chopped fresh root ginger

4 tbsp fish sauce

2 tbsp palm sugar or caster sugar

8 lime leaves, roughly torn

1.2 litres/2 pints vegetable stock

100 g/3½ oz carrots, thinly sliced

225 g/8 oz button mushrooms, halved

350 g/12 oz shredded white cabbage

100 g/3½ oz fine green beans, halved

3 tbsp roughly chopped fresh coriander

100 g/3½ oz cherry tomatoes, halved

COOK'S TIP

Tamarind is the dried fruit of the tamarind tree. Sold as a pulp or paste, it is used to give a special sweet and sour flavour to Oriental dishes.

1 Place the tamarind paste, red chillies, garlic, ginger, fish sauce, palm or caster sugar, lime leaves and vegetable stock in a large preheated wok or heavy-based frying pan. Bring the mixture to the boil, stirring occasionally.

2 Reduce the heat and add the carrots, mushrooms, white cabbage and green beans. Leave the soup to simmer, uncovered, for about 10 minutes, or until the vegetables are tender, but not soft.

3 Stir the fresh coriander and cherry tomatoes into the mixture in the wok and heat through for another 5 minutes.

4 Transfer the soup to a warm tureen or individual serving bowls and serve immediately.

Crab & Sweetcorn Soup

Crab and sweetcorn are classic ingredients in Chinese cookery. Here egg noodles are added for a filling dish.

NUTRITIONAL INFORMATION

Calories 324	Sugars 6g
Protein 27g	Fat 8g
Carbohydrate ...39g	Saturates 2g

 5 mins   🕐 20 mins

SERVES 4

INGREDIENTS

1 tbsp sunflower oil

1 tsp Chinese five-spice powder

225 g/8 oz carrots, cut into sticks

150 g/5½ oz canned or frozen sweetcorn

75 g/2¾ oz cup peas

6 spring onions, trimmed and sliced

1 red chilli, seeded and very thinly sliced

400g/14oz canned white crab meat

175 g/6 oz egg noodles

1.7 litres/3 pints fish stock

3 tbsp soy sauce

1 Heat the sunflower oil in a large preheated wok or heavy-based frying pan.

2 Add the Chinese five-spice powder, carrots, sweetcorn, peas, spring onions and red chilli to the wok and cook for about 5 minutes, stirring constantly.

3 Add the crab meat to the wok and stir-fry the mixture for 1 minute, distributing the crab meat evenly.

4 Roughly break up the egg noodles and add to the wok.

5 Pour the fish stock and soy sauce into the mixture in the wok and bring to the boil.

6 Cover the wok or frying pan and leave the soup to simmer for 5 minutes.

7 Stir once more, then transfer the soup to a warm soup tureen or individual serving bowls and serve at once.

COOK'S TIP

Chinese five-spice powder is a mixture of star anise, fennel, cloves, cinnamon and Szechuan pepper. It has an unmistakeable flavour. Use it sparingly, as it is very pungent.

Spicy Prawn Soup

Lime leaves are used as a flavouring in this soup to add tartness.

NUTRITIONAL INFORMATION

Calories . . . . .217 Sugars 16g
Protein . . . . .16g Fat 4g
Carbohydrate . . .31g Saturates 1g

 10 mins   20 mins

SERVES 4

I N G R E D I E N T S

2 tbsp tamarind paste

4 red chillies, very finely chopped

2 cloves garlic, crushed

2 tsp finely chopped fresh root ginger

4 tbsp fish sauce

2 tbsp palm sugar or caster sugar

1.25 litres/2 pints fish stock

8 lime leaves

100 g/3½ oz carrots, thinly sliced

350 g/12 oz sweet potato, diced

100 g/3½ oz baby corn cobs, halved

3 tbsp roughly chopped fresh coriander

100g/3½ oz cherry tomatoes, halved

225 g/8 oz fan-tail prawns

1 Place the tamarind paste, red chillies, garlic, ginger, fish sauce, sugar and fish stock in a preheated wok or large, heavy frying pan. Roughly tear the lime leaves and add to the wok. Bring to the boil, stirring constantly to blend the flavours.

2 Reduce the heat and add the carrot, sweet potato and baby corn cobs to the mixture in the wok.

3 Leave the soup to simmer, uncovered, for about 10 minutes, or until the vegetables are just tender.

4 Stir the coriander, cherry tomatoes and prawns into the soup and heat through for 5 minutes.

5 Transfer the soup to a warm soup tureen or individual serving bowls and serve hot.

COOK'S TIP

Thai ginger or galangal is a member of the ginger family, but it is yellow in colour with pink sprouts. The flavour is aromatic and less pungent than ginger.

Coconut & Crab Soup

Thai red curry paste is quite fiery, but adds a superb flavour to this dish. It is available in jars or packets from supermarkets.

NUTRITIONAL INFORMATION

Calories	122	Sugar	.........9g
Protein	........11g	Fats	...........4g
Carbohydrates	...11g	Saturates	......1g

5 mins   10 mins

SERVES 4

INGREDIENTS

1 tbsp groundnut oil

2 tbsp Thai red curry paste

1 red pepper, seeded and sliced

600 ml/1 pint coconut milk

600 ml/1 pint fish stock

2 tbsp fish sauce

225 g/8 oz canned or fresh white crab meat

225 g/8 oz fresh or frozen crab claws

2 tbsp chopped fresh coriander

3 spring onions, trimmed and sliced

1 Heat the oil in a large preheated wok.

2 Add the red curry paste and red pepper to the wok and stir-fry for 1 minute.

3 Add the coconut milk, fish stock and fish sauce and bring to the boil.

4 Add the crab meat, crab claws, coriander and spring onions to the wok.

5 Stir the mixture well and heat thoroughly for 2–3 minutes or until everything is warmed through.

6 Transfer the soup to warm bowls and serve hot.

COOK'S TIP

Clean the wok after use by washing it with water, using a mild detergent if necessary, and a soft cloth or brush. Do not scrub or use any abrasive cleaner as this will scratch the surface. Dry thoroughly then wipe the surface all over with a little oil to protect the surface.

Chilli Fish Soup

Chinese mushrooms add an intense flavour to this soup which is unique. If they are unavailable, use open-cap mushrooms, sliced.

NUTRITIONAL INFORMATION

Calories ....166 Sugars 1g
Protein ....23g Fat 7g
Carbohydrate ....4g Saturates 1g

15 mins   15 mins

SERVES 4

INGREDIENTS

15 g/½ oz Chinese dried mushrooms

2 tbsp sunflower oil

1 onion, sliced

100 g/3½ oz mangetout

100 g/3½ oz bamboo shoots

3 tbsp sweet chilli sauce

1.2 litres/2 pints fish or vegetable stock

3 tbsp light soy sauce

2 tbsp fresh coriander, plus extra to garnish

450 g/1 lb cod fillet, skinned and cubed

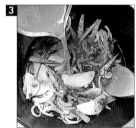
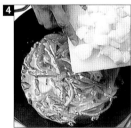

COOK'S TIP

Cod is used in this recipe as it is a meaty white fish. For real luxury, use monkfish tail instead.

There are many different varieties of dried mushrooms, but shiitake are best. They are not cheap, but a small amount will go a long way.

1 Place the mushrooms in a large bowl. Pour over enough boiling water to cover and leave to stand for 5 minutes. Drain the mushrooms thoroughly in a colander. Using a sharp knife, roughly chop the mushrooms.

2 Heat the sunflower oil in a preheated wok or large frying pan. Add the sliced onion to the wok and stir-fry for 5 minutes, or until softened.

3 Add the mangetout, bamboo shoots, chilli sauce, stock and soy sauce to the wok and bring to the boil.

4 Add the coriander and cod and leave to simmer for 5 minutes or until the fish is cooked through.

5 Transfer the soup to warm bowls, garnish with extra coriander, if wished, and serve hot.

Fish Soup with Wontons

This soup is topped with small wontons filled with prawns, making it both very tasty and satisfying.

NUTRITIONAL INFORMATION

Calories 115   Sugars 0g
Protein . . . . .16g   Fat 5g
Carbohydrate . . . .1g   Saturates 1g

 10 mins   15 mins

SERVES 4

I N G R E D I E N T S

125 g/4½ oz large, cooked, peeled prawns

1 tsp chopped chives

1 small garlic clove, finely chopped

1 tbsp vegetable oil

12 wonton wrappers

1 small egg, beaten

900 ml/1½ pints fish stock

175 g/6 oz white fish fillet, diced

dash of chilli sauce

TO GARNISH

sliced fresh red chilli and snipped chives

1 Roughly chop a quarter of the prawns and mix together with the chopped chives and garlic.

2 Heat the oil in a preheated wok or large frying pan until it is really hot.

3 Stir-fry the prawn mixture for 1–2 minutes. Remove from the heat and set aside to cool completely.

4 Spread out the wonton wrappers on a work surface. Spoon a little of the prawn filling into the centre of each wrapper. Brush the edges of the wrappers with beaten egg and press the edges together, scrunching them to form a 'moneybag' shape. Set aside while you are preparing the soup.

5 Pour the fish stock into a large saucepan and bring to the boil. Add the diced white fish and the remaining prawns and cook for 5 minutes.

6 Season to taste with the chilli sauce. Add the wontons and cook for a further 5 minutes.

7 Spoon into warmed serving bowls, garnish with sliced red chilli and chives and serve immediately.

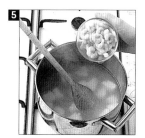

VARIATION

Replace the prawns with cooked crabmeat for an alternative flavour.

Fish & Vegetable Soup

A chunky fish soup with strips of vegetables, all flavoured with ginger and lemon, makes a meal in itself.

NUTRITIONAL INFORMATION

Calories ....88 Sugars 1g
Protein ....12g Fat 3g
Carbohydrate ....3g Saturates 0.5g

 40 mins   20 mins

SERVES 4

INGREDIENTS

250 g/9 oz white fish fillets (cod, halibut, haddock, sole)

½ tsp ground ginger

½ tsp salt

1 small leek, trimmed

2–4 crab sticks, defrosted if frozen (optional)

1 tbsp sunflower oil

1 large carrot, cut into julienne strips

8 canned water chestnuts, thinly sliced

1.25 litres/2 pints fish or vegetable stock

1 tbsp lemon juice

1 tbsp light soy sauce

1 large courgette, cut into matchsticks

black pepper

1 Remove any skin from the fish and cut into cubes of about 2.5 cm/1 inch. Combine the ground ginger and salt and use to rub into the pieces of fish. Leave to marinate for at least 30 minutes.

2 Meanwhile, divide the green and white parts of the leek. Cut each part into 2.5-cm/1-inch lengths and then into matchsticks down the length of each piece, keeping the two parts separate. Slice the crab sticks into 1-cm/½-inch pieces.

3 Heat the oil in the wok, swirling it around so it is really hot. Add the white part of the leek and stir-fry for a couple of minutes, then add the carrots and water chestnuts and continue to cook for 1–2 minutes, stirring thoroughly.

4 Add the stock and bring to the boil, then add the lemon juice and soy sauce and simmer for 2 minutes.

5 Add the fish and continue to cook for about 5 minutes until the fish begins to break up a little, then add the green part of the leek and the courgettes and simmer for about 1 minute. Add the sliced crab sticks, if using, and season to taste with black pepper. Simmer for a further minute or so and serve piping hot.

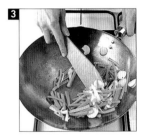

COOK'S TIP

To skin fish, place the fillet skin-side down and insert a sharp, flexible knife at one end between the flesh and the skin. Hold the skin tightly at the end and push the knife along, keeping the blade flat against the skin.

Prawn Soup

This soup is an interesting mix of colours and textures. The egg may be made into a flat omelette and added as thin strips if preferred.

NUTRITIONAL INFORMATION

Calories 123   Sugars 0.2g
Protein . . . . .13g   Fat 8g
Carbohydrate . . . .1g   Saturates 1g

5 mins   20 mins

SERVES 4

I N G R E D I E N T S

2 tbsp sunflower oil

2 spring onions, thinly sliced diagonally

1 carrot, roughly grated

125 g/4½ oz large closed cup mushrooms, thinly sliced

1 litre/1¾ pints fish or vegetable stock

½ tsp Chinese five-spice powder

1 tbsp light soy sauce

125 g/4½ oz large peeled prawns or peeled tiger prawns, defrosted if frozen

½ bunch watercress, trimmed and roughly chopped

1 egg, well beaten

salt and pepper

4 large prawns in shells, to garnish (optional)

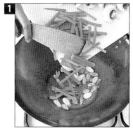

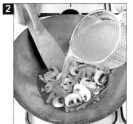

1   Heat the oil in a wok, swirling it around until really hot. Add the spring onions and stir-fry for a minute then add the carrots and mushrooms and continue to cook for about 2 minutes.

2   Add the stock and bring to the boil then season to taste with salt and pepper, Chinese five-spice powder and soy sauce and simmer for 5 minutes.

3   If the prawns are really large, cut them in half before adding to the wok and simmer for 3–4 minutes.

4   Add the watercress to the wok and mix well, then slowly pour in the beaten egg in a circular movement so that it cooks in threads in the soup. Adjust the seasoning and serve each portion topped with a whole prawn.

COOK'S TIP

The large open mushrooms with black gills give the best flavour but they tend to spoil the colour of the soup, making it very dark. Oyster mushrooms can also be used.

Spicy Chicken Noodle Soup

This filling soup is filled with spicy flavours and bright colours for a really attractive and hearty dish.

NUTRITIONAL INFORMATION

Calories	286	Sugars	........21g
Protein	........22g	Fat	...........6g
Carbohydrate	...37g	Saturates	.......1g

 15 mins 20 mins

SERVES 4

I N G R E D I E N T S

2 tbsp tamarind paste

4 red chillies, finely chopped

2 cloves garlic, crushed

2 tsp finely chopped fresh root ginger

4 tbsp fish sauce

2 tbsp palm sugar or caster sugar

8 lime leaves, roughly torn

1.2 litres/2 pints chicken stock

350 g/12 oz boneless chicken breast

100 g/3½ oz carrots, thinly sliced

350 g/12 oz sweet potato, diced

100 g/3½ oz baby corn cobs, halved

3 tbsp roughly chopped fresh coriander

100 g/3½ oz cherry tomatoes, halved

150 g/5½ oz flat rice noodles

chopped fresh coriander to garnish

1 Preheat a large wok or frying pan. Place the tamarind paste, chillies, garlic, ginger, fish sauce, sugar, lime leaves and chicken stock in the wok and bring to the boil, stirring constantly. Reduce the heat and cook for about 5 minutes.

2 Using a sharp knife, thinly slice the chicken. Add the chicken to the wok and cook for a further 5 minutes, stirring the mixture well.

3 Reduce the heat and add the carrots, sweet potato and baby corn cobs to the wok. Leave to simmer, uncovered, for 5 minutes, or until the vegetables are just tender and the chicken is completely cooked through.

4 Stir in the chopped fresh coriander, cherry tomatoes and flat rice noodles.

5 Leave the soup to simmer for about 5 minutes, or until the noodles are tender.

6 Garnish the spicy chicken noodle soup with chopped fresh coriander and serve hot.

Chicken Noodle Soup

Quick to make, this hot and spicy soup is hearty and warming. If you like your food really fiery, add a chopped dried or fresh chilli with its seeds.

NUTRITIONAL INFORMATION

Calories 196	Sugars 4g	
Protein 16g	Fat 11g	
Carbohydrate 8g	Saturates 2g	

10 mins   25 mins

SERVES 4–6

I N G R E D I E N T S

1 sheet of dried egg noodles
from a 250 g/9 oz packet

1 tbsp oil

4 skinless, boneless
chicken thighs, diced

1 bunch spring onions, sliced

2 garlic cloves, chopped

2 tsp finely chopped fresh root ginger

900 ml/1½ pints chicken stock

200 ml/7 fl oz coconut milk

3 tsp red curry paste

3 tbsp peanut butter

2 tbsp light soy sauce

1 small red pepper, chopped

60 g/2 oz frozen peas

salt and pepper

1 Put the noodles in a shallow dish and soak in boiling water as the packet directs.

2 Heat the oil in a large preheated saucepan or wok.

3 Add the diced chicken to the pan or wok and fry for 5 minutes, stirring until lightly browned.

4 Add the white part of the spring onions, the garlic and ginger and fry for 2 minutes, stirring.

5 Stir in the chicken stock, coconut milk, red curry paste, peanut butter and soy sauce.

6 Season with salt and pepper to taste. Bring to the boil, stirring, then simmer for 8 minutes, stirring occasionally.

7 Add the red pepper, peas and green spring onion tops and cook for 2 minutes.

8 Add the drained noodles and heat through. Spoon the chicken noodle soup into warmed bowls and serve with a spoon and fork.

VARIATION

Green curry paste can be used instead of red curry paste for a less fiery flavour.

Spicy Sweetcorn Fritters

Polenta can be found in most supermarkets or health food shops. Yellow in colour, it acts as a binding agent in this recipe.

NUTRITIONAL INFORMATION

Calories 213   Sugars 6g
Protein . . . . .5g   Fat 8g
Carbohydrate . . .30g   Saturates 1g

5 mins

15 mins

SERVES 4

I N G R E D I E N T S

225 g/8 oz canned or frozen sweetcorn kernels

2 red chillies, seeded and finely chopped

2 cloves garlic, crushed

10 lime leaves, finely chopped

2 tbsp chopped fresh coriander

1 large egg

75 g/2¾ oz polenta

100 g/3½ oz fine green beans, finely sliced

groundnut oil, for frying

1 Place the sweetcorn, chillies, garlic, lime leaves, coriander, egg and polenta in a large mixing bowl, and stir to combine.

2 Add the green beans to the ingredients in the bowl and mix well, using a wooden spoon.

3 Divide the mixture into small, evenly sized balls. Flatten the balls of mixture between the palms of your hands to form rounds.

4 Heat a little groundnut oil in a preheated wok or large frying pan until really hot. Cook the fritters, in batches, until brown and crispy on the outside, turning occasionally.

5 Leave the fritters to drain on absorbent kitchen paper while frying the remaining fritters.

6 Transfer the drained fritters to warm serving plates and serve immediately.

COOK'S TIP

Kaffir lime leaves are dark green, glossy leaves that have a lemony-lime flavour. They can be bought from specialist Asian stores either fresh or dried. Fresh leaves impart the most delicious flavour.

Vegetable Spring Rolls

There are many different versions of spring rolls throughout the Far East, a vegetable filling being the classic.

NUTRITIONAL INFORMATION

Calories 189   Sugars 4g
Protein ....2g   Fat 16g
Carbohydrate ....11g   Saturates 5g

10 mins   15 mins

SERVES 4

INGREDIENTS

225 g/8 oz carrots

1 red pepper

1 tbsp sunflower oil, plus extra for frying

75 g/2¾ oz beansprouts

finely grated zest and juice of 1 lime

1 red chilli, seeded and finely chopped

1 tbsp soy sauce

½ tsp arrowroot

2 tbsp chopped fresh coriander

8 sheets filo pastry

25 g/1 oz butter

2 tsp sesame oil

TO SERVE

chilli sauce

spring onion tassels

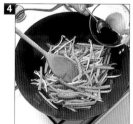

1 Using a sharp knife, cut the carrots into thin sticks. Seed the pepper and cut into thin slices.

2 Heat the sunflower oil in a large preheated wok.

3 Add the carrot, red pepper and beansprouts and cook, stirring, for 2 minutes, or until softened. Remove the wok from the heat and toss in the lime zest and juice, and the red chilli.

4 Mix the soy sauce with the arrowroot. Stir the mixture into the wok, return to the heat and cook for 2 minutes or until the juices thicken.

5 Add the chopped fresh coriander to the wok and mix well.

6 Lay the sheets of filo pastry out on a board. Melt the butter and sesame oil and brush each sheet with the mixture.

7 Spoon a little of the vegetable filling at the top of each sheet, fold over each long side, and roll up.

8 Add a little oil to the wok and cook the spring rolls in batches, for 2–3 minutes, or until crisp and golden.

9 Transfer the spring rolls to a serving dish, garnish and serve hot with chilli dipping sauce.

Seven-Spice Aubergines

This is a really simple dish which is perfect served with a chilli dip.

NUTRITIONAL INFORMATION

Calories 169   Sugars 2g
Protein . . . . .2g   Fat 12g
Carbohydrate . . .15g   Saturates 1g

 35 mins   20 mins

SERVES 4

I N G R E D I E N T S

450 g/1 lb aubergines, wiped

1 egg white

3½ tbsp cornflour

1 tsp salt

1 tbsp seven-spice seasoning

oil, for deep-frying

1 Using a sharp knife, thinly slice the aubergines. Place the aubergine in a colander, sprinkle with salt and leave to stand for 30 minutes. This will remove all the bitter juices.

2 Rinse the aubergine thoroughly and pat dry with absorbent kitchen paper.

3 Place the egg white in a small bowl and whip until light and foamy.

4 Using a spoon, mix together the cornflour, salt and seven-spice powder on a large plate.

5 Heat the oil for deep-frying in a large preheated wok or a frying pan with a heavy base.

6 Dip the aubergines into the egg white, and then into the cornflour and seven-spice mixture to coat evenly.

7 Deep-fry the coated aubergine slices, in batches, for 5 minutes, or until pale golden and crispy.

8 Transfer the aubergines to kitchen paper and leave to drain. Transfer the seven-spice aubergines to serving plates and serve hot.

COOK'S TIP

The best oil to use for deep-frying is groundnut oil which has a high smoke point and mild flavour, so it will neither burn or taint the food. About 600 ml/1 pint oil is sufficient.

Fried Tofu with Peanut Sauce

This is a very sociable dish if put in the centre of the table where people can help themselves with cocktail sticks.

NUTRITIONAL INFORMATION

Calories ....338 Sugars 9g
Protein ....16g Fat 22g
Carbohydrate ...21g Saturates 4g

5 mins   20 mins

SERVES 4

INGREDIENTS

500 g/1 lb 2 oz marinated or plain tofu

2 tbsp rice vinegar

2 tbsp sugar

1 tsp salt

3 tbsp smooth peanut butter

½ tsp chilli flakes

3 tbsp barbecue sauce

1 litre/1¾ pints sunflower oil

2 tbsp sesame oil

BATTER

4 tbsp plain flour

2 eggs, beaten

4 tbsp milk

½ tsp baking powder

½ tsp chilli powder

COOK'S TIP

Tofu is made from puréed soya beans. It is white, with a soft cheese-like texture, and is sold in blocks, either fresh or vacuum-packed. Although it has a bland flavour, it blends well with other ingredients, and absorbs the flavours of spices and sauces.

1 Cut the tofu into 2.5-cm/1-inch triangles. Set aside until required.

2 Combine the rice vinegar, sugar and salt in a saucepan. Bring to the boil and then simmer for 2 minutes.

3 Remove the sauce from the heat and add the smooth peanut butter, chilli flakes and barbecue sauce, stirring well until thoroughly blended.

4 To make the batter, sift the plain flour into a bowl, make a well in the centre and add the eggs. Draw in the flour, adding the milk slowly. Stir in the baking powder and chilli powder.

5 Heat both the sunflower oil and sesame oil in a deep-fryer or large saucepan until a light haze appears on top.

6 Dip the tofu triangles into the batter and deep-fry until golden brown. You may need to do this in batches. Drain on kitchen paper.

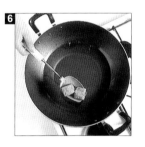

7 Transfer the tofu triangles to a serving dish and serve with the peanut sauce.

Chicken Balls with Sauce

Serve these bite-sized chicken starters warm as a snack, with drinks or packed cold for a picnic or lunchbox treat.

NUTRITIONAL INFORMATION

Calories 214   Sugars 29g
Protein . . . . .20g   Fat 13g
Carbohydrate . . . .5g   Saturates 2g

🕙 10 mins   ⏱ 25 mins

SERVES 4

I N G R E D I E N T S

2 large boneless, skinless chicken breasts

3 tbsp vegetable oil

2 shallots, finely chopped

½ celery stick, finely chopped

1 garlic clove, crushed

2 tbsp light soy sauce

1 small egg

1 bunch spring onions

salt and pepper

spring onion tassels, to garnish

D I P P I N G   S A U C E

3 tbsp dark soy sauce

1 tbsp rice wine

1 tsp sesame seeds

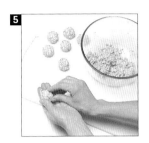

1 Cut the chicken into 2-cm/¾-inch pieces. Heat half of the oil in a frying pan or wok and stir-fry the chicken over a high heat for 2–3 minutes until golden. Remove from the pan with a perforated spoon; set aside.

2 Add the shallots, celery and garlic to the pan and stir-fry for 1–2 minutes until softened but not browned.

3 Place the chicken, shallots, celery and garlic in a food processor and process until finely minced. Add 1 tablespoon of the light soy sauce, just enough egg to make a fairly firm mixture, and salt and pepper.

4 Trim the spring onions and cut into 5-cm/2-inch lengths. Make the dipping sauce by mixing together the dark soy sauce, rice wine and sesame seeds; set aside.

5 Shape the chicken mixture into 16–18 walnut-sized balls. Heat the remaining oil in the frying pan or wok and stir-fry the balls in small batches for 4–5 minutes until golden brown. As each batch is cooked drain on paper towels and keep hot.

6 Stir-fry the spring onions for 1–2 minutes until they begin to soften, then stir in the remaining light soy sauce. Serve with the chicken balls and a bowl of dipping sauce on a platter, garnished with the spring onion tassels.

Crispy Pork & Peanut Baskets

These tasty little appetite-teasers are an adaptation of a traditional recipe made with a light batter, but filo pastry is just as good.

NUTRITIONAL INFORMATION

Calories 243   Sugars 1g
Protein . . . . .12g   Fat 16g
Carbohydrate . . .12g   Saturates 3g

10 mins   15 mins

SERVES 4

I N G R E D I E N T S

2 sheets filo pastry, each about
    42 x 28 cm/16½ x 11 inches

2 tbsp vegetable oil

1 garlic clove, crushed

125 g/4½ oz minced pork

1 tsp Thai red curry paste

2 spring onions, finely chopped

3 tbsp crunchy peanut butter

1 tbsp light soy sauce

1 tbsp chopped fresh coriander

salt and pepper

fresh coriander sprigs, to garnish

1 Cut each sheet of filo pastry into 24 squares, 7-cm/2¾-inches across, to make a total of 48 squares. Brush each square lightly with oil, and arrange the squares in stacks of 4 in 12 small patty tins, pointing outwards. Press the pastry down into the patty tins.

2 Bake the pastry cases in the oven preheated to 200°C/400°F/Gas Mark 6 for 6–8 minutes until golden brown.

3 Meanwhile, heat 1 tablespoon oil in a wok. Add the garlic and fry for 30 seconds, then stir in the pork and stir-fry over a high heat for 4–5 minutes until the meat is golden brown.

4 Add the curry paste and spring onions and continue to stir-fry for a further minute, then stir in the peanut butter, soy sauce and coriander. Season to taste with salt and pepper.

5 Spoon the pork mixture into the filo baskets and serve hot, garnished with coriander.

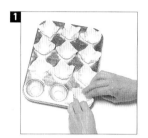

COOK'S TIP

When using filo pastry, remember that it dries out very quickly and becomes brittle and difficult to handle. Work quickly and keep any sheets of pastry you're not using covered with clingfilm and a dampened cloth.

Crispy Seaweed

This tasty Chinese starter is not all that it seems – the 'seaweed' is in fact pak choi which is then fried, salted and tossed with pine kernels.

NUTRITIONAL INFORMATION

Calories 214   Sugars 14g
Protein . . . . .6g   Fat 15g
Carbohydrate . . .15g   Saturates 2g

10 mins   5 mins

SERVES 4

I N G R E D I E N T S

1 kg/2 lb 4 oz pak choi

900 ml/1½ pints groundnut oil, for deep-frying

1 tsp salt

1 tbsp caster sugar

2½ tbsp toasted pine kernels

1 Rinse the pak choi leaves under cold running water and then pat dry thoroughly with absorbent kitchen paper.

2 Discarding any tough outer leaves, roll each pak choi leaf up, then slice through thinly so that the leaves are finely

shredded. Alternatively, use a food processor to shred the pak choi.

3 Heat the groundnut oil in a large wok or heavy-based frying pan.

4 Carefully add the shredded pak choi leaves to the wok or frying pan and fry for about 30 seconds or until they shrivel up and become crispy (you will probably need to do this in several

batches, depending on the size of your wok).

5 Remove the crispy seaweed from the wok with a slotted spoon and drain on absorbent kitchen paper.

6 Transfer the crispy seaweed to a large bowl and toss with the salt, sugar and pine kernels. Serve immediately on warm serving plates.

COOK'S TIP

The tough, outer leaves of pak choi are discarded as these will spoil the overall taste and texture of the dish.

Use savoy cabbage instead of the pak choi if it is unavailable, drying the leaves thoroughly before frying.

Thai-Stuffed Omelette

This makes a substantial starter, or a light lunch or supper dish. Serve with a colourful, crisp salad to accompany the dish.

NUTRITIONAL INFORMATION

Calories 250   Sugars 1g
Protein . . . . .21g   Fat 18g
Carbohydrate . . . .2g   Saturates 4g

5–10 mins   25 mins

SERVES 4

I N G R E D I E N T S

2 garlic cloves, chopped

4 black peppercorns

4 sprigs fresh coriander

2 tbsp vegetable oil

200 g/7 oz minced pork

2 spring onions, chopped

1 large, firm tomato, chopped

6 large eggs

1 tbsp fish sauce

½ tsp turmeric

mixed salad leaves, tossed, to serve

1 Place the garlic, peppercorns and coriander in a pestle and mortar and crush until a smooth paste forms.

2 Heat 1 tablespoon of the oil in a wok over a medium heat. Add the paste and fry for 1–2 minutes until it just changes colour.

3 Stir in the pork and stir-fry until it is lightly browned. Add the spring onions and tomato, and stir-fry for a further minute, then remove the wok from the heat.

4 Heat the remaining oil in a small, heavy-based frying pan. Beat the eggs with the fish sauce and turmeric, then pour a quarter of the egg mixture into the pan. As the mixture begins to set, stir lightly to ensure that all the liquid egg has set sufficiently.

5 Spoon a quarter of the pork mixture down the centre of the omelette, then fold the sides inwards towards the centre, enclosing the filling. Make 3 more omelettes with the remaining egg and fill with the remaining pork mixture.

6 Slide the omelettes on to a warm serving plate and serve with the tossed, mixed salad leaves.

COOK'S TIP

If you prefer, spread half the pork mixture evenly over one omelette, then place a second omelette on top, without folding. Cut into slim wedges to serve.

Thai-Style Fish Cakes

These small fish cakes are quick to make and are delicious served with a chilli dip.

NUTRITIONAL INFORMATION

Calories 214   Sugars 14g
Protein . . . . .6g   Fat 15g
Carbohydrate . . .15g   Saturates 2g

 10 mins   20 mins

SERVES 4

INGREDIENTS

450 g/1 lb cod fillets, skinned

2 tbsp fish sauce

2 red Thai chillies, seeded and finely
  chopped

2 cloves garlic, crushed

10 lime leaves, finely chopped

2 tbsp chopped fresh coriander

1 large egg

25 g/1 oz plain flour

100 g/3½ oz fine green beans, finely sliced

groundnut oil, for frying

1 Using a sharp knife, roughly cut the cod fillets into bite-sized pieces.

COOK'S TIP

Fish sauce is a salty, brown liquid which is a must for authentic flavour. It is used to salt dishes but is milder in flavour than soy sauce. It is available from Asian food stores or health food shops.

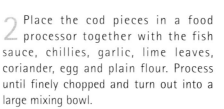

2 Place the cod pieces in a food processor together with the fish sauce, chillies, garlic, lime leaves, coriander, egg and plain flour. Process until finely chopped and turn out into a large mixing bowl.

3 Add the green beans to the cod mixture and combine.

4 Divide the mixture into small balls. Flatten the balls between the palms of your hands to form rounds.

5 Heat a little oil in a preheated wok. Fry the fish cakes on both sides until brown and crispy on the outside.

6 Transfer the fish cakes to serving plates and serve hot.

Chilli & Peanut Prawns

Peanut flavours are widely used in Far East and South East Asian cooking and complement many ingredients.

NUTRITIONAL INFORMATION

Calories 478	Sugars 2g
Protein 32g	Fat 30g
Carbohydrate . . .19g	Saturates 11g

15 mins   10 mins

SERVES 4

I N G R E D I E N T S

450 g/1 lb king prawns, peeled apart from tail end

3 tbsp crunchy peanut butter

1 tbsp chilli sauce

10 sheets filo pastry

25 g/1 oz butter, melted

50 g/1¾ oz fine egg noodles

oil, for frying

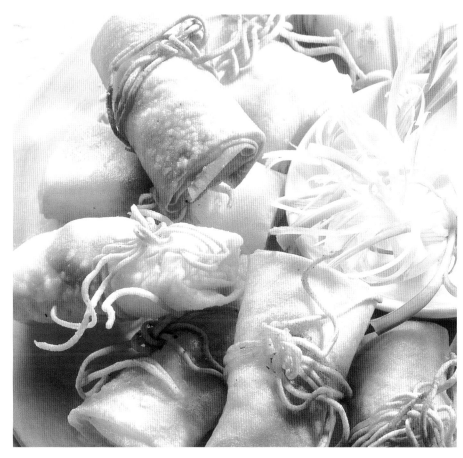

1 Using a sharp knife, make a small horizontal slit across the back of each prawn. Press down on the prawns so that they lie flat.

2 Mix together the peanut butter and chilli sauce in a small bowl until well blended. Using a pastry brush, spread a little of the sauce on to each prawn so they are evenly coated.

3 Cut each pastry sheet in half and brush with melted butter.

4 Wrap each prawn in a piece of pastry, tucking the edges under to fully enclose the prawn.

5 Place the fine egg noodles in a bowl, pour over enough boiling water to cover and leave to stand for 5 minutes. Drain the noodles thoroughly. Use 2–3 cooked noodles to tie around each prawn parcel.

6 Heat the oil in a preheated wok. Cook the prawns for 3–4 minutes, or until golden and crispy.

7 Remove the prawns with a slotted spoon, transfer to kitchen paper and leave to drain. Transfer to serving plates and serve warm.

COOK'S TIP

When using filo pastry, keep any unused pastry covered to prevent it drying out and becoming brittle.

Prawn Parcels

These small prawn bites are packed with the flavour of lime and coriander for a quick and tasty starter.

NUTRITIONAL INFORMATION

Calories 305   Sugars 2g
Protein . . . . .15g   Fat 21g
Carbohydrate . . .14g   Saturates 8g

   15 mins   20 mins

SERVES 4

INGREDIENTS

1 tbsp sunflower oil

1 red pepper, seeded and thinly sliced

75 g/2¾ oz beansprouts

finely grated rind and juice of 1 lime

1 red chilli, seeded and finely chopped

1tsp grated fresh root ginger

225 g/8 oz peeled prawns

1 tbsp fish sauce

½ tsp arrowroot

2 tbsp chopped fresh coriander

8 sheets filo pastry

2 tbsp butter

2 tsp sesame oil

oil, for frying

spring onion tassels, to garnish

chilli sauce, to serve

COOK'S TIP

If using cooked prawns, cook for 1 minute only, otherwise the prawns will toughen.

1 Heat the sunflower oil in a large preheated wok. Add the red pepper and beansprouts and stir-fry for 2 minutes, or until the vegetables have softened.

2 Remove the wok from the heat and toss in the lime zest and juice, red chilli, ginger and prawns, stirring well.

3 Mix the fish sauce with the arrowroot and stir the mixture into the wok juices. Return the wok to the heat and cook, stirring, for 2 minutes, or until the juices thicken. Toss in the coriander and mix well.

4 Lay the sheets of filo pastry out on a board. Melt the butter and sesame oil and brush each pastry sheet with the mixture.

5 Spoon a little of the prawn filling on to the top of each sheet, fold over each end, and roll up to enclose the filling.

6 Heat the oil in a large wok. Cook the parcels, in batches, for 2–3 minutes, or until crisp and golden. Garnish with spring onion tassels and serve hot with a chilli dipping sauce.

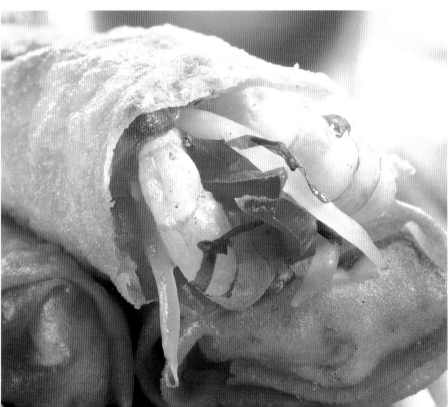

Chinese Prawn Salad

Noodles and bean sprouts form the basis of this refreshing salad which combines the flavours of fruit and prawns.

NUTRITIONAL INFORMATION

Calories 359   Sugars 4g
Protein . . . . .31g   Fat 15g
Carbohydrate . . .25g   Saturates 2g

15 mins   5 mins

SERVES 4

I N G R E D I E N T S

250 g/9 oz fine egg noodles

3 tbsp sunflower oil

1 tbsp sesame oil

1 tbsp sesame seeds

150 g/5½ oz bean sprouts

1 ripe mango, sliced

6 spring onions, sliced

75 g/2¾ oz radishes, sliced

350 g/12 oz peeled cooked prawns

2 tbsp light soy sauce

1 tbsp sherry

1 Place the egg noodles in a large bowl and pour over enough boiling water to cover. Leave to stand for 10 minutes.

2 Drain the noodles thoroughly and pat dry with kitchen paper.

3 Heat the sunflower oil in a large wok or frying pan and stir-fry the noodles for 5 minutes, tossing frequently.

4 Remove the wok from the heat and add the sesame oil, sesame seeds and bean sprouts, tossing to mix well.

5 In a separate bowl, mix together the sliced mango, spring onions, radish and prawns. Stir in the light soy sauce and sherry and mix until the ingredients are thoroughly combined.

6 Toss the prawn mixture with the noodles and transfer to a serving dish. Alternatively, arrange the noodles around the edge of a serving plate and pile the prawn mixture into the centre. Serve immediately as this salad is best eaten warm.

COOK'S TIP

If fresh mango is unavailable, use canned mango slices, rinsed and drained, instead.

Prawn Omelette

This is called *Foo Yung* in China and is a classic dish which may be flavoured with any ingredients you have to hand.

NUTRITIONAL INFORMATION

Calories 320   Sugars 1g
Protein ....31g   Fat 18g
Carbohydrate ....8g   Saturates 4g

5 mins   10 mins

SERVES 4

INGREDIENTS

3 tbsp sunflower oil

2 leeks, trimmed and sliced

350 g/12 oz raw tiger prawns

25 g/1 oz/4 tbsp cornflour

1 tsp salt

175 g/6 oz mushrooms, sliced

175 g/6 oz beansprouts

6 eggs

deep-fried leeks, to garnish (optional)

1 Heat the sunflower oil in a preheated wok or large frying pan. Add the sliced leeks and stir-fry for 3 minutes.

2 Rinse the prawns under cold running water and then pat them dry with kitchen paper.

3 Mix together the cornflour and salt in a large bowl.

4 Add the prawns to the cornflour and salt mixture and toss to coat all over.

5 Add the prawns to the wok or frying pan and stir-fry for 2 minutes, or until the prawns are almost cooked through.

6 Add the mushrooms and bean sprouts to the wok and stir-fry for a further 2 minutes.

7 Beat the eggs with 3 tablespoons of cold water. Pour the egg mixture into the wok and cook until the egg sets, carefully turning over once. Turn the omelette out on to a clean board, divide into 4 and serve hot, garnished with deep-fried leeks (if using).

VARIATION

If liked, divide the mixture into 4 once the initial cooking has taken place in step 6 and cook 4 individual omelettes.

Salt & Pepper Prawns

Szechuan peppercorns are very hot, adding heat and a red colour to the prawns. They are effectively offset by the sugar in this recipe.

NUTRITIONAL INFORMATION

Calories ....174 Sugars 1g
Protein ....25g Fat 8g
Carbohydrate ....1g Saturates 1g

5 mins   10 mins

SERVES 4

INGREDIENTS

2 tsp salt

1 tsp black pepper

2 tsp Szechuan peppercorns

1 tsp sugar

450 g/1 lb peeled raw tiger prawns

2 tbsp groundnut oil

1 red chilli, seeded and finely chopped

1 tsp grated fresh root ginger

3 cloves garlic, crushed

spring onions, sliced, to garnish

prawn crackers, to serve

1 Grind the salt, black pepper and Szechuan peppercorns in a pestle and mortar.

2 Mix the salt and pepper mixture with the sugar and set aside until required.

3 Rinse the tiger prawns under cold running water and pat dry with kitchen paper.

4 Heat the oil in a preheated wok or large frying pan.

5 Add the prawns, chopped red chilli, ginger and garlic to the wok or frying pan and stir-fry for 4–5 minutes, or until the prawns are cooked through.

6 Add the salt and pepper mixture to the wok and stir-fry for 1 minute, stirring constantly so it does not burn on the base of the wok.

7 Transfer the prawns to warm serving bowls and garnish with spring onions. Serve hot with prawn crackers.

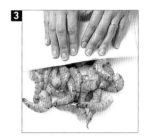
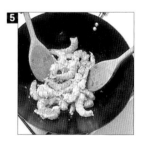

COOK'S TIP

Tiger prawns are widely available and have a lovely meaty texture. If using cooked tiger prawns, add them with the salt and pepper mixture in step 5 – if the cooked prawns are added any earlier they will toughen up and be inedible.

Sesame Prawn Toasts

These are one of the most recognised and popular starters in Chinese restaurants in the Western world. They are also quick and easy to make.

NUTRITIONAL INFORMATION

Calories	237	Sugars	.........1g
Protein	........18g	Fat	..........12g
Carbohydrate	...15g	Saturates	.......2g

5 mins 10 mins

SERVES 4

INGREDIENTS

4 slices medium, thick-sliced white bread

225 g/8 oz cooked peeled prawns

1 tbsp soy sauce

2 cloves garlic, crushed

1 tbsp sesame oil

1 egg

2 tbsp sesame seeds

oil, for deep-frying

sweet chilli sauce, to serve

1 Remove the crusts from the bread, if desired, then set aside until required.

2 Place the peeled prawns, soy sauce, crushed garlic, sesame oil and egg into a food processor and blend until a smooth paste has formed.

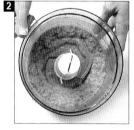 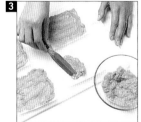 

3 Spread the prawn paste evenly over the 4 slices of bread. Sprinkle the sesame seeds over the top of the prawn mixture and press the seeds down with your hands so that they stick to the mixture. Cut each slice in half and in half again to form 4 triangles.

4 Heat the oil in a large wok or frying pan and deep-fry the toasts, sesame seed-side up, for 4–5 minutes, or until they are golden and crispy.

5 Remove the toasts with a slotted spoon and transfer to kitchen paper and leave to drain thoroughly.

6 Serve the sesame prawn toasts warm with sweet chilli sauce for dipping.

VARIATION

Add 2 chopped spring onions to the mixture in step 2 for added flavour and crunch.

Sweet & Sour Prawns

Prawns are marinated in a soy sauce mixture then coated in a light batter, fried and served with a delicious sweet-and-sour dip.

NUTRITIONAL INFORMATION

Calories 294   Sugars 11g
Protein . . . . .14g   Fat 12g
Carbohydrate . . .34g   Saturates 2g

🐚 🐚 🐚 🐚

🍲 40 mins   🕐 20 mins

SERVES 4

INGREDIENTS

16 large raw prawns, peeled

1 tsp grated fresh root ginger

1 garlic clove, crushed

2 spring onions, sliced

2 tbsp dry sherry

2 tsp sesame oil

1 tbsp light soy sauce

vegetable oil, for deep-frying

shredded spring onion,
   to garnish

BATTER

4 egg whites

4 tbsp cornflour

2 tbsp plain flour

SAUCE

2 tbsp tomato purée

3 tbsp white wine vinegar

4 tsp light soy sauce

2 tbsp lemon juice

3 tbsp light brown sugar

1 green pepper, seeded and cut into
   matchsticks

½ tsp chilli sauce

300 ml10 fl oz vegetable stock

2 tsp cornflour

1 Using tweezers, de-vein the prawns, then flatten them with a large knife.

2 Place the prawns in a dish and add the ginger, garlic, spring onions, dry sherry, sesame oil and soy sauce. Cover with clingfilm and leave to marinate for 30 minutes.

3 Make the batter by beating the egg whites until thick. Fold in the cornflour and plain flour to form a light batter.

4 Place all of the sauce ingredients in a saucepan and bring to the boil. Reduce the heat and leave to simmer for 10 minutes.

5 Remove the prawns from the marinade and dip them into the batter to coat.

6 Heat the vegetable oil in a preheated wok or large frying pan until almost smoking. Reduce the heat and fry the prawns for 3–4 minutes, until crisp and golden brown.

7 Garnish the prawns with shredded spring onion and serve with the sauce.

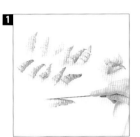

Rice Paper Parcels

These special rice paper wrappers are available in Chinese supermarkets and health shops. Do not use the rice paper sold for making cakes.

NUTRITIONAL INFORMATION

Calories ....133 Sugars 2g
Protein ....10g Fat 8g
Carbohydrate ....5g Saturates 1g

5 mins   15 mins

SERVES 4

INGREDIENTS

1 egg white

2 tsp cornflour

2 tsp dry sherry

1 tsp caster sugar

2 tsp hoisin sauce

225 g/8 oz peeled, cooked prawns

4 spring onions, sliced

25 g/1 oz canned water chestnuts, drained, rinsed and chopped

8 Chinese rice paper wrappers

vegetable oil, for deep-frying

hoisin sauce or plum sauce, to serve

1 Lightly beat the egg white in a bowl. Mix in the cornflour, dry sherry, sugar and hoisin sauce. Add the prawns, spring onions and water chestnuts, mixing thoroughly.

COOK'S TIP

Use this filling inside wonton wrappers (see page 47) if the rice paper wrappers are unavailable.

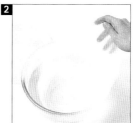

2 Soften the rice papers first by dipping them in a bowl of water one at a time. Spread them out on a clean work surface.

3 Using a dessert spoon, place a little of the prawn mixture into the centre of each rice paper. Carefully wrap the rice paper around the filling to make a secure parcel. Repeat to make 8 parcels.

4 Heat the oil in a wok until it is almost smoking. Reduce the heat slightly, add the parcels, in batches if necessary, and deep-fry for 4–5 minutes, until crisp. Remove from the oil with a slotted spoon and drain on absorbent kitchen paper.

5 Transfer the parcels to a warmed serving dish and serve immediately with a little hoisin or plum sauce.

Crispy Crab Wontons

These delicious wontons are a superb starter. Deep-fried until crisp and golden, they are delicious with a chilli dipping sauce.

NUTRITIONAL INFORMATION

Calories 266   Sugars 0.4g
Protein . . . . .10g   Fat 17g
Carbohydrate . . .18g   Saturates 5g

10 mins   15 mins

SERVES 4

I N G R E D I E N T S

175 g/6 oz white crabmeat, flaked

50 g/1¾ oz canned water chestnuts, drained, rinsed and chopped

1 small fresh red chilli, chopped

1 spring onion, chopped

1 tbsp cornflour

1 tsp dry sherry

1 tsp light soy sauce

½ tsp lime juice

24 wonton wrappers

vegetable oil, for deep-frying

sliced lime, to garnish

1 To make the filling, mix together the crabmeat, water chestnuts, chilli, spring onion, cornflour, sherry, soy sauce and lime juice.

2 Spread out the wonton wrappers on a work surface and spoon one portion of the filling into the centre of each wonton wrapper.

3 Dampen the edges of the wonton wrappers with a little water and fold them in half to form triangles. Fold the two pointed ends in towards the centre, moisten with a little water to secure and then pinch together to seal to prevent the wontons unwrapping.

4 Heat the oil for deep-frying in a wok or deep-fryer to 180°C–190°C/350°F–375°F, or until a cube of bread browns in 30 seconds. Fry the wontons, in batches, for 2–3 minutes, until golden brown and crisp. Remove the wontons from the oil and leave to drain on kitchen paper.

5 Serve the wontons hot, garnished with slices of lime.

COOK'S TIP

Handle wonton wrappers carefully as they can be easily damaged. Make sure that the wontons are sealed well and secured before deep-frying to prevent the filling coming out and the wontons unwrapping.

Crab Ravioli

These small parcels are made from wonton wrappers, filled with mixed vegetables and crabmeat for a melt-in-the-mouth starter.

NUTRITIONAL INFORMATION

Calories 292   Sugars 1g
Protein ....25g   Fat 17g
Carbohydrate ....11g   Saturates 5g

20 mins   25 mins

SERVES 4

I N G R E D I E N T S

450 g/1 lb fresh or canned crabmeat, drained

½ red pepper, seeded and finely diced

125 g/4½ oz Chinese leaves, shredded

25 g/1 oz beansprouts, roughly chopped

1 tbsp light soy sauce

1 tsp lime juice

16 wonton wrappers

1 small egg, beaten

2 tbsp peanut oil

1 tsp sesame oil

salt and pepper

1 Mix together the crabmeat, pepper, Chinese leaves, beansprouts, soy sauce and lime juice. Season and leave to stand for 15 minutes.

2 Spread out the wonton wrappers on a work surface. Spoon a little of the crabmeat mixture into the centre of each wrapper. Brush the edges with egg and fold in half, pushing out any air. Press the edges together to seal.

3 Heat the peanut oil in a preheated wok or frying pan. Fry the ravioli, in batches, for 3–4 minutes, turning, until browned. Remove with a slotted spoon and drain on kitchen paper.

4 Heat any remaining filling in the wok or frying pan over a gentle heat until hot. Serve the ravioli with the hot filling and sprinkled with sesame oil.

COOK'S TIP

Make sure that the edges of the ravioli are sealed well and that all of the air is pressed out to prevent them from opening during cooking.

Spicy Chicken Livers

This is a richly flavoured dish with a dark, slightly tangy sauce which is popular in China.

NUTRITIONAL INFORMATION

Calories ....195 Sugars 2g
Protein ....20g Fat 8g
Carbohydrate ....9g Saturates 1g

🕙 5 mins 🕐 5–10 mins

SERVES 4

I N G R E D I E N T S

350 g/12 oz chicken livers

2 tbsp sunflower oil

1 red chilli, seeded and finely chopped

1 tsp grated fresh root ginger

2 cloves garlic, crushed

2 tbsp tomato ketchup

3 tbsp sherry

3 tbsp soy sauce

1 tsp cornflour

450 g/1 lb pak choi

egg noodles, to serve

1 Using a sharp knife, trim the fat from the chicken livers and slice into small pieces.

2 Heat the oil in a large wok. Add the chicken liver pieces and stir-fry over a high heat for 2–3 minutes.

3 Add the chilli, ginger and garlic and stir-fry for about 1 minute.

4 Mix together the tomato ketchup, sherry, soy sauce and cornflour in a small bowl and set aside.

5 Add the pak choi to the wok and stir-fry until it just wilts.

6 Add the reserved tomato ketchup mixture to the wok and cook, stirring to mix, until the juices start to bubble.

7 Transfer to serving bowls and serve hot with noodles.

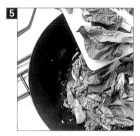

COOK'S TIP

Fresh root ginger will keep for several weeks in a dry, cool place.

Chicken livers are available fresh or frozen from most supermarkets.

Honeyed Chicken Wings

Chicken wings are ideal for a starter as they are small and perfect for eating with the fingers.

NUTRITIONAL INFORMATION

Calories	131	Sugars	.........4g
Protein	........10g	Fat	...........8g
Carbohydrate	....4g	Saturates	.......2g

 2 hrs 5 mins 40 mins

SERVES 4

INGREDIENTS

450 g/1 lb chicken wings

2 tbsp peanut oil

2 tbsp light soy sauce

2 tbsp hoisin sauce

2 tbsp clear honey

2 garlic cloves, crushed

1 tsp sesame seeds

MARINADE

1 dried red chilli

½–1 tsp chilli powder

½–1 tsp ground ginger

finely grated rind of 1 lime

1 To make the marinade, crush the dried chilli in a pestle and mortar. Mix together the crushed dried chilli, chilli powder, ground ginger and lime rind in a small mixing bowl.

2 Thoroughly rub the spice mixture into the chicken wings with your fingertips. Set aside for at least 2 hours to allow the flavours to penetrate the chicken wings.

3 Heat the peanut oil in a large wok or frying pan.

4 Add the chicken wings and fry, turning frequently, for about 10–12 minutes, until golden and crisp. Drain off any excess oil.

5 Add the soy sauce, hoisin sauce, honey, garlic and sesame seeds to the wok, turning the chicken wings to coat.

6 Reduce the heat and cook for 20–25 minutes, turning the chicken wings frequently, until completely cooked through. Serve hot.

COOK'S TIP

Make the dish in advance and freeze the chicken wings. Defrost thoroughly, cover with foil and heat right through in a moderate oven.

Steamed Duck Buns

The dough used in this recipe may also be wrapped around chicken, pork or prawns, or sweet fillings as an alternative.

NUTRITIONAL INFORMATION

Calories 307   Sugars 11g
Protein . . . . .17g   Fat 6g
Carbohydrate . . .50g   Saturates 1g

 1½ hrs   🕐 1 hr

SERVES 4

I N G R E D I E N T S

D U M P L I N G   D O U G H

300 g/10½ oz plain flour

15 g/½ oz dried yeast

1 tsp caster sugar

2 tbsp warm water

175 ml/6 fl oz warm milk

F I L L I N G

300 g/10½ oz duck breast

1 tbsp light brown sugar

1 tbsp light soy sauce

2 tbsp clear honey

1 tbsp hoisin sauce

1 tbsp vegetable oil

1 leek, finely chopped

1 garlic clove, crushed

1 tsp grated fresh root ginger

1 Place the duck breast in a large bowl. Mix together the light brown sugar, soy sauce, honey and hoisin sauce. Pour the mixture over the duck and marinate for 20 minutes.

2 Remove the duck from the marinade and cook on a rack set over a roasting tin in a preheated oven, 200°C/ 400°F/Gas

Mark 6, for 35–40 minutes, or until cooked through. Leave to cool, remove the meat from the bones and cut into small cubes.

3 Heat the vegetable oil in a preheated wok or frying pan until really hot.

4 Add the leek, garlic and ginger to the wok and fry for 3 minutes. Mix with the duck meat.

5 Sift the plain flour into a large bowl. Mix the yeast, caster sugar and warm water in a separate bowl and leave in a warm place for 15 minutes.

6 Pour the yeast mixture into the flour, together with the warm milk, mixing to form a firm dough. Knead the dough on a floured surface for 5 minutes. Roll into a sausage shape, 2.5 cm/1 inch in diameter. Cut into 16 pieces, cover and let stand for 20–25 minutes.

7 Flatten the dough pieces into 10-cm/4-inch rounds. Place a spoonful of filling in the centre of each, draw up the sides to form a "moneybag" shape and twist to seal.

8 Place the dumplings on a clean, damp tea towel in the base of a steamer, cover and steam for 20 minutes. Serve immediately.

Spring Rolls

This classic Chinese dish is very popular in the West. Serve hot or chilled with a soy sauce or hoisin dip.

NUTRITIONAL INFORMATION

Calories 442   Sugars 4g
Protein . . . . .23g   Fat 21g
Carbohydrate . . .42g   Saturates 3g

 45 mins   45 mins

SERVES 4

I N G R E D I E N T S

175 g/6 oz cooked pork, chopped

75 g/2¾ oz cooked chicken, chopped

1 tsp light soy sauce

1 tsp light brown sugar

1 tsp sesame oil

1 tsp vegetable oil

225 g/8 oz beansprouts

25 g/1 oz canned bamboo shoots, drained, rinsed and chopped

1 green pepper, seeded and chopped

2 spring onions, sliced

1 tsp cornflour

2 tsp water

vegetable oil, for deep-frying

SKINS

125 g/4½ oz plain flour

5 tbsp cornflour

450 ml/15 fl oz water

3 tbsp vegetable oil

1 Mix the pork, chicken, soy sauce, sugar and sesame oil. Cover and marinate for 30 minutes.

2 Heat the vegetable oil in a preheated wok. Add the bean sprouts, bamboo shoots, pepper and spring onions to the wok and stir-fry for 2–3 minutes. Add the meat and the marinade to the wok and stir-fry for 2–3 minutes.

3 Blend the cornflour with the water and stir the mixture into the wok. Set aside to cool completely.

4 To make the skins, mix the flour and cornflour and gradually stir in the water, to make a smooth batter.

5 Heat a small, oiled frying pan. Swirl one-eighth of the batter over the base and cook for 2–3 minutes. Repeat with the remaining batter. Cover the skins with a damp tea towel while frying the remaining skins.

6 Spread out the skins and spoon one-eighth of the filling along the centre of each. Brush the edges with water and fold in the sides, then roll up.

7 Heat the oil for deep-frying in a wok to 180°C/350°F. Cook the spring rolls, in batches, for 2–3 minutes, or until golden and crisp. Remove from the oil with a slotted spoon, drain and serve immediately.

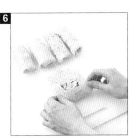

Pancake Rolls

This classic *dim sum* dish is adaptable to almost any filling of your choice. Here the traditional mixture of pork and pak choi is used.

NUTRITIONAL INFORMATION

Calories 488   Sugars 19g
Protein . . . . .16g   Fat 24g
Carbohydrate . . .55g   Saturates 4g

20 mins   20 mins

SERVES 4

INGREDIENTS

4 tsp vegetable oil

1–2 garlic cloves, crushed

225 g/8 oz minced pork

225 g/8 oz pak choi, shredded

4½ tsp light soy sauce

½ tsp sesame oil

8 spring roll skins, 25 cm/10 inches square, defrosted if frozen

oil, for deep-frying

CHILLI SAUCE

60 g/2 oz caster sugar

50 ml/2 fl oz rice vinegar

2 tbsp water

2 red chillies, finely chopped

1 Heat the oil in a preheated wok. Add the garlic and stir-fry for 30 seconds. Add the pork and stir-fry for 2–3 minutes, until lightly coloured.

2 Add the pak choi, soy sauce and sesame oil to the wok and stir-fry for 2–3 minutes. Remove from the heat and set aside to cool.

3 Spread out the spring roll skins on a work surface and spoon 2 tablespoons of the pork mixture along one edge of each. Roll the skin over once and fold in the sides. Roll up completely to make a sausage shape, brushing the edges with a little water to seal. Set the pancake rolls aside for 10 minutes to seal firmly.

4 To make the chilli sauce, heat the sugar, vinegar and water in a small saucepan, stirring until the sugar dissolves. Bring the mixture to the boil and boil rapidly until a light syrup forms. Remove from the heat and stir in the chopped red chillies. Leave the sauce to cool before serving.

5 Heat the oil for deep-frying in a wok until almost smoking. Reduce the heat slightly and fry the pancake rolls, in batches if necessary, for 3–4 minutes, until golden brown. Remove from the oil with a slotted spoon and drain on kitchen paper. Serve on warm serving plates with the chilli sauce.

Poultry & Meat

Meat is expensive in Far Eastern countries and is eaten in smaller proportions than in the Western world. However, when meat is used, it is done so to its full potential – it is marinated or spiced and combined with other delicious

native flavourings to create a wide array of mouthwatering dishes.

In Malaysia, a wide variety of spicy meats is offered, reflecting the many ethnic origins of the population. In China, poultry, lamb, beef or pork are stir-fried or steamed in the wok and combined with sauces and seasonings such as soy, black bean and oyster sauce. In Japan, meat is usually marinated and quickly stir-fried in a wok over a very high heat or simmered in miso stock. Thai dishes use meat that is leaner and more flavoursome due to its 'free-range' rearing.

Stir-Fried Ginger Chicken

The oranges add colour and piquancy to this refreshing dish, which complements the chicken well.

NUTRITIONAL INFORMATION

Calories 289	Sugars 15g	
Protein 20g	Fat 9g	
Carbohydrate ...17g	Saturates 2g	

 5 mins   20 mins

SERVES 4

INGREDIENTS

2 tbsp sunflower oil

1 onion, sliced

175 g/6 oz carrots, cut into matchsticks

1 clove garlic, crushed

350 g/12 oz boneless skinless chicken breasts

2 tbsp grated fresh root ginger

1 tsp ground ginger

4 tbsp sweet sherry

1 tbsp tomato purée

1 tbsp demerara sugar

100 ml/3½ fl oz orange juice

1 tsp cornflour

1 orange, peeled and segmented

fresh snipped chives, to garnish

1 Heat the oil in a large preheated wok. Add the onion, carrots and garlic and stir-fry over a high heat for 3 minutes or until the vegetables begin to soften.

2 Slice the chicken into thin strips. Add to the wok with the fresh and ground ginger. Stir-fry for a further 10 minutes, or until the chicken is well cooked through and golden in colour.

3 Mix together the sherry, tomato purée, sugar, orange juice and cornflour in a bowl. Stir the mixture into the wok and heat through until the mixture bubbles and the juices start to thicken.

4 Add the orange segments and carefully toss to mix.

5 Transfer the stir-fried chicken to warm serving bowls and garnish with freshly snipped chives. Serve immediately.

COOK'S TIP

Make sure that you do not continue cooking the dish once the orange segments have been added in step 4, otherwise they will break up.

Coconut Chicken Curry

Okra or ladies fingers are slightly bitter in flavour. The pineapple and coconut in this recipe offsets them in both colour and flavour.

NUTRITIONAL INFORMATION

Calories 456   Sugars 21g
Protein ....29g   Fat 29g
Carbohydrate ...22g   Saturates 17g

5 mins   45 mins

SERVES 4

I N G R E D I E N T S

2 tbsp sunflower oil

450 g/1 lb boneless, skinless chicken thighs or breasts

150 g/5½ oz okra

1 large onion, sliced

2 cloves garlic, crushed

3 tbsp mild curry paste

300 ml/½ pint chicken stock

1 tbsp fresh lemon juice

100 g/3½ oz creamed coconut, roughly grated

175 g/6 oz fresh or canned pineapple, cubed

150 ml/¼ pint thick, natural yogurt

2 tbsp chopped fresh coriander

freshly boiled rice, to serve

TO GARNISH

lemon wedges

fresh coriander sprigs

 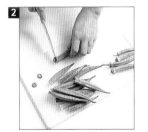 

1 Heat the oil in a wok. Cut the chicken into bite-sized pieces, add to the wok and stir-fry until evenly browned.

2 Using a sharp knife, trim the okra. Add the onion, garlic and okra to the wok and cook for a further 2–3 minutes, stirring constantly.

3 Mix the curry paste with the chicken stock and lemon juice and pour into the wok. Bring to the boil, cover and leave to simmer for 30 minutes.

4 Stir the grated coconut into the curry and cook for about 5 minutes.

5 Add the pineapple, yogurt and coriander and cook for 2 minutes, stirring. Garnish and serve on warm serving plates.

COOK'S TIP

Score around the top of the okra with a knife before cooking to release the sticky glue-like substance which is bitter in taste.

Cashew Chicken

Yellow bean sauce is available from large supermarkets. Try to buy a chunky sauce rather than a smooth sauce for texture.

NUTRITIONAL INFORMATION

Calories 398   Sugars 2g
Protein . . . . .31g   Fat 27g
Carbohydrate . . . .8g   Saturates 4g

10 mins   15 mins

SERVES 4

INGREDIENTS

450 g/1 lb boneless chicken breasts

2 tbsp vegetable oil

1 red onion, sliced

175 g/6 oz flat mushrooms, sliced

100 g/3½ oz cashew nuts

75 g/2¾ oz jar yellow bean sauce

fresh coriander, to garnish

egg fried rice or plain boiled rice, to serve

1 Using a sharp knife, remove the excess skin from the chicken breasts, if desired. Cut the chicken into small, bite-sized chunks.

2 Heat the vegetable oil in a preheated wok or frying pan.

3 Add the chicken to the wok and stir-fry for 5 minutes.

4 Add the red onion and mushrooms to the wok and continue to stir-fry for a further 5 minutes.

5 Place the cashew nuts on a baking tray and toast under a preheated medium grill until just browning – toasting nuts brings out their flavour.

6 Toss the toasted cashew nuts into the wok together with the yellow bean sauce and heat through.

7 Allow the sauce to bubble for 2–3 minutes.

8 Transfer the chop suey to warm serving bowls and garnish with fresh coriander. Serve hot with egg fried rice or plain boiled rice.

VARIATION

Chicken thighs could be used instead of the chicken breasts for a more economical dish.

Lemon Chicken

This is on everyone's list of favourite Chinese dishes, and it is so simple to make. Serve with stir-fried vegetables for a truly delicious meal.

NUTRITIONAL INFORMATION

Calories 272   Sugars 1g
Protein . . . . .36g   Fat 11g
Carbohydrate . . . .5g   Saturates 2g

5 mins   15 mins

SERVES 4

INGREDIENTS

vegetable oil, for deep-frying

650 g/1 lb 7 oz skinless, boneless
    chicken, cut into strips

SAUCE

1 tbsp cornflour

6 tbsp cold water

3 tbsp fresh lemon juice

2 tbsp sweet sherry

½ tsp caster sugar

TO GARNISH

lemon slices

shredded spring onion

1 Heat the oil for deep-frying in a preheated wok or frying pan to 180°C/350°F or until a cube of bread browns in 30 seconds.

COOK'S TIP

If you would prefer to use chicken portions rather than strips, cook them in the oil, covered, over a low heat for about 30 minutes, or until cooked through.

2 Reduce the heat and stir-fry the chicken strips for 3–4 minutes, until cooked through.

3 Remove the chicken with a slotted spoon, set aside and keep warm. Drain the oil from the wok.

4 To make the sauce, mix the cornflour with 2 tablespoons of the water to form a paste.

5 Pour the lemon juice and remaining water into the mixture in the wok.

6 Add the sweet sherry and caster sugar and bring to the boil, stirring until the sugar has completely dissolved.

7 Stir in the cornflour mixture and return to the boil. Reduce the heat and simmer, stirring constantly, for 2–3 minutes, until the sauce is thickened and clear.

8 Transfer the chicken to a warm serving plate and pour the sauce over the top.

9 Garnish the chicken with the lemon slices and shredded spring onion and serve immediately.

Sweet Mango Chicken

The sweet, scented flavour of mango gives this dish its characteristic sweetness.

NUTRITIONAL INFORMATION

Calories 244   Sugars 18g
Protein . . . . .27g   Fat 7g
Carbohydrate . . .2.1g   Saturates 2g

10 mins   15 mins

SERVES 4

I N G R E D I E N T S

1 tbsp sunflower oil

6 skinless, boneless chicken thighs

1 ripe mango

2 cloves garlic, crushed

225 g/8 oz leeks, shredded

100 g/3½ oz bean sprouts

150 ml/¼ pint mango juice

1 tbsp white wine vinegar

2 tbsp clear honey

2 tbsp tomato ketchup

1 tsp cornflour

COOK'S TIP

Mango juice is available in jars from most supermarkets and is quite thick and sweet. If it is unavailable, purée and sieve a ripe mango and add a little water to make up the required quantity.

1 Heat the sunflower oil in a large preheated wok.

2 Cut the chicken into bite-sized cubes, add to the wok and stir-fry over a high heat for 10 minutes, tossing frequently until the chicken is cooked through and golden in colour.

3 Peel and slice the mango and add to the wok with the garlic, leeks and

beansprouts. Stir-fry for a further 2–3 minutes, or until softened.

4 Mix together the mango juice, white wine vinegar, honey, tomato ketchup and cornflour. Pour into the wok and stir-fry for a further 2 minutes, or until the juices start to thicken.

5 Transfer to a warmed serving plate and serve immediately.

Chicken with Cashew Nuts

This is a popular dish in Chinese restaurants in the West, although nothing beats making it yourself.

NUTRITIONAL INFORMATION

Calories 330   Sugars 5g
Protein . . . . .22g   Fat 18g
Carbohydrate . . .19g   Saturates 3g

5 mins   15 mins

SERVES 4

I N G R E D I E N T S

300 g/10½ oz boneless, skinless chicken breasts

1 tbsp cornflour

1 tsp sesame oil

1 tbsp hoisin sauce

1 tsp light soy sauce

3 garlic cloves, crushed

2 tbsp vegetable oil

75 g/2¾ oz unsalted cashew nuts

25 g/1 oz mangetout

1 celery stick, sliced

1 onion, cut into 8 pieces

60 g/2 oz beansprouts

1 red pepper, seeded and diced

S A U C E

2 tsp cornflour

2 tbsp hoisin sauce

200 ml/7 fl oz chicken stock

1 Trim any fat from the chicken breasts and cut the meat into thin strips. Place the chicken in a large mixing bowl. Sprinkle with the cornflour and toss to coat the chicken strips in it, shaking off any excess. Mix together the sesame oil, hoisin sauce, soy sauce and 1 garlic clove. Pour this mixture over the chicken, turning to coat thoroughly. Leave to marinate for 20 minutes.

2 Heat half of the vegetable oil in a preheated wok. Add the cashew nuts and stir-fry for 1 minute, until browned. Add the mangetout, celery, the remaining garlic, the onion, beansprouts and red pepper and cook, stirring occasionally, for 2–3 minutes. Remove the vegetables from the wok with a slotted spoon, set aside and keep warm.

3 Heat the remaining oil in the wok. Remove the chicken from the marinade and stir-fry for 3–4 minutes. Return the vegetables to the wok.

4 To make the sauce, mix the cornflour, hoisin sauce and chicken stock together and pour into the wok. Bring to the boil, stirring until thickened and clear. Serve immediately on warm serving plates.

Chicken Chop Suey

Chop suey is a well known and popular dish based on bean sprouts and soy sauce with a meat or vegetable flavouring.

NUTRITIONAL INFORMATION

Calories	337	Sugars	.........7g
Protein	........32g	Fat	..........18g
Carbohydrate	...14g	Saturates	.......3g

25 mins   15 mins

SERVES 4

INGREDIENTS

4 tbsp light soy sauce

2 tsp light brown sugar

500 g/1 lb 2 oz skinless, boneless chicken breasts

3 tbsp vegetable oil

2 onions, quartered

2 garlic cloves, crushed

350 g/12 oz beansprouts

3 tsp sesame oil

1 tbsp cornflour

3 tbsp water

425 ml/¾ pint chicken stock

shredded leek, to garnish

VARIATION

This recipe may be made with strips of lean steak, pork or with mixed vegetables. Change the type of stock accordingly.

1 Mix the soy sauce and sugar together, stirring until the sugar has dissolved.

2 Trim any fat from the chicken and cut into thin strips. Place the meat in a shallow dish and spoon the soy mixture over them, turning to coat. Marinate in the refrigerator for 20 minutes.

3 Heat the oil in a wok and stir-fry the chicken for 2–3 minutes, until golden brown. Add the onions and garlic and cook for a further 2 minutes. Add the beansprouts, cook for 4–5 minutes, then add the sesame oil.

4 Mix the cornflour and water to form a smooth paste. Pour the stock into the wok, add the cornflour paste and bring to the boil, stirring until the sauce is thickened and clear. Serve, garnished with shredded leek.

Chicken with Chilli & Basil

Chicken drumsticks are cooked in a delicious sauce and served with deep-fried basil for colour and flavour.

NUTRITIONAL INFORMATION

Calories	196	Sugars	........2g
Protein	........23g	Fat	..........10g
Carbohydrate	....3g	Saturates	.......2g

5 mins   30 mins

SERVES 4

INGREDIENTS

8 chicken drumsticks

2 tbsp soy sauce

1 tbsp sunflower oil

1 red chilli

100 g/3½ oz carrots, cut into matchsticks

6 celery sticks, cut into matchsticks

3 tbsp sweet chilli sauce

oil, for frying

about 50 fresh basil leaves

1 Remove the skin from the chicken drumsticks if desired. Make 3 slashes in each drumstick. Brush the drumsticks with the soy sauce.

2 Heat the sunflower oil in a preheated wok and fry the drumsticks for 20 minutes, turning frequently, until they are cooked through.

3 Seed and finely chop the chilli. Add the chilli, carrots and celery to the wok and cook for a further 5 minutes. Stir in the chilli sauce, cover and allow to bubble gently whilst preparing the basil leaves.

4 Heat a little oil in a heavy based pan. Carefully add the basil leaves – stand well away from the pan and protect your hand with a tea towel as they may spit a little. Cook the basil leaves for about 30 seconds or until they begin to curl up but not brown. Leave the leaves to drain on kitchen paper.

5 Arrange the cooked chicken, vegetables and pan juices on to a warm serving plate, garnish with the deep-fried crispy basil leaves and serve immediately.

COOK'S TIP

Basil has a very strong flavour which is perfect with chicken and Chinese flavourings. You could use baby spinach instead of the basil, if you prefer.

Crispy Chicken

In this recipe, the chicken is brushed with a syrup and deep-fried until golden. It is a little time consuming, but well worth the effort.

NUTRITIONAL INFORMATION

Calories	283	Sugars	.........8g
Protein	........29g	Fat	..........15g
Carbohydrate	....8g	Saturates	.......3g

15 hrs   35 mins

SERVES 4

INGREDIENTS

1.5 kg/3 lb 5 oz oven-ready chicken

2 tbsp clear honey

2 tsp Chinese five-spice powder

2 tbsp rice wine vinegar

900 ml/1½ pints vegetable oil,
    for deep-frying

chilli sauce, to serve

1 Rinse the chicken inside and out under cold running water and pat dry with kitchen paper.

2 Bring a large saucepan of water to the boil and remove from the heat. Place the chicken in the water, cover and set aside for 20 minutes.

3 Remove the chicken from the boiled water and pat dry with kitchen paper.

Cool and leave to chill in the refrigerator overnight.

4 To make the glaze, mix the honey, Chinese five-spice powder and rice wine vinegar.

5 Brush some of the glaze all over the chicken and return to the refrigerator for 20 minutes.

6 Repeat this process of glazing and refrigerating the chicken until all of the glaze has been used up. Return the chicken to the refrigerator for at least 2 hours after the final coating.

7 Using a cleaver or heavy kitchen knife, open the chicken out by splitting it through the centre through the breast and then cut each half into 4 pieces.

8 Heat the oil for deep-frying in a wok until almost smoking. Reduce the heat and fry each piece of chicken for 5–7 minutes, until golden and cooked through. Remove from the oil with a slotted spoon and drain on kitchen paper.

9 Transfer to a serving dish and serve hot with a little chilli sauce.

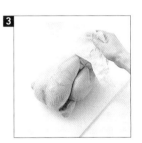

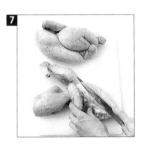

COOK'S TIP

If it is easier, use chicken portions instead of a whole chicken. You could also use chicken legs for this recipe, if you prefer.

Spicy Peanut Chicken

This quick dish has many variations, but this version includes the classic combination of peanuts, chicken and chillies.

NUTRITIONAL INFORMATION

Calories	342	Sugars	.........3g
Protein	........25g	Fat	..........24g
Carbohydrate	....6g	Saturates	.......5g

🍗 🍗 🍗 🍗

🍲 5 mins   🕐 10 mins

SERVES 4

I N G R E D I E N T S

300 g/10½ oz skinless, boneless
   chicken breast

2 tbsp peanut oil

125 g/4½ oz shelled peanuts

1 fresh red chilli, sliced

1 green pepper, seeded and
   cut into strips

fried rice, to serve

S A U C E

150 ml/5 fl oz chicken stock

1 tbsp Chinese rice wine or
   dry sherry

1 tbsp light soy sauce

1½ tsp light brown sugar

2 garlic cloves, crushed

1 tsp grated fresh root ginger

1 tsp rice wine vinegar

1 tsp sesame oil

1 Trim any fat from the chicken and cut the meat into 2.5-cm/1-inch cubes. Set aside until required.

2 Heat the peanut oil in a preheated wok or frying pan.

3 Add the peanuts to the wok and stir-fry for 1 minute. Remove the peanuts with a slotted spoon and set aside.

4 Add the chicken to the wok and cook for 1–2 minutes.

5 Stir in the chilli and green pepper and cook for 1 minute. Remove from the wok with a slotted spoon and set aside.

6 Put half of the peanuts in a food processor and process until almost smooth. If necessary, add a little stock to form a softer paste. Alternatively, place them in a plastic bag and crush them with a rolling pin.

7 To make the sauce, add the chicken stock, Chinese rice wine or dry sherry, light soy sauce, light brown sugar, crushed garlic cloves, grated fresh root ginger and rice wine vinegar to the wok.

8 Heat the sauce without boiling and stir in the peanut purée, remaining peanuts, chicken, sliced red chilli and green pepper strips. Mix well until all the ingredients are thoroughly combined.

9 Sprinkle the sesame oil into the wok, stir and cook for 1 minute. Transfer the spicy peanut chicken to a warm serving dish and serve hot with fried rice.

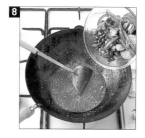

Chinese Chicken Salad

This is a refreshing dish suitable for a summer meal or light lunch.

NUTRITIONAL INFORMATION

Calories 162   Sugars 3g
Protein . . . . .15g   Fat 10g
Carbohydrate . . . .5g   Saturates 2g

25 mins   10 mins

SERVES 4

INGREDIENTS

225 g/8 oz skinless, boned chicken breasts

2 tsp light soy sauce

1 tsp sesame oil

1 tsp sesame seeds

2 tbsp vegetable oil

125 g/4½ oz beansprouts

1 red pepper, seeded and thinly sliced

1 carrot, cut into matchsticks

3 baby corn cobs, sliced

SAUCE

2 tsp rice wine vinegar

1 tbsp light soy sauce

dash of chilli oil

TO GARNISH

snipped chives

carrot matchsticks

1 Place the chicken breasts in a shallow glass dish.

2 Mix together the soy sauce and sesame oil and pour over the chicken. Sprinkle with the sesame seeds and let stand for 20 minutes, turning the chicken over occasionally.

3 Remove the chicken from the marinade and cut the meat into thin slices.

4 Heat the vegetable oil in a preheated wok or large frying pan. Add the chicken and fry for 4–5 minutes, until cooked through and golden brown on both sides. Remove the chicken from the wok with a slotted spoon, set aside and leave to cool.

5 Add the beansprouts, pepper, carrot and baby corn cobs to the wok and stir-fry for 2–3 minutes. Remove from the wok with a slotted spoon, set aside and leave to cool.

6 To make the sauce, mix together the rice wine vinegar, light soy sauce and chilli oil.

7 Arrange the chicken and vegetables together on a serving plate. Spoon the sauce over the salad, garnish with chives and carrot matchsticks and serve.

Speedy Peanut Pan-Fry

Thread egg noodles are the ideal accompaniment to this quick dish because they can be cooked quickly and easily while the stir-fry sizzles.

NUTRITIONAL INFORMATION

Calories . . . . . . .563 Sugars 7g
Protein . . . . .45g Fat 33g
Carbohydrate . . .22g Saturates 7g

5 mins   15 mins

SERVES 4

I N G R E D I E N T S

300 g/10½ oz courgettes

250 g/9 oz baby corn cobs

250 g/9 oz thread egg noodles

2 tbsp corn oil

1 tbsp sesame oil

8 boneless chicken thighs or 4 breasts, thinly sliced

300 g/10½ oz button mushrooms

350 g/12 oz beansprouts

4 tbsp smooth peanut butter

2 tbsp soy sauce

2 tbsp lime or lemon juice

60 g/2 oz roasted peanuts

salt and pepper

coriander, to garnish

1 Using a sharp knife, trim and thinly slice the courgettes and baby corn cobs. Set the vegetables aside until required.

2 Cook the noodles in lightly salted boiling water for 3–4 minutes.

3 Meanwhile, heat the corn oil and sesame oil in a large wok or frying pan and fry the chicken over a fairly high heat for 1 minute.

4 Add the courgettes, corn and mushrooms and stir-fry for 5 minutes.

5 Add the beansprouts, peanut butter, soy sauce, lime or lemon juice and pepper, then cook for a further 2 minutes.

6 Drain the noodles thoroughly. Scatter with the roasted peanuts and serve with the courgette and mushroom mixture. Garnish and serve.

COOK'S TIP

Try serving this stir-fry with rice sticks. These are broad, pale, translucent ribbon noodles made from ground rice.

Chicken & Corn Sauté

Stir-fries are quick and healthy dishes, because you need use only the minimum of fat.

NUTRITIONAL INFORMATION

Calories 280   Sugars 7g
Protein . . . . .31g   Fat 11g
Carbohydrate . . . .9g   Saturates 2g

 5 mins   10 mins

SERVES 4

INGREDIENTS

4 skinless, boneless chicken breasts

250 g/9 oz baby corn cobs

250 g/9 oz mangetout

2 tbsp sunflower oil

1 tbsp sherry vinegar

1 tbsp honey

1 tbsp light soy sauce

1 tbsp sunflower seeds

pepper

rice or Chinese egg noodles, to serve

1 Using a sharp knife, slice the chicken breasts into long, thin strips.

2 Cut the baby corn cobs in half lengthways and top and tail the mangetout.

3 Heat the sunflower oil in a preheated wok or a wide frying pan.

4 Add the chicken and fry over a fairly high heat, stirring, for 1 minute.

5 Add the baby corn cobs and mangetout and stir-fry over a moderate heat for 5–8 minutes, until evenly cooked. The vegetables should still be slightly crunchy.

6 Mix together the sherry vinegar, honey and soy sauce in a small bowl.

7 Stir the vinegar mixture into the pan with the sunflower seeds.

8 Season well with pepper. Cook, stirring, for 1 minute.

9 Serve the dish hot with rice or Chinese egg noodles.

VARIATION

Rice vinegar or balsamic vinegar makes a good substitute for the sherry vinegar.

Spicy Chicken Tortillas

The chicken filling for these easy-to-prepare tortillas has a mild, mellow spicy heat and a fresh salad makes a perfect accompaniment.

NUTRITIONAL INFORMATION

Calories 650   Sugars 15g
Protein . . . . .48g   Fat 31g
Carbohydrate . . .47g   Saturates 10g

10 mins   35 mins

SERVES 4

INGREDIENTS

2 tbsp oil

8 skinless, boneless chicken thighs, sliced

1 onion, chopped

2 garlic cloves, chopped

1 tsp cumin seeds, roughly crushed

2 large dried chillies, sliced

400 g/14 oz canned tomatoes

400 g/14 oz canned red kidney beans, drained

150 ml/¼ pint/5 fl oz chicken stock

2 tsp sugar

salt and pepper

lime wedges, to garnish

TO SERVE

1 large ripe avocado

1 lime

8 soft tortillas

225 ml/8 fl oz thick yogurt

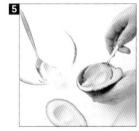

1 Heat the oil in a large frying pan or wok, add the chicken and fry for 3 minutes.

2 Add the chopped onion and fry for 5 minutes, stirring until browned.

3 Add the chopped garlic, cumin and chillies, with their seeds, and cook for about 1 minute.

4 Add the tomatoes, kidney beans, stock, sugar and salt and pepper. Bring to the boil, breaking up the tomatoes. Cover and simmer for 15 minutes. Remove the lid and cook for 5 minutes, stirring occasionally until the sauce has thickened.

5 Halve the avocado, discard the stone and scoop out the flesh onto a plate. Mash the avocado with a fork.

6 Cut half of the lime into 8 thin wedges. Now squeeze the juice from the remaining lime over the mashed avocado.

7 Warm the tortillas according to the directions on the pack. Put two tortillas on each serving plate, fill with the chicken mixture and top with spoonfuls of avocado and yogurt. Garnish the tortillas with lime wedges.

Chicken & Mango Stir-Fry

A colourful, exotic mix of flavours that works surprisingly well, this dish is easy and quick to cook – ideal for a mid-week family meal.

NUTRITIONAL INFORMATION

Calories	0	Sugars	.........0g
Protein	.........0g	Fat	...........0g
Carbohydrate	....0g	Saturates	.......0g

5 mins   12 mins

SERVES 4

INGREDIENTS

6 boneless, skinless chicken thighs

2 tsp grated fresh root ginger

1 garlic clove, crushed

1 small red chilli, seeded

1 large red pepper

4 spring onions

200 g/7 oz mangetout

100 g/3½ oz baby corn cobs

1 large, firm, ripe mango

2 tbsp sunflower oil

1 tbsp light soy sauce

3 tbsp rice wine or sherry

1 tsp sesame oil

salt and pepper

snipped chives, to garnish

1 Cut the chicken into long, thin strips and place in a bowl. Mix together the ginger, garlic and chilli, then stir in to the chicken strips to coat them evenly.

2 Slice the pepper thinly, cutting diagonally. Trim and diagonally slice the spring onions. Cut the mangetouts and corn in half diagonally. Peel the mango, remove the stone and slice thinly.

3 Heat the oil in a large frying pan or wok over a high heat. Add the chicken and stir-fry for 4–5 minutes until just turning golden brown. Add the peppers and stir-fry over a medium heat for 4–5 minutes to soften them.

4 Add the spring onions, mangetout and corn and stir-fry for a further minute.

5 Mix together the soy sauce, rice wine or sherry and sesame oil and stir it into the wok. Add the mango and stir gently for 1 minute to heat thoroughly.

6 Adjust the seasoning with salt and pepper to taste and serve immediately. Garnish with chives.

Thai Stir-Fried Chicken

Coconut adds a creamy texture and delicious flavour to this Thai-style stir-fry, which is spiked with green chilli.

NUTRITIONAL INFORMATION

Calories 184   Sugars 6g
Protein ....24g   Fat 5g
Carbohydrate ....8g   Saturates 2g

15 mins   10 mins

SERVES 4

I N G R E D I E N T S

3 tbsp sesame oil

350 g/12 oz chicken breast, sliced thinly

8 shallots, sliced

2 garlic cloves, finely chopped

2 tsp grated fresh root ginger

1 green chilli, finely chopped

1 each red and green pepper, thinly sliced

3 courgettes, thinly sliced

2 tbsp ground almonds

1 tsp ground cinnamon

1 tbsp oyster sauce

20 g/¾ oz creamed coconut, grated

salt and pepper

1 Heat the sesame oil in a wok, add the chicken, season with salt and pepper, and stir fry for about 4 minutes.

2 Add the shallots, garlic, ginger and chilli and stir-fry for 2 minutes.

3 Add the peppers and courgettes and cook for about 1 minute.

4 Finally, add the remaining ingredients and seasoning. Stir-fry for 1 minute and serve.

COOK'S TIP

Creamed coconut is sold in blocks by supermarkets and oriental stores. It is a useful store-cupboard standby as it adds richness and depth of flavour.

Chicken with Black Bean Sauce

This tasty chicken stir-fry is quick and easy to make and is full of fresh flavours and crunchy vegetables.

NUTRITIONAL INFORMATION

Calories	205	Sugars	.........4g
Protein	........25g	Fat	..........9g
Carbohydrate	....6g	Saturates	.......2g

40 mins   10 mins

SERVES 4

I N G R E D I E N T S

425 g/15 oz chicken breasts, thinly sliced

pinch of salt

pinch of cornflour

2 tbsp oil

1 garlic clove, crushed

1 tbsp black bean sauce

1 each small red and green seeded pepper, seeded and cut into strips

1 red chilli, chopped finely

75 g/2¾ oz mushrooms, sliced

1 onion, chopped

6 spring onions, chopped

salt and pepper

S E A S O N I N G

½ tsp salt

½ tsp sugar

3 tbsp chicken stock

1 tbsp dark soy sauce

2 tbsp beef stock

2 tbsp rice wine

1 tsp cornflour, blended with a little rice wine

1 Put the chicken strips in a bowl. Add a pinch of salt and a pinch of cornflour and cover with water. Leave to stand for 30 minutes.

2 Heat 1 tablespoon of the oil in a wok or deep-sided frying pan and stir-fry the chicken for 4 minutes.

3 Remove the chicken to a warm serving dish and clean the wok.

4 Add the remaining oil to the wok and add the garlic, black bean sauce, green and red peppers, chilli, mushrooms, onion and spring onions. Stir-fry for 2 minutes then return the chicken to the wok.

5 Add the seasoning ingredients, fry for 3 minutes and thicken with a little of the cornflour blend. Serve with fresh noodles.

Chilli Coconut Chicken

This tasty dish combines the flavours of lime, peanut, coconut and chilli.
You'll find coconut cream in most supermarkets or delicatessens.

NUTRITIONAL INFORMATION

Calories	348	Sugars	.........2g
Protein	........36g	Fat	..........21g
Carbohydrate	....3g	Saturates	.......8g

5 mins   15 mins

SERVES 4

INGREDIENTS

150 ml/5 fl oz hot chicken stock

25 g/1 oz creamed coconut

1 tbsp sunflower oil

8 skinless, boneless chicken thighs,
   cut into long, thin strips

1 small red chilli, thinly sliced

4 spring onions, thinly sliced

4 tbsp smooth or crunchy peanut butter

finely grated rind and juice of 1 lime

boiled rice, to serve

TO GARNISH

1 fresh red chilli

spring onion tassel

1 Pour the chicken stock into a measuring jug or small bowl. Crumble the creamed coconut into the chicken stock and stir the mixture until the coconut dissolves.

2 Heat the oil in a preheated wok or large heavy pan.

3 Add the chicken strips and cook, stirring, until the chicken turns a golden colour.

4 Stir in the chopped red chilli and spring onions and cook gently for a few minutes.

5 Add the peanut butter, coconut and chicken stock mixture, lime rind, lime juice and simmer, uncovered, for about 5 minutes, stirring frequently to prevent the mixture sticking to the base of the wok or pan.

6 Transfer the chilli coconut chicken to a warm serving dish, garnish with the red chilli and spring onion tassel and serve with boiled rice.

COOK'S TIP

Serve jasmine rice with this spicy dish. It has a fragrant aroma that is well-suited to the flavours in this dish.

Turkey with Cranberry Glaze

Traditional Christmas ingredients are given a Chinese twist in this stir-fry which containing cranberries, ginger, chestnuts and soy sauce!

NUTRITIONAL INFORMATION

Calories	167	Sugars	........11g
Protein	.........8g	Fat	...........7g
Carbohydrate	...20g	Saturates	.......1g

  5 mins   15 mins

SERVES 4

I N G R E D I E N T S

1 turkey breast

2 tbsp sunflower oil

15 g/½ oz stem ginger

50 g/1¾ oz fresh or frozen cranberries

100 g/3½ oz canned chestnuts

4 tbsp cranberry sauce

3 tbsp light soy sauce

salt and pepper

1 Remove any skin from the turkey breast. Using a sharp knife, thinly slice the turkey breast.

2 Heat the sunflower oil in a large preheated wok or heavy-based frying pan.

3 Add the turkey to the wok and stir-fry for 5 minutes, or until cooked through.

4 Using a sharp knife, finely chop the stem ginger.

5 Add the ginger and the cranberries to the wok or frying pan and stir-fry for 2–3 minutes or until the cranberries have softened.

6 Add the chestnuts, cranberry sauce and soy sauce, season to taste with salt and pepper and allow to bubble for 2–3 minutes.

7 Transfer the turkey stir-fry to warm serving dishes and serve immediately.

COOK'S TIP

It is very important that the wok is very hot before you stir-fry. Test by by holding your hand flat about 7.5 cm/3 inches above the base of the interior – you should be able to feel the heat radiating from it.

Duck in Spicy Sauce

Chinese five-spice powder gives a lovely flavour to this sliced duck, and the chilli adds a little subtle heat.

NUTRITIONAL INFORMATION

Calories	162	Sugars	.........2g
Protein	........20g	Fat	...........7g
Carbohydrate	....3g	Saturates	.......2g

5 mins   25 mins

SERVES 4

INGREDIENTS

1 tbsp vegetable oil

1 tsp grated fresh root ginger

1 garlic clove, crushed

1 fresh red chilli, chopped

350 g/12 oz skinless, boneless duck meat, cut into strips

125 g/4½ oz cauliflower, cut into florets

60 g/2 oz mangetout

60 g/2 oz baby corn cobs, halved lengthways

300 ml/10 fl oz chicken stock

1 tsp Chinese five-spice powder

2 tsp Chinese rice wine or dry sherry

1 tsp cornflour

2 tsp water

1 tsp sesame oil

1 Heat the oil in a wok. Lower the heat slightly, add the ginger, garlic, chilli and duck and stir-fry for 2–3 minutes. Remove from the wok and set aside.

2 Add the vegetables to the wok and stir-fry for 2–3 minutes. Pour off any excess oil from the wok and push the vegetables to one side.

3 Return the duck to the wok and pour in the stock. Sprinkle the Chinese five-spice powder over the top, stir in the wine or sherry and cook over a low heat for 15 minutes, or until the duck is tender.

4 Blend the cornflour with the water to form a paste and stir into the wok with the sesame oil. Bring to the boil, stirring until the sauce has thickened and cleared. Transfer the duck and spicy sauce to a warm serving dish and serve immediately.

COOK'S TIP

Omit the chilli for a milder dish, or seed the chilli before adding it to remove some of the heat.

Duck with Mangoes

Use fresh mangoes in this recipe for a terrific flavour and colour. If they are unavailable, use canned mangoes and rinse them before using.

NUTRITIONAL INFORMATION

Calories 235   Sugars 6g
Protein ....23g   Fat 14g
Carbohydrate ....6g   Saturates 2g

5 mins   35 mins

SERVES 4

INGREDIENTS

2 ripe mangoes

300 ml/10 fl oz chicken stock

2 garlic cloves, crushed

1 tsp grated fresh root ginger

3 tbsp vegetable oil

2 large skinless duck breasts, 225 g/8 oz each

1 tsp wine vinegar

1 tsp light soy sauce

1 leek, sliced

freshly chopped parsley, to garnish

1 Peel the mangoes and cut the flesh from each side of the stones. Cut the flesh into strips.

2 Put half of the mango pieces and the chicken stock in a food processor and process until smooth. Alternatively, press half of the mangoes through a fine sieve and mix with the stock.

3 Rub the garlic and ginger over the duck. Heat the vegetable oil in a preheated wok and cook the duck breasts, turning, until sealed. Reserve the oil in the wok and remove the duck.

4 Place the duck on a rack set over a roasting tin and cook in a preheated oven, at 220°C/425°F/Gas Mark 7, for 20 minutes, until the duck is cooked through.

5 Meanwhile, place the mango and stock mixture in a saucepan and add the wine vinegar and light soy sauce.

6 Bring the mixture in the saucepan to the boil and cook over a high heat, stirring, until reduced by half.

7 Heat the oil reserved in the wok and stir-fry the sliced leek and remaining mango for 1 minute. Remove from the wok, transfer to a serving dish and keep warm until required.

8 Slice the cooked duck breasts and arrange the slices on top of the leek and mango mixture. Pour the sauce over the duck slices, garnish and serve.

Duck with Broccoli & Peppers

This is a colourful dish using different coloured peppers
and broccoli to make it both tasty and appealing to the eye.

NUTRITIONAL INFORMATION

Calories 261   Sugars 3g
Protein . . . . .26g   Fat 13g
Carbohydrate . . . .11g   Saturates 2g

🍲 35 mins   ⏱ 15 mins

SERVES 4

INGREDIENTS

1 egg white

2 tbsp cornflour

450 g/1 lb skinless, boneless duck meat

vegetable oil, for deep-frying

1 red pepper, seeded and diced

1 yellow pepper, seeded and diced

125 g/4½ oz small broccoli florets

1 garlic clove, crushed

2 tbsp light soy sauce

2 tsp Chinese rice wine or dry sherry

1 tsp light brown sugar

125 ml/4 fl oz chicken stock

2 tsp sesame seeds

1 In a mixing bowl, beat together the egg white and cornflour.

2 Using a sharp knife, cut the duck into 2.5-cm/1-inch cubes and stir into the egg white mixture. Leave to stand for 30 minutes.

3 Heat the oil for deep-frying in a preheated wok or heavy-based frying pan until almost smoking.

4 Remove the duck from the egg white mixture, add to the wok and fry in the oil for 4–5 minutes, until crisp. Remove the duck from the oil with a slotted spoon and drain on kitchen paper (paper towels).

5 Add the peppers and broccoli to the wok and fry for 2–3 minutes. Remove with a slotted spoon and let them drain on kitchen paper.

6 Pour all but 2 tablespoons of the oil from the wok and return to the heat. Add the garlic and stir-fry for 30 seconds. Stir in the soy sauce, Chinese rice wine or sherry, sugar and chicken stock and bring to the boil.

7 Stir in the duck and reserved vegetables and cook for 1–2 minutes.

8 Carefully spoon the duck and vegetables on to a warmed serving dish and sprinkle with the sesame seeds. Serve immediately.

Duck with Leek & Cabbage

Duck is a strongly-flavoured meat which benefits from the added citrus peel to counteract this rich taste.

NUTRITIONAL INFORMATION

Calories 192   Sugars 5g
Protein . . . . .26g   Fat 7g
Carbohydrate . . . .6g   Saturates 2g

10 mins   40 mins

SERVES 4

I N G R E D I E N T S

4 duck breasts

350 g/12 oz green cabbage,
   thinly shredded

225 g/8 oz leeks, sliced

finely grated rind of 1 orange

6 tbsp oyster sauce

1 tsp toasted sesame seeds,
   to serve

1 Heat a large wok and dry-fry the duck breasts, with the skin on, for about 5 minutes on each side (you may need to do this in 2 batches).

2 Remove the duck breasts from the wok and transfer to a clean board.

3 Using a sharp knife, cut the duck breasts into thin slices.

4 Remove all but 1 tablespoon of the fat from the duck left in the wok; discard the rest.

5 Using a sharp knife, thinly shred the green cabbage.

6 Add the leeks, green cabbage and orange rind to the wok and stir-fry for about 5 minutes, or until the vegetables have softened.

7 Return the duck to the wok and heat through for 2–3 minutes.

8 Drizzle the oyster sauce over the mixture in the wok, toss well until all the ingredients are combined and then heat through.

9 Scatter the stir-fry with toasted sesame seeds, transfer to a warm serving dish and serve hot.

VARIATION

Use Chinese leaves for a lighter, sweeter flavour instead of the green cabbage, if you prefer.

Fruity Duck Stir-Fry

The pineapple and plum sauce add a sweetness and fruity flavour to this colourful recipe which blends well with the duck.

NUTRITIONAL INFORMATION

Calories 241   Sugars 7g
Protein . . . . .26g   Fat 8g
Carbohydrate . . .16g   Saturates 2g

 5 mins   25 mins

SERVES 4

INGREDIENTS

4 duck breasts

1 tsp Chinese five-spice powder

1 tbsp cornflour

1 tbsp chilli oil

225 g/8 oz baby onions, peeled

2 cloves garlic, crushed

100 g/3½ oz baby corn cobs

175 g/6 oz canned pineapple chunks

6 spring onions, sliced

100 g/3½ oz beansprouts

2 tbsp plum sauce

1 Remove any skin from the duck breasts. Cut the duck into thin slices.

2 Mix the Chinese five-spice powder and the cornflour. Toss the duck in the mixture until well coated.

3 Heat the oil in a preheated wok. Stir-fry the duck for 10 minutes, or until just beginning to crispen around the edges. Remove from wok and set aside.

4 Add the onions and garlic to the wok and stir-fry for 5 minutes, or until softened. Add the baby corn cobs and stir-fry for a further 5 minutes. Add the pineapple, spring onions and beansprouts and stir-fry for 3–4 minutes. Stir in the plum sauce.

5 Return the cooked duck to the wok and toss until well mixed. Transfer to warm serving dishes and serve hot.

COOK'S TIP

Buy pineapple chunks in natural juice rather than syrup for a fresher flavour. If you can only obtain pineapple in syrup, rinse it in cold water and drain thoroughly before using.

Pork Satay Stir-Fry

Satay sauce is easy to make and is one of the best known and loved sauces in Oriental cooking. It is perfect with beef, chicken or pork.

NUTRITIONAL INFORMATION

Calories . . . . . . .506 Sugars 11g
Protein . . . . .31g Fat 36g
Carbohydrate . . .15g Saturates 8g

10 mins   15 mins

SERVES 4

INGREDIENTS

150 g/5½ oz carrots

2 tbsp sunflower oil

350 g/12 oz pork neck fillet, thinly sliced

1 onion, sliced

2 cloves garlic, crushed

1 yellow pepper, seeded and sliced

150 g/5½ oz mangetout

75 g/2¾ oz fine asparagus

chopped salted peanuts, to serve

SATAY SAUCE

6 tbsp crunchy peanut butter

6 tbsp coconut milk

1 tsp chilli flakes

1 clove garlic, crushed

1 tsp tomato purée

COOK'S TIP

Cook the sauce just before serving as it tends to thicken very quickly and will not be spoonable if you cook it too far in advance.

1 Using a sharp knife, slice the carrots into thin sticks.

2 Heat the oil in a large, preheated wok. Add the pork, onion and garlic and stir-fry for 5 minutes or until the lamb is cooked through.

3 Add the carrots, pepper, mangetout and asparagus to the wok and stir-fry for 5 minutes.

4 To make the satay sauce, place the peanut butter, coconut milk, chilli flakes, garlic and tomato purée in a small pan and heat gently, stirring, until well combined. Be careful not to let the sauce stick to the bottom of the pan.

5 Transfer the stir-fry to warm serving plates. Spoon the satay sauce over the stir-fry and scatter with chopped peanuts. Serve immediately.

Spicy Pork & Rice

Pork is coated in a spicy mixture before being fried until crisp in this recipe and then stirred into a delicious egg rice for a very filling meal.

NUTRITIONAL INFORMATION

Calories ....599 Sugars 11g
Protein ....30g Fat 22g
Carbohydrate ...76g Saturates 7g

 10 mins   35 mins

SERVES 4

I N G R E D I E N T S

275 g/9½ oz long-grain
    white rice

600 ml/1 pint cold water

350 g/12 oz pork fillet

2 tsp Chinese five-spice powder

4 tbsp cornflour

3 large eggs, beaten

25 g/1 oz demerara sugar

2 tbsp sunflower oil

1 onion

2 cloves garlic, crushed

100 g/3½ oz carrots, diced

1 red pepper, seeded and diced

100 g/3½ oz peas

2 tbsp butter

salt and pepper

1 Rinse the rice under cold running water. Place the rice in a large saucepan, add the cold water and a pinch of salt. Bring to the boil, cover, then reduce the heat and leave to simmer for about 9 minutes, or until all of the liquid has been absorbed and the rice is tender.

2 Meanwhile, slice the pork fillet into very thin even-sized pieces, using a sharp knife or meat cleaver. Set the pork strips aside until required.

3 Whisk together the Chinese five-spice powder, cornflour, 1 egg and the demerara sugar. Toss the pork in the mixture until coated.

4 Heat the sunflower oil in a large wok or frying pan. Add the pork and cook over a high heat until the pork is cooked through and crispy. Remove the pork from the wok with a slotted spoon and set aside until required.

5 Using a sharp knife, cut the onion into dice.

6 Add the onion, garlic, carrots, pepper and peas to the wok and stir-fry for 5 minutes.

7 Return the pork to the wok together with the cooked rice and stir-fry for 5 minutes.

8 Heat the butter in a frying pan. Add the remaining beaten eggs and cook until set. Turn out on to a clean board and slice thinly. Toss the strips of egg into the rice mixture and serve immediately.

Spicy Pork Balls

These small meatballs are packed with flavour and cooked in a crunchy tomato sauce for a very quick dish.

NUTRITIONAL INFORMATION

Calories ....299 Sugars 3g
Protein ....28g Fat 15g
Carbohydrate ...14g Saturates 4g

10 mins   40 mins

SERVES 4

INGREDIENTS

450 g/1 lb minced pork

2 shallots, finely chopped

2 cloves garlic, crushed

1 tsp cumin seeds

½ tsp chilli powder

25 g/1 oz wholemeal breadcrumbs

1 cgg, beaten

2 tbsp sunflower oil

400 g/14 oz canned chopped tomatoes, flavoured with chilli

2 tbsp soy sauce

200 g/7 oz canned water chestnuts, drained

3 tbsp chopped fresh coriander

COOK'S TIP

Add a few teaspoons of chilli sauce to a tin of chopped tomatoes, if you can't find the flavoured variety.

1 Place the minced pork in a large mixing bowl. Add the shallots, garlic, cumin seeds, chilli powder, breadcrumbs and beaten egg and mix together well.

2 Form the mixture into balls between the palms of your hands.

3 Heat the oil in a large preheated wok. Add the pork balls and stir-fry, in batches, over a high heat for about 5 minutes or until sealed on all sides.

4 Add the tomatoes, soy sauce and water chestnuts and bring to the boil. Return the pork balls to the wok, reduce the heat and leave to simmer for 15 minutes.

5 Scatter with chopped fresh coriander and serve hot.

Sweet & Sour Pork

In this classic Chinese dish, tender pork pieces are fried and served in a crunchy sauce. This dish is perfect served with plain rice.

NUTRITIONAL INFORMATION

Calories	357	Sugars	........25g
Protein	........28g	Fat	..........14g
Carbohydrate	...30g	Saturates	.......4g

🥟 10 mins   🕐 20 mins

SERVES 4

INGREDIENTS

450 g/1 lb pork fillet

2 tbsp sunflower oil

225 g/8 oz courgettes

1 red onion, cut into matchsticks

2 cloves garlic, crushed

225 g/8 oz carrots, cut into thin sticks

1 red pepper, seeded and sliced

100 g/3½ oz baby corn cobs

100 g/3½ oz button mushrooms, halved

175 g/6 oz fresh pineapple, cubed

100 g/3½ oz beansprouts

150 ml/5 fl oz pineapple juice

1 tbsp cornflour

2 tbsp soy sauce

3 tbsp tomato ketchup

1 tbsp white wine vinegar

1 tbsp clear honey

COOK'S TIP

If you prefer a crisper coating, toss the pork in a mixture of cornflour and egg white and deep fry in the wok in step 2.

1 Using a sharp knife, thinly slice the pork fillet into even-sized pieces.

2 Heat the sunflower oil in a large preheated wok. Add the pork to the wok and stir-fry for 10 minutes, or until the pork is completely cooked through and beginning to turn crispy at the edges.

3 Meanwhile, cut the courgettes into thin sticks.

4 Add the onion, garlic, carrots, courgettes, pepper, corn cobs and mushrooms to the wok and stir-fry for a further 5 minutes.

5 Add the pineapple cubes and beansprouts to the wok and stir-fry for 2 minutes.

6 Mix together the pineapple juice, cornflour, soy sauce, tomato ketchup, white wine vinegar and honey.

7 Pour the sweet and sour mixture into the wok and cook over a high heat, tossing frequently, until the juices thicken. Transfer the sweet and sour pork to serving bowls and serve hot.

Twice-Cooked Pork

Twice-cooked is a popular way of cooking meat in China. The meat is first boiled to tenderize it, then cut into strips or slices and stir-fried.

NUTRITIONAL INFORMATION

Calories 199   Sugars 3g
Protein . . . . .15g   Fat 13g
Carbohydrate . . . .4g   Saturates 3g

3¼ hrs   30 mins

SERVES 4

I N G R E D I E N T S

250–300 g/9–10½ oz shoulder or leg of pork, in one piece

1 small green pepper, cored and seeded

1 small red pepper, cored and seeded

125 g/4½ oz canned sliced bamboo shoots, rinsed and drained

3 tbsp vegetable oil

1 spring onion, cut into short sections

1 tsp salt

½ tsp sugar

1 tbsp light soy sauce

1 tsp chilli bean sauce or freshly minced chilli

1 tsp rice wine or dry sherry

a few drops of sesame oil

1 Immerse the pork in a pot of boiling water to cover. Return to the boil and skim the surface. Reduce the heat, cover and simmer for 15–20 minutes. Turn off the heat and leave the pork in the water to cool for at least 2–3 hours.

2 Remove the pork and drain well. Trim off any excess fat, then cut into small, thin slices. Cut the peppers into pieces about the same size as the pork and the sliced bamboo shoots.

3 Heat the vegetable oil in a preheated wok and add the vegetables together with the spring onion. Stir-fry for about 1 minute.

4 Add the pork, followed by the salt, sugar, light soy sauce, chilli bean sauce and wine or sherry. Blend well and continue stirring for another minute. Transfer the stir-fry to a warm serving dish, sprinkle with sesame oil and serve.

COOK'S TIP

For ease of handling, buy a boned piece of meat, and roll into a compact shape. Tie securely with string before placing in the boiling water.

Pork with Mooli

Pork and mooli are a perfect combination, especially with the added heat of the sweet chilli sauce.

NUTRITIONAL INFORMATION

Calories . . . . . . .280 Sugars 1g
Protein . . . . .25g Fat 19g
Carbohydrate . . . .2g Saturates 4g

  10 mins   15 mins

SERVES 4

I N G R E D I E N T S

4 tbsp vegetable oil

450 g/1 lb pork tenderloin

1 aubergine

225 g/8 oz mooli

2 cloves garlic, crushed

3 tbsp soy sauce

2 tbsp sweet chilli sauce

boiled rice or noodles, to serve

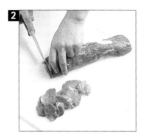

1 Heat 2 tablespoons of the vegetable oil in a large preheated wok or frying pan.

2 Using a sharp knife, thinly slice the pork into even-size pieces.

3 Add the slices of pork to the wok or frying pan and stir-fry for about 5 minutes.

4 Using a sharp knife, trim and dice the aubergine. Peel and slice the mooli.

5 Add the remaining vegetable oil to the wok.

6 Add the diced aubergine to the wok or frying pan together with the garlic and stir-fry for 5 minutes.

7 Add the mooli to the wok and stir-fry for about 2 minutes.

8 Stir the soy sauce and sweet chilli sauce into the mixture in the wok and cook until heated through.

9 Transfer the pork and mooli to warm serving bowls and serve immediately with boiled rice or noodles.

COOK'S TIP

Mooli are long white vegetables common in Chinese cooking. Usually grated, they have a milder flavour than red radish. They are generally available in most large supermarkets.

Pork Fry with Vegetables

This is a very simple dish which lends itself to almost any combination of vegetables that you have to hand.

NUTRITIONAL INFORMATION

Calories 216   Sugars 3g
Protein . . . . .19g   Fat 12g
Carbohydrate . . . .5g   Saturates 3g

5 mins   15 mins

SERVES 4

I N G R E D I E N T S

350 g/12 oz lean pork fillet

2 tbsp vegetable oil

2 garlic cloves, crushed

1-cm/½-inch piece fresh root ginger, cut into slivers

1 carrot, cut into thin strips

1 red pepper, seeded and diced

1 fennel bulb, sliced

25 g/1 oz water chestnuts, halved

75 g/2 ¾ oz beansprouts

2 tbsp Chinese rice wine

300 ml/10 fl oz pork or chicken stock

pinch of dark brown sugar

1 tsp cornflour

2 tsp water

1 Cut the pork into thin slices. Heat the oil in a preheated wok. Add the garlic, ginger and pork and stir-fry for 1–2 minutes, until the meat is sealed.

2 Add the carrot, pepper, fennel and water chestnuts to the wok and stir-fry for about 2–3 minutes.

3 Add the beansprouts and stir-fry for 1 minute. Remove the pork and vegetables from the wok and keep warm.

4 Add the Chinese rice wine, pork or chicken stock and sugar to the wok. Blend the cornflour to a smooth paste with the water and stir it into the sauce. Bring to the boil, stirring constantly until thickened and clear.

5 Return the meat and vegetables to the wok and cook for 1–2 minutes, until heated through and coated with the sauce. Serve immediately.

VARIATION

Use dry sherry instead of the Chinese rice wine if you have difficulty obtaining it.

Sweet & Sour Pork

This dish is a popular choice in Western diets, and must be one of the best known of Chinese recipes.

NUTRITIONAL INFORMATION

Calories 471   Sugars 47g
Protein . . . . .16g   Fat 13g
Carbohydrate . . .77g   Saturates 2g

10 mins   20 mins

SERVES 4

I N G R E D I E N T S

150 ml/5 fl oz vegetable oil, for
　deep-frying

225 g/8 oz pork fillet, cut into 1-cm/½-inch
　cubes

1 onion, sliced

1 green pepper, seeded and sliced

225 g/8 oz pineapple pieces

1 small carrot, cut into thin strips

25 g/1 oz canned bamboo shoots,
　drained, rinsed and halved

rice or noodles, to serve

B A T T E R

125 g/4½ oz plain flour

1 tbsp cornflour

1½ tsp baking powder

1 tbsp vegetable oil

S A U C E

125 g/4½ oz light brown sugar

2 tbsp cornflour

125 ml/4 fl oz white wine vinegar

2 garlic cloves, crushed

4 tbsp tomato purée

6 tbsp pineapple juice

1 To make the batter, sift the plain flour into a mixing bowl, together with the cornflour and baking powder. Add the vegetable oil and stir in enough water to make a thick, smooth batter (about 175 ml/6 fl oz).

2 Pour the vegetable oil into a preheated wok and heat until almost smoking.

3 Dip the cubes of pork into the batter, and cook in the hot oil, in batches, until the pork is cooked through. Remove the pork from the wok with a slotted spoon and drain on kitchen paper. Set aside and keep warm until required.

4 Drain all but 1 tablespoon of oil from the wok and return it to the heat. Add the onion, pepper, pineapple pieces, carrot and bamboo shoots and stir-fry for 1–2 minutes. Remove from the wok with a slotted spoon and set aside.

5 Mix all of the sauce ingredients together and pour into the wok. Bring to the boil, stirring until thickened and clear. Cook for 1 minute, then return the pork and vegetables to the wok. Cook for a further 1–2 minutes, then transfer to a serving plate and serve with rice or noodles.

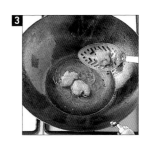

Pork with Plums

Plum sauce is often used in Chinese cooking with duck or rich, fattier meat to counteract the flavour

NUTRITIONAL INFORMATION

Calories 281   Sugars 6g
Protein . . . . .25g   Fat 14g
Carbohydrate . . .10g   Saturates 4g

🍧 35 mins   🕐 25 mins

SERVES 4

INGREDIENTS

450 g/1 lb pork fillet

1 tbsp cornflour

2 tbsp light soy sauce

2 tbsp Chinese rice wine

4 tsp light brown sugar

pinch of ground cinnamon

5 tsp vegetable oil

2 garlic cloves, crushed

2 spring onions, chopped

4 tbsp plum sauce

1 tbsp hoisin sauce

150 ml/5 fl oz water

dash of chilli sauce

TO GARNISH

fried plum quarters

spring onions

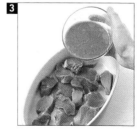  

1 Cut the pork fillet into thin slices.

2 Combine the cornflour, soy sauce, rice wine, sugar and cinnamon in a small bowl.

3 Place the pork in a shallow dish and pour the cornflour mixture over it. Toss the meat in the marinade until it is completely coated. Cover and leave to marinate for at least 30 minutes.

4 Remove the pork from the dish, reserving the marinade.

5 Heat the oil in a preheated wok or large frying pan. Add the pork and stir-fry for 3–4 minutes, until a light golden colour.

6 Stir in the garlic, spring onions, plum sauce, hoisin sauce, water and chilli sauce. Bring the sauce to the boil. Reduce the heat, cover and leave to simmer for 8–10 minutes, or until the pork is cooked through and tender.

7 Stir in the reserved marinade and cook, stirring, for about 5 minutes.

8 Transfer the pork stir-fry to a warm serving dish and garnish with fried plum quarters and spring onions. Serve immediately.

Deep-Fried Pork Fritters

Small pieces of pork are coated in a light batter and deep-fried in this recipe – they are delicious dipped in a soy and honey sauce.

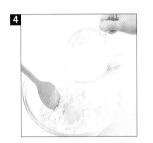

NUTRITIONAL INFORMATION

Calories 528   Sugars 12g
Protein . . . . .32g   Fat 22g
Carbohydrate . . .52g   Saturates 6g

10 mins   15 mins

SERVES 4

I N G R E D I E N T S

450 g/1 lb pork fillet

2 tbsp peanut oil

200 g/7 oz plain flour

2 tsp baking powder

1 egg, beaten

225 ml/8 fl oz milk

pinch of chilli powder

vegetable oil, for deep-frying

S A U C E :

2 tbsp dark soy sauce

3 tbsp clear honey

1 tbsp wine vinegar

1 tbsp chopped chives

1 tbsp tomato purée

chives, to garnish

1 Using a sharp knife, cut the pork into 2.5-cm/1-inch cubes.

2 Heat the peanut oil in a preheated wok. Add the pork to the wok and stir-fry for 2–3 minutes, until sealed.

3 Remove the pork with a slotted spoon and set aside until required.

4 Sift the flour and baking powder into a mixing bowl and make a well in the centre. Gradually beat in the egg, milk and chilli powder to make a thick batter.

5 Heat the oil for deep-frying in a wok until almost smoking, then reduce the heat slightly.

6 Toss the pork pieces in the batter to coat thoroughly. Add the pork to the wok and deep-fry until golden brown and cooked through. Remove with a slotted spoon and drain well on kitchen paper.

7 Meanwhile, mix together the soy sauce, honey, wine vinegar, chives and tomato purée and spoon into a small serving bowl.

8 Transfer the pork fritters to serving dishes, garnish with chives and serve with the sauce.

Spicy Fried Minced Pork

A warmly spiced dish, this is ideal for a quick family meal. Just cook fine egg noodles for an accompaniment while the meat sizzles.

NUTRITIONAL INFORMATION

Calories 278	Sugars 4g
Protein 28g	Fat 16
Carbohydrate 7g	Saturates 4g

 5 mins 15 mins

SERVES 4

INGREDIENTS

2 garlic cloves

3 shallots

2 tsp finely chopped fresh root ginger

2 tbsp sunflower oil

500 g/1 lb 2 oz lean minced pork

2 tbsp fish sauce

1 tbsp dark soy sauce

1 tbsp red curry paste

4 dried kaffir lime leaves, crumbled

4 plum tomatoes, chopped

3 tbsp fresh coriander, chopped

salt and pepper

boiled fine egg noodles, to serve

TO GARNISH

fresh coriander sprigs

1 Peel and finely chop the garlic and shallots. Heat the oil in a wok over a medium heat. Add the garlic, shallots and ginger and stir-fry for about 2 minutes. Stir in the pork and continue stir-frying until golden brown.

2 Stir in the fish sauce, soy sauce, curry paste and lime leaves, and stir-fry for a further 1–2 minutes over a high heat.

3 Add the tomatoes and cook for a further 5–6 minutes, stirring occasionally.

4 Stir in the chopped coriander and season to taste with salt and pepper. Serve hot, spooned on to boiled fine egg noodles, garnished with coriander sprigs.

COOK'S TIP

Dried kaffir lime leaves are a useful store-cupboard ingredient as they can be crumbled easily straight into quick dishes such as this. If you prefer to use fresh kaffir lime leaves, shred them finely and add to the dish.

Stir-Fried Pork and Corn

A speedy dish, typical of Thai street food, though sweetcorn was introduced in Thailand relatively recently.

NUTRITIONAL INFORMATION

Calories	336	Sugars	........49g
Protein	........30g	Fat	..........16g
Carbohydrate	...18g	Saturates	.......4g

 2 mins   8–10 mins

SERVES 4

I N G R E D I E N T S

2 tbsp vegetable oil

500 g/1 lb 2 oz lean boneless pork, cut in thin strips

1 garlic clove, chopped

350 g/12 oz fresh sweetcorn kernels

200 g/7 oz green beans, cut into short lengths

2 spring onions, chopped

1 small red chilli, chopped

1 tsp sugar

1 tbsp light soy sauce

3 tbsp chopped fresh coriander

egg noodles or boiled rice, to serve

COOK'S TIP

In Thailand, long beans would be used for dishes such as this, but you can substitute green beans, which are more easily available. But look out for long beans in Oriental food stores – they are like long string beans and have a similar flavour, but their texture is crisp, and they cook more quickly.

1 Heat the oil in a large frying pan or wok and stir-fry the pork quickly over a high heat until lightly browned.

2 Stir in the garlic, sweetcorn, beans, spring onions and chilli, and continue stir-frying over a high heat for 2–3 minutes, until the vegetables are heated through and almost tender.

3 Stir in the sugar and soy sauce and stir-fry for a further 30 seconds, over a high heat.

4 Sprinkle with the coriander and serve immediately either with egg noodles or rice.

Lamb with Satay Sauce

This recipe demonstrates the classic serving of lamb satay – lamb marinated in chilli and coconut and threaded on to wooden skewers.

NUTRITIONAL INFORMATION

Calories 501   Sugars 6g
Protein . . . . .34g   Fat 37g
Carbohydrate . . . .9g   Saturates 10g

 35 mins   25 mins

SERVES 4

I N G R E D I E N T S

450 g/1 lb lamb loin fillet

1 tbsp mild curry paste

150 ml/5 fl oz coconut milk

2 cloves garlic, crushed

½ tsp chilli powder

½ tsp cumin

S A T A Y   S A U C E

1 tbsp corn oil

1 onion, diced

6 tbsp crunchy peanut butter

1 tsp tomato purée

1 tsp fresh lime juice

100 ml/3½ fl oz cold water

1 Using a sharp knife, thinly slice the lamb and place in a large dish.

2 Mix together the curry paste, coconut milk, garlic, chilli powder and cumin in a bowl. Pour over the lamb, toss well, cover and marinate for 30 minutes.

3 To make the satay sauce. Heat the oil in a large wok and stir-fry the onion for 5 minutes, then reduce the heat and cook for 5 minutes.

4 Stir in the peanut butter, tomato purée, lime juice and water.

5 Thread the lamb on to wooden skewers, reserving the marinade.

6 Grill the lamb skewers under a hot grill for 6–8 minutes, turning once.

7 Add the reserved marinade to the wok, bring to the boil and cook for 5 minutes. Serve the lamb skewers with the satay sauce.

COOK'S TIP

Soak the wooden skewers in cold water for 30 minutes before grilling to prevent the skewers from burning.

Lamb with Black Bean Sauce

Red onions add great colour to recipes and are perfect in this dish, combining with the colours of the peppers.

NUTRITIONAL INFORMATION

Calories . . . . . . .328 Sugars 5g
Protein . . . . .26g Fat 20g
Carbohydrate . . .12g Saturates 6g

10 mins   15 mins

SERVES 4

I N G R E D I E N T S

450 g/1 lb lamb neck fillet or boneless
    leg of lamb chops

1 egg white, lightly beaten

4 tbsp cornflour

1 tsp Chinese five-spice powder

3 tbsp sunflower oil

1 red onion

1 red pepper, seeded
    and sliced

1 green pepper, seeded
    and sliced

1 yellow or orange pepper, seeded
    and sliced

5 tbsp black bean sauce

boiled rice or noodles, to serve

1 Using a sharp knife, slice the lamb into very thin strips.

2 Mix together the egg white, cornflour and Chinese five-spice powder. Toss the lamb strips in the mixture until evenly coated.

3 Heat the oil in a wok and stir-fry the lamb over a high heat for 5 minutes or until it crispens around the edges.

4 Slice the red onion. Add the onion and pepper slices to the wok and stir-fry for 5–6 minutes, or until the vegetables just begin to soften.

5 Stir the black bean sauce into the mixture in the wok and heat through.

6 Transfer the lamb and sauce to warm serving plates and serve hot with freshly boiled rice or noodles.

COOK'S TIP

Take care when frying the lamb as the cornflour mixture may cause it to stick to the wok. Move the lamb around the wok constantly during stir-frying.

Oyster Sauce Lamb

This really is a speedy dish, lamb leg steaks being perfect for the short cooking time.

NUTRITIONAL INFORMATION

Calories 243   Sugars 0.4g
Protein ....26g   Fat 14
Carbohydrate ....3g   Saturates 5g

 5 mins   10 mins

SERVES 4

INGREDIENTS

450 g/1 lb lamb leg steaks

1 tsp ground Szechuan peppercorns

1 tbsp groundnut oil

2 cloves garlic, crushed

8 spring onions, sliced

2 tbsp dark soy sauce

6 tbsp oyster sauce

175 g/6 oz Chinese leaves

prawn crackers, to serve (optional)

1 Using a sharp knife, remove any excess fat from the lamb. Slice the lamb thinly.

2 Sprinkle the ground Szechuan peppercorns over the meat and toss together until well combined.

3 Heat the groundnut oil in a preheated wok or large heavy-based frying pan.

4 Add the lamb to the wok or frying pan and stir-fry for about 5 minutes.

5 Meanwhile, crush the garlic cloves in a pestle and mortar and slice the spring onions. Add the garlic and spring onions to the wok together with the dark soy sauce and stir-fry for 2 minutes.

6 Add the oyster sauce and Chinese leaves and stir-fry for a further 2 minutes, or until the leaves have wilted and the juices are bubbling.

7 Transfer the stir-fry to warm serving bowls and serve hot with prawn crackers (if using).

COOK'S TIP

Oyster sauce is made from oysters which are cooked in brine and soy sauce. Sold in bottles, it will keep in the refrigerator for months.

Garlic Lamb with Soy Sauce

The long marinating time allows the garlic to really penetrate the meat, creating a much more flavourful dish.

NUTRITIONAL INFORMATION

Calories 309   Sugars 0.2g
Protein . . . . .25g   Fat 21g
Carbohydrate . . . .3g   Saturates 9g

  1¼ hrs   15 mins

SERVES 4

I N G R E D I E N T S

450 g/1 lb lamb loin fillet

2 cloves garlic

2 tbsp groundnut oil

3 tbsp dry sherry or rice wine

3 tbsp dark soy sauce

1 tsp cornflour

2 tbsp cold water

2 tbsp butter

1 Using a sharp knife, make small slits in the flesh of the lamb.

2 Carefully peel the cloves of garlic and cut them into slices, using a sharp knife.

3 Push the slices of garlic into the slits in the lamb. Place the garlic-infused lamb in a shallow dish.

4 In a small bowl, mix together 1 tablespoon each of the groundnut oil, dry sherry or rice wine and dark soy sauce. Drizzle this mixture over the lamb, cover with clingfilm and leave to marinate for at least 1 hour, preferably overnight.

5 Using a sharp knife or meat cleaver, thinly slice the marinated lamb.

6 Heat the remaining oil in a preheated wok or large frying pan. Add the marinated lamb and stir-fry for 5 minutes.

7 Add the marinade juices and the remaining sherry and soy sauce to the wok and allow the juices to bubble for 5 minutes.

8 Blend the cornflour to a smooth paste with the cold water. Add the cornflour mixture to the wok and cook, stirring occasionally, until the juices start to thicken.

9 Cut the butter into small pieces. Add the butter to the wok or frying pan and stir until the butter melts. Transfer the lamb to serving dishes and serve immediately.

COOK'S TIP

Adding the butter at the end of the recipe gives a glossy, rich sauce which is ideal with the lamb.

Lamb with Lime Leaves

Groundnut oil is used here for flavour – it is a common oil used for stir-frying.

NUTRITIONAL INFORMATION

Calories ....302 Sugars 15g
Protein ....24g Fat 16g
Carbohydrate ...17g Saturates 6g

5 mins   35 mins

SERVES 4

INGREDIENTS

2 red chillies

2 tbsp groundnut oil

2 cloves garlic, crushed

4 shallots, chopped

2 stalks lemon grass, sliced

6 lime leaves

1 tbsp tamarind paste

25 g/1 oz palm sugar

450 g/1 lb lean lamb (leg or loin fillet)

600 ml/1 pint coconut milk

175 g/6 oz cherry tomatoes, halved

1 tbsp chopped fresh coriander

fragrant rice, to serve

1 Using a sharp knife, seed and very finely chop the red chillies.

2 Heat the oil in a large preheated wok or frying pan.

3 Add the garlic, shallots, lemon grass, lime leaves, tamarind paste, palm sugar and chillies to the wok and stir-fry for about 2 minutes.

4 Using a sharp knife, cut the lamb into thin strips or cubes. Add the lamb to the wok or frying pan and stir-fry for about 5 minutes, tossing well so that the lamb is evenly coated in the spice mixture.

5 Pour the coconut milk into the wok and bring to the boil. Reduce the heat and leave to simmer for 20 minutes.

6 Add the tomatoes and coriander to the wok and leave to simmer for 5 minutes. Transfer to serving plates and serve hot with fragrant rice.

COOK'S TIP

When buying fresh coriander, look for bright green, unwilted leaves. To store it, wash and dry the leaves, leaving them on the stem. Wrap the leaves in damp kitchen paper and keep them in a plastic bag in the refrigerator.

Stir-Fried Lamb with Orange

Oranges and lamb are a great combination because the citrus flavour offsets the fattier, fuller flavour of the lamb.

NUTRITIONAL INFORMATION

Calories 209   Sugars 4g
Protein . . . . .25g   Fat 10g
Carbohydrate . . . .5g   Saturates 5g

5 mins   30 mins

SERVES 4

INGREDIENTS

450 g/1 lb minced lamb

2 cloves garlic, crushed

1 tsp cumin seeds

1 tsp ground coriander

1 red onion, sliced

finely grated rind and juice of 1 orange

2 tbsp soy sauce

1 orange, peeled and segmented

salt and pepper

snipped fresh chives, to garnish

1 Heat a wok or large, heavy-based frying pan, without adding any oil.

2 Add the minced lamb to the wok. Dry fry the minced lamb for 5 minutes, or until the lamb is evenly browned. Drain away any excess fat from the wok.

3 Add the garlic, cumin seeds, coriander and red onion to the wok and stir-fry for a further 5 minutes.

4 Stir in the finely grated orange rind and juice and the soy sauce, mixing until thoroughly combined. Cover, reduce the heat and leave to simmer, stirring occasionally, for 15 minutes.

5 Remove the lid, increase the heat and add the orange segments. Stir to mix.

6 Season with salt and pepper to taste and heat through for a further 2–3 minutes.

7 Transfer the stir-fry to warm serving plates and garnish with snipped fresh chives. Serve immediately.

COOK'S TIP

If you wish to serve wine with your meal, try light, dry white wines and lighter Burgundy-style red wines as they blend well with Oriental food.

Lamb's Liver with Peppers

This is a richly flavoured dish which is great served with plain rice or noodles to soak up the delicious juices.

NUTRITIONAL INFORMATION

Calories 369   Sugars 5g
Protein . . . . .25g   Fat 18g
Carbohydrate . . .27g   Saturates 4g

  15 mins   10 mins

SERVES 4

INGREDIENTS

450 g/1 lb lamb's liver

2 tbsp cornflour

2 tbsp groundnut oil

1 onion, sliced

2 cloves garlic, crushed

2 green peppers, seeded and sliced

2 tbsp tomato purée

3 tbsp dry sherry

1 tbsp cornflour

2 tbsp soy sauce

1 Using a sharp knife, trim any excess fat from the lamb's liver. Slice the lamb's liver into thin strips.

2 Place the cornflour in a large bowl.

3 Add the strips of lamb's liver to the cornflour and toss well until coated evenly all over.

4 Heat the groundnut oil in a large preheated wok.

5 Add the lamb's liver, onion, garlic and green pepper to the wok and stir-fry for 6–7 minutes, or until the lamb's liver is just cooked through and the vegetables are tender.

6 Mix together the tomato purée, sherry, cornflour and soy sauce. Stir the mixture into the wok and cook for a further 2 minutes or until the juices have thickened. Transfer to warm serving bowls and serve immediately.

VARIATION

Use rice wine instead of the sherry for a really authentic Oriental flavour. Chinese rice wine is made from glutinous rice and is also known as 'yellow wine' because of it's golden colour. The best variety, from south-east China, is called Shao Hsing or Shaoxing.

Lamb Meatballs

These small meatballs are made with minced lamb and flavoured with chilli, garlic, parsley and Chinese curry powder.

NUTRITIONAL INFORMATION

Calories	320	Sugars	.........1g
Protein	........28g	Fat	..........20g
Carbohydrate	....8g	Saturates	.......6g

🍦 5 mins   🕐 20 mins

SERVES 4

I N G R E D I E N T S

450 g/1 lb minced lamb

3 garlic cloves, crushed

2 spring onions, finely chopped

½ tsp chilli powder

1 tsp Chinese curry powder

1 tbsp chopped fresh parsley

25 g/1 oz fresh white breadcrumbs

1 egg, beaten

3 tbsp vegetable oil

125 g/4½ oz Chinese leaves, shredded

1 leek, sliced

1 tbsp cornflour

2 tbsp water

300 ml/10 fl oz lamb stock

1 tbsp dark soy sauce

shredded leek, to garnish

1 Mix the lamb, garlic, spring onions, chilli powder, Chinese curry powder, parsley and breadcrumbs together in a bowl. Work the egg into the mixture, bringing it together to form a firm mixture. Roll into 16 small, even-sized balls.

2 Heat the oil in a preheated wok. Add the Chinese leaves and leek and stir-fry for 1 minute. Remove from the wok with a slotted spoon and set aside.

3 Add the meatballs to the wok and fry in batches, turning gently, for 3–4 minutes, or until golden brown all over.

4 Mix the cornflour and water together to form a smooth paste and set aside. Pour the lamb stock and soy sauce into the wok and cook for 2–3 minutes. Stir in the cornflour paste. Bring to the boil and cook, stirring constantly, until the sauce is thickened and clear.

5 Return the Chinese leaves and leek to the wok and cook for 1 minute, until heated through. Arrange the Chinese leaves and leek on a warm serving dish, top with the meatballs, garnish with shredded leek and serve immediately.

VARIATION

Use minced pork or beef instead of the lamb as an alternative.

Lamb with Mushroom Sauce

Use a lean cut of lamb, such as fillet, for this recipe for both flavour and tenderness.

NUTRITIONAL INFORMATION

Calories 219   Sugars 1g
Protein . . . . .21g   Fat 14g
Carbohydrate . . . .4g   Saturates 4g

🕒 5 mins   🕐 10 mins

SERVES 4

I N G R E D I E N T S

350 g/12 oz lean boneless lamb, such as fillet or loin

2 tbsp vegetable oil

3 garlic cloves, crushed

1 leek, sliced

175 g/6 oz large mushrooms, sliced

½ tsp sesame oil

fresh red chillies, to garnish

S A U C E

1 tsp cornflour

4 tbsp light soy sauce

3 tbsp Chinese rice wine or dry sherry

3 tbsp water

½ tsp chilli sauce

1 Using a sharp knife or meat cleaver, cut the lamb into thin strips.

2 Heat the vegetable oil in a preheated wok or large frying pan.

3 Add the lamb strips, garlic and leek and stir-fry for about 2–3 minutes.

4 To make the sauce, mix together the cornflour, soy sauce, Chinese rice wine or dry sherry, water and chilli sauce and set aside.

5 Add the sliced mushrooms to the wok and stir-fry for 1 minute.

6 Stir in the prepared sauce and cook for 2–3 minutes, or until the lamb is cooked through and tender.

7 Sprinkle the sesame oil over the top and transfer the lamb and mushrooms to a warm serving dish. Garnish with red chillies and serve immediately.

VARIATION

The lamb can be replaced with lean steak or pork fillet in this classic recipe from Beijing. You could also use 2–3 spring onions, 1 shallot or 1 small onion instead of the leek, if you prefer.

Red Lamb Curry

This curry uses the typically red-hot chilli flavour of Thai red curry paste, made with dried red chillies, to give it a warm, russet-red colour.

NUTRITIONAL INFORMATION

Calories . . . . . . .363 Sugars 11g
Protein . . . . .29g Fat 19g
Carbohydrate . . .21g Saturates 6g

5 mins   35–40 mins

SERVES 4

I N G R E D I E N T S

500 g/1 lb 2 oz boneless lean

leg of lamb

2 tbsp vegetable oil

1 large onion, sliced

2 garlic cloves, crushed

2 tbsp red curry paste

150 ml/5 fl oz coconut milk

1 tbsp soft light brown sugar

1 large red pepper, seeded and thickly
    sliced

120 ml/4 fl oz lamb or beef stock

1 tbsp fish sauce

2 tbsp lime juice

227 g/8 oz can water chestnuts, drained

2 tbsp fresh coriander, chopped

2 tbsp fresh basil, chopped

salt and pepper

boiled jasmine rice, to serve

fresh basil leaves, to garnish

1 Trim the meat and cut it into 3-cm/1¼-inch cubes. Heat the oil in a large frying pan or wok over a high heat and stir-fry the onion and garlic for 2–3 minutes to soften. Add the meat and fry the mixture quickly until lightly browned.

2 Stir in the curry paste and cook for a few seconds, then add the coconut milk and sugar and bring to the boil. Reduce the heat and simmer for 15 minutes, stirring occasionally.

3 Stir in the red pepper, stock, fish sauce and lime juice, cover and continue simmering for a further 15 minutes, or until the meat is tender.

4 Add the water chestnuts, coriander and basil, adjust the seasoning to taste. Serve with jasmine rice garnished with fresh basil leaves.

COOK'S TIP

This curry can also be made with other lean red meats. Try replacing the lamb with trimmed duck breasts or pieces of lean braising beef.

Lamb with Garlic Sauce

This dish contains Szechuan pepper which is quite hot and may be replaced with black pepper, if preferred.

NUTRITIONAL INFORMATION

Calories	320	Sugars	.........2g
Protein	........25g	Fat	..........21g
Carbohydrate	....4g	Saturates	.......6g

35 mins   10 mins

SERVES 4

I N G R E D I E N T S

450 g/1 lb lamb fillet or loin

2 tbsp dark soy sauce

2 tsp sesame oil

2 tbsp Chinese rice wine or dry sherry

½ tsp Szechuan pepper

4 tbsp vegetable oil

4 garlic cloves, crushed

60 g/2 oz water chestnuts, quartered

1 green pepper, seeded and sliced

1 tbsp wine vinegar

1 tbsp sesame oil

rice or noodles, to serve

1 Cut the lamb into 2.5-cm/1-inch pieces and place in a shallow dish.

2 Mix together 1 tablespoon of the soy sauce, the sesame oil, Chinese rice wine or sherry and Szechuan pepper. Pour the mixture over the lamb, turning to coat, and leave to marinate for 30 minutes.

3 Heat the vegetable oil in a preheated wok. Remove the lamb from the marinade and add to the wok, together with the garlic. Stir-fry for 2–3 minutes.

4 Add the water chestnuts and pepper to the wok and stir-fry for 1 minute.

5 Add the remaining soy sauce and the wine vinegar, mixing together well.

6 Add the sesame oil and cook, stirring constantly, for 1–2 minutes, or until the lamb is cooked through.

7 Transfer the lamb and garlic sauce to a warm serving dish and serve immediately with rice or noodles.

COOK'S TIP

Chinese chives, also known as garlic chives, would make an appropriate garnish for this dish.

Sesame oil is used as a flavouring, rather than for frying, as it burns readily, hence it is added at the end of cooking.

Hot Lamb

This is quite a spicy dish, using 2 chillies in the sauce. Halve the number of chillies to reduce the heat or seed the chillies before using if desired.

NUTRITIONAL INFORMATION

Calories ....323 Sugars 4g
Protein ....26g Fat 22g
Carbohydrate ....5g Saturates 7g

 25 mins 15 mins

SERVES 4

INGREDIENTS

450 g/1 lb lean, boneless lamb

2 tbsp hoisin sauce

1 tbsp dark soy sauce

1 garlic clove, crushed

2 tsp grated fresh root ginger

2 tbsp vegetable oil

2 onions, sliced

1 fennel bulb, sliced

4 tbsp water

SAUCE

1 large fresh red chilli, cut into thin strips

1 fresh green chilli, cut into thin strips

2 tbsp rice wine vinegar

2 tsp light brown sugar

2 tbsp peanut oil

1 tsp sesame oil

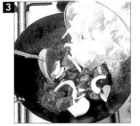

1 Cut the lamb into 2.5-cm/1-inch cubes and place in a glass dish.

2 Mix together the hoisin sauce, soy sauce, garlic and ginger and pour over the lamb, turning to coat well. Leave to marinate for 20 minutes.

3 Heat the oil in a preheated wok and stir-fry the lamb for 1–2 minutes. Add the onions and fennel and cook for a further 2 minutes, or until they are just beginning to brown. Stir in the water, cover and cook for 2–3 minutes.

4 To make the sauce, place all the ingredients in a pan and cook over a low heat for 3-4 minutes, stirring.

5 Transfer the lamb and onions to a serving dish, toss lightly in the sauce and serve immediately.

VARIATION

Try using beef, pork or duck instead of the lamb, and vary the vegetables, using leeks or celery instead of the onion and fennel.

Sesame Lamb Stir-Fry

This is a very simple, but delicious dish, in which lean pieces of lamb are cooked in sugar and soy sauce and then sprinkled with sesame seeds.

NUTRITIONAL INFORMATION

Calories . . . . . . .276 Sugars 4g
Protein . . . . .25g Fat 18g
Carbohydrate . . . .5g Saturates 6g

🍲 5 mins 🕐 10 mins

SERVES 4

INGREDIENTS

450 g/1 lb boneless lean lamb

2 tbsp peanut oil

2 leeks, sliced

1 carrot, cut into matchsticks

2 garlic cloves, crushed

85 ml/3 fl oz lamb or vegetable stock

2 tsp light brown sugar

1 tbsp dark soy sauce

4½ tsp sesame seeds

1 Using a sharp knife, cut the lamb into thin strips.

2 Heat the peanut oil in a preheated wok or large frying pan until it is really hot.

3 Add the lamb and stir-fry for 2–3 minutes. Remove the lamb from the wok with a slotted spoon and set aside until required.

4 Add the leeks, carrot and garlic to the wok or frying pan and stir-fry in the remaining oil for 1–2 minutes.

5 Remove the vegetables from the wok with a slotted spoon and set aside.

6 Drain any remaining oil from the wok. Place the lamb or vegetable stock,

light brown sugar and dark soy sauce in the wok and add the lamb. Cook, stirring constantly to coat the lamb, for 2–3 minutes.

7 Sprinkle the sesame seeds over the top, turning the lamb to coat.

8 Spoon the leek, carrot and garlic mixture on to a warm serving dish and top with the lamb. Serve immediately.

COOK'S TIP

Be careful not to burn the sugar in the wok when heating and coating the meat, otherwise the flavour of the dish will be spoiled.

Beef with Lemon Grass

A delicately flavoured stir-fry infused with lemon grass and ginger.
Colourful peppers help to complete the dish.

NUTRITIONAL INFORMATION

Calories	230	Sugars	.........4g
Protein	........26g	Fat	..........12g
Carbohydrate	....6g	Saturates	.......3g

5 mins   8 mins

SERVES 4

I N G R E D I E N T S

500 g/1 lb 2 oz lean beef fillet

2 tbsp vegetable oil

1 garlic clove, finely chopped

1 lemon grass stalk, finely shredded

2 tsp finely chopped fresh root ginger

1 red pepper, seeded and thickly sliced

1 green pepper, seeded and thickly sliced

1 onion, thickly sliced

2 tbsp lime juice

boiled noodles or rice, to serve

1   Cut the beef into long, thin strips, cutting across the grain.

2   Heat the oil in a large frying pan or wok over a high heat. Add the garlic and stir-fry for 1 minute.

3   Add the beef and stir-fry for a further 2–3 minutes until lightly coloured. Stir in the lemon grass and ginger and remove the wok from the heat.

4   Remove the beef from the pan or wok and keep to one side. Next add the peppers and onion to the pan or wok and stir-fry over a high heat for 2–3 minutes until the onions are just turning golden brown and slightly softened.

5   Return the beef to the pan, stir in the lime juice and season to taste with salt and pepper. Serve with noodles or rice.

COOK'S TIP

When preparing lemon grass, take care to remove the outer layers which can be tough and fibrous. Use only the centre, tender part, which has the finest flavour.

Stir-Fried Beef & Vegetables

Fillet of beef is perfect for stir-frying as it is so tender and lends itself to quick cooking.

NUTRITIONAL INFORMATION

Calories 521   Sugars 7g
Protein . . . . .31g   Fat 35g
Carbohydrate . . .18g   Saturates 8g

10 mins   20 mins

SERVES 4

I N G R E D I E N T S

2 tbsp sunflower oil

350 g/12 oz fillet of beef, sliced

1 red onion, sliced

175 g/6 oz courgettes

175 g/6 oz carrots, thinly sliced

1 red pepper, seeded and sliced

1 small head Chinese leaves, shredded

150 g/5½ oz beansprouts

225 g/8 oz canned bamboo shoots, drained

150 g/5½ oz cashew nuts, toasted

S A U C E

3 tbsp medium sherry

3 tbsp light soy sauce

1 tsp ground ginger

1 clove garlic, crushed

1 tsp cornflour

1 tbsp tomato purée

3 Add the carrots, pepper, and courgettes to the wok and stir-fry for 5 minutes.

4 Toss in the Chinese leaves, bean sprouts and bamboo shoots and heat through for 2–3 minutes, or until the leaves are just beginning to wilt.

5 Scatter the cashews nuts over the stir-fry and toss well to mix.

6 To make the sauce, mix together the sherry, soy sauce, ground ginger, garlic, cornflour and tomato purée until well combined.

7 Pour the sauce over the stir-fry and toss to mix. Allow the sauce to bubble for 2–3 minutes or until the juices thicken.

8 Transfer to warm serving dishes and serve at once.

1 Heat the sunflower oil in a large preheated wok. Add the sliced beef and red onion to the wok and stir-fry for about 4–5 minutes or until the onion begins to soften and the meat is just browning.

2 Trim the courgettes and slice diagonally.

Chilli Beef Stir-Fry Salad

This dish has a Mexican feel to it, combining all of the classic flavours.

NUTRITIONAL INFORMATION

Calories 243   Sugars 2g
Protein ....21g   Fat 18g
Carbohydrate ....7g   Saturates 4g

5 mins   10 mins

SERVES 4

INGREDIENTS

450 g/1 lb lean rump steak

2 cloves garlic, crushed

1 tsp chilli powder

½ tsp salt

1 tsp ground coriander

1 ripe avocado

2 tbsp sunflower oil

425 g/15 oz canned red kidney beans, drained

175 g/6 oz cherry tomatoes, halved

1 large packet tortilla chips

shredded Iceberg lettuce

chopped fresh coriander, to serve

1 Using a sharp knife, slice the beef into thin strips.

2 Place the garlic, chilli powder, salt and ground coriander in a large bowl and mix until well combined.

3 Add the strips of beef to the marinade and toss well to coat all over.

4 Using a sharp knife, peel the avocado. Slice the avocado lengthways and then crossways to form small dice.

5 Heat the oil in a large preheated wok. Add the beef and stir-fry for 5 minutes, tossing frequently.

6 Add the kidney beans, tomatoes and avocado and heat through for 2 minutes.

7 Arrange a bed of tortilla chips and Iceberg lettuce around the edge of a large serving plate and spoon the beef mixture into the centre. Alternatively, serve the tortilla chips and iceberg lettuce separately.

8 Garnish with chopped fresh coriander and serve immediately.

COOK'S TIP

Serve this dish immediately as avocado tends to discolour quickly. Once you have cut the avocado into dice, sprinkle it with a little lemon juice to prevent discoloration.

Beef with Bamboo Shoots

Tender beef, marinated in a soy and tomato sauce, is stir-fried with crisp bamboo shoots and mangetout in this simple recipe.

NUTRITIONAL INFORMATION

Calories . . . . . . .275 Sugars 3g
Protein . . . . .21g Fat 19g
Carbohydrate . . . .6g Saturates 6g

1¼ hrs   10 mins

SERVES 4

INGREDIENTS

350 g/12 oz rump steak

3 tbsp dark soy sauce

1 tbsp tomato ketchup

2 cloves garlic, crushed

1 tbsp fresh lemon juice

1 tsp ground coriander

2 tbsp vegetable oil

175 g/6 oz mangetout

200 g/7 oz canned bamboo shoots

1 tsp sesame oil

COOK'S TIP

Leave the meat to marinate for at least 1 hour in order for the flavours to penetrate and increase the tenderness of the meat. If possible, leave for a little longer for a fuller flavour to develop.

1 Thinly slice the meat and place in a non metallic dish together with the dark soy sauce, tomato ketchup, garlic, lemon juice and ground coriander. Mix well so that all of the meat is coated in the marinade, cover and leave for at least 1 hour.

2 Heat the vegetable oil in a preheated wok. Add the meat to the wok and stir-fry for 2–4 minutes (depending on how well cooked you like your meat) or until cooked through.

3 Add the mangetout and bamboo shoots to the mixture in the wok and stir-fry over a high heat, tossing frequently, for a further 5 minutes.

4 Drizzle with the sesame oil and toss well to combine. Transfer to serving dishes and serve hot.

Caramelised Beef

Palm sugar or brown sugar is used in this recipe to give the beef a slightly caramelised flavour.

NUTRITIONAL INFORMATION

Calories ....335 Sugars 8g
Protein ....23g Fat 21g
Carbohydrate ...14g Saturates 7g

1¼ hrs   10 mins

SERVES 4

INGREDIENTS

450 g/1 lb fillet beef

2 tbsp soy sauce

1 tsp chilli oil

1 tbsp tamarind paste

2 tbsp palm sugar or demerara sugar

2 cloves garlic, crushed

2 tbsp sunflower oil

225 g/8 oz baby onions

2 tbsp chopped fresh coriander

1 Using a sharp knife, thinly slice the beef.

2 Place the slices of beef in a large, shallow non-metallic dish.

3 Mix together the soy sauce, chilli oil, tamarind paste, palm sugar and garlic.

4 Spoon the palm sugar mixture over the beef. Toss well to coat the beef in the mixture, cover with clingfilm and leave to marinate for at least 1 hour.

5 Heat the sunflower oil in a preheated wok or large frying pan.

6 Peel the onions and cut them in half. Add the onions to the wok and stir-fry for 2–3 minutes, or until just browning.

7 Add the beef and marinade juices to the wok and stir-fry over a high heat for about 5 minutes.

8 Scatter with chopped fresh coriander and serve at once.

COOK'S TIP

Use the chilli oil carefully as it is very hot and could easily spoil the dish if too much is added.

Beef & Black Bean Sauce

It is not necessary to use the expensive cuts of beef steak for this recipe: the meat will be tender as it is cut into small thin slices and marinated.

NUTRITIONAL INFORMATION

Calories 392   Sugars 2g
Protein ....13g   Fat 36g
Carbohydrate ....3g   Saturates 7g

3¼ hrs   10 mins

SERVES 4

INGREDIENTS

250-300 g/9-10½ oz beef steak (such as rump)

1 small onion

1 small green pepper, cored and seeded

about 300 ml/10 fl oz vegetable oil

1 spring onion, cut into short sections

a few small slices of fresh root ginger

1–2 small green or red chillies, seeded and sliced

2 tbsp crushed black bean sauce

MARINADE

½ tsp bicarbonate of soda or baking powder

½ tsp sugar

1 tbsp light soy sauce

2 tsp rice wine or dry sherry

2 tsp cornflour

2 tsp sesame oil

1 Using a sharp knife or meat cleaver, cut the beef into small, thin strips.

2 To make the marinade, mix together all the ingredients in a shallow dish. Add the beef strips, turn to coat and leave to marinate for at least 2–3 hours.

3 Cut the onion and green pepper into small cubes.

4 Heat the vegetable oil in a pre-heated wok or large frying pan. Add the beef strips and stir-fry for about 1 minute, or until the colour changes. Remove the beef strips with a slotted spoon and drain on kitchen paper. Keep warm and set aside until required.

5 Pour off the excess oil, leaving about 1 tablespoon in the wok. Add the spring onion, ginger, chillies, onion and green pepper and stir-fry for about 1 minute.

6 Add the black bean sauce and stir until smooth. Return the beef strips to the wok, blend well and stir-fry for another minute. Transfer the stir-fry to a warm serving dish and serve hot.

Soy & Sesame Beef

Soy sauce and sesame seeds are classic ingredients in Chinese cookery. Use a dark soy sauce for fuller flavour and richness.

NUTRITIONAL INFORMATION

Calories	324	Sugars	.........2g
Protein	........25g	Fat	..........22g
Carbohydrate	....3g	Saturates	.......6g

5 mins   10 mins

SERVES 4

INGREDIENTS

2 tbsp sesame seeds

450 g/1 lb beef fillet

2 tbsp vegetable oil

1 green pepper, seeded and thinly sliced

4 cloves garlic, crushed

2 tbsp dry sherry

4 tbsp soy sauce

6 spring onions, sliced

noodles, to serve

1 Heat a large wok or heavy-based frying pan until it is very hot.

2 Add the sesame seeds to the wok or frying pan and dry fry, stirring, for 1–2 minutes or until they just begin to brown. Remove the sesame seeds from the wok and set aside until required.

3 Using a sharp knife or meat cleaver, thinly slice the beef.

4 Heat the vegetable oil in the wok or frying pan. Add the beef and stir-fry for 2–3 minutes or until sealed on all sides.

5 Add the sliced pepper and crushed garlic to the wok and continue stir-frying for 2 minutes.

6 Add the dry sherry and soy sauce to the wok together with the spring onions. Allow the mixture in the wok to bubble, stirring occasionally, for about 1 minute, but do not let the mixture burn

7 Transfer the garlic beef stir-fry to warm serving bowls and scatter with the dry-fried sesame seeds. Serve hot with boiled noodles.

COOK'S TIP

You can spread the sesame seeds out on a baking tray and toast them under a preheated grill until browned all over, if you prefer.

Beef & Broccoli Stir-Fry

This is a great combination of ingredients in terms of colour and flavour, and it is so simple to prepare.

NUTRITIONAL INFORMATION

Calories ....232 Sugars 1g
Protein ....12g Fat 19g
Carbohydrate ....4g Saturates 6g

4¼ hrs   15 mins

SERVES 4

INGREDIENTS

225 g/8 oz lean steak, trimmed

2 garlic cloves, crushed

dash of chilli oil

1 tsp grated fresh root ginger

½ tsp Chinese five-spice powder

2 tbsp dark soy sauce

2 tbsp vegetable oil

150 g/5½ oz broccoli florets

1 tbsp light soy sauce

150 ml/5 fl oz beef stock

2 tsp cornflour

4 tsp water

carrot strips, to garnish

1 Using a sharp knife, cut the steak into thin strips and place in a shallow glass dish.

2 Mix together the garlic, chilli oil, grated ginger, Chinese five-spice powder and dark soy sauce in a small bowl and pour over the beef, tossing to coat the strips evenly.

3 Cover the bowl and leave the meat to marinate in the refrigerator for several hours to allow the flavours to develop fully.

4 Heat 1 tablespoon of the vegetable oil in a preheated wok or large frying pan. Add the broccoli and stir-fry over a medium heat for 4–5 minutes. Remove from the wok with a slotted spoon and set aside until required.

5 Heat the remaining oil in the wok. Add the steak together with the marinade, and stir-fry for 2-3 minutes, until the steak is browned and sealed.

6 Return the broccoli to the wok and stir in the light soy sauce and stock.

7 Blend the cornflour with the water to form a smooth paste and stir into the wok. Bring to the boil, stirring, until thickened and clear. Cook for 1 minute. Transfer the beef & broccoli stir-fry to a warm serving dish, arrange the carrot strips in a lattice on top and serve immediately.

Oyster Sauce Beef

Like other stir-fry dishes, the vegetables used in this recipe can be varied as you wish.

NUTRITIONAL INFORMATION

Calories 462   Sugars 2g
Protein . . . . .16g   Fat 42g
Carbohydrate . . . .4g   Saturates 8g

40 mins   10 mins

SERVES 4

INGREDIENTS

300 g/10½ oz beef steak

1 tsp sugar

1 tbsp light soy sauce

1 tsp rice wine or dry sherry

1 tsp cornflour

½ small carrot

60 g/2 oz mangetout

60 g/2 oz canned bamboo shoots

60 g/2 oz canned straw mushrooms

about 300 ml/10 fl oz vegetable oil

1 spring onion, cut into short sections

2–3 small slices ginger root

½ tsp salt

2 tbsp oyster sauce

2–3 tbsp vegetable stock or water

1 Cut the beef into small, thin slices. Place in a shallow dish with the sugar, soy sauce, wine and cornflour and leave to marinate for 25-30 minutes.

2 Slice the carrot, mangetout, bamboo shoots and straw mushrooms into roughly the same size pieces as each other.

3 Heat the oil in a wok and add the beef slices. Stir-fry for 1 minute, then remove and keep warm.

4 Pour off the oil, leaving about 1 tablespoon in the wok. Add the sliced vegetables with the spring onion and ginger and stir-fry for about 2 minutes. Add the salt, beef and oyster sauce with stock or water. Blend well until heated through and serve.

VARIATION

You can use whatever vegetables are available for this dish, but it is important to get a good contrast of colour – don't use all red or all green for example.

Spicy Beef

In this recipe, beef is marinated in a five-spice and chilli marinade for a spicy flavour.

NUTRITIONAL INFORMATION

Calories 246   Sugars 2g
Protein ....21g   Fat 13g
Carbohydrate ...10g   Saturates 3g

1¼ hrs   10 mins

SERVES 4

INGREDIENTS

225 g/8 oz fillet steak

2 garlic cloves, crushed

1 tsp powdered star anise

1 tbsp dark soy sauce

spring onion tassels, to garnish

SAUCE

2 tbsp vegetable oil

1 bunch spring onions, halved lengthways

1 tbsp dark soy sauce

1 tbsp dry sherry

¼ tsp chilli sauce

150 m/5 fl oz water

2 tsp cornflour

4 tsp water

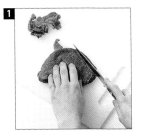

1 Cut the steak into thin strips and place in a shallow dish.

2 Mix together the garlic, star anise and dark soy sauce in a bowl.

3 Pour the sauce mixture over the steak strips, turning them to coat thoroughly. Cover and leave to marinate in the refrigerator for at least 1 hour.

4 To make the sauce, heat the oil in a preheated wok or large frying pan.

Reduce the heat and stir-fry the spring onions for 1–2 minutes.

5 Remove the spring onions from the wok with a slotted spoon, drain on kitchen paper and set aside until required.

6 Add the beef to the wok, together with the marinade, and stir-fry for 3–4 minutes. Return the spring onions to the wok and add the soy sauce, sherry, chilli sauce and two thirds of the water.

7 Blend the cornflour with the remaining water and stir into the wok. Bring to the boil, stirring until the sauce thickens and clears.

8 Transfer to a warm serving dish, garnish and serve immediately.

Beef & Beans

The green of the beans complements the dark colour of the beef, served in a rich sauce.

NUTRITIONAL INFORMATION

Calories 381   Sugars 3g
Protein . . . . .25g   Fat 27g
Carbohydrate . . .10g   Saturates 8g

35 mins   15 mins

SERVES 4

INGREDIENTS

450 g/1 lb rump or fillet steak, cut into 2.5-cm/1-inch pieces

MARINADE

2 tsp cornflour

2 tbsp dark soy sauce

2 tsp peanut oil

SAUCE

2 tbsp vegetable oil

3 garlic cloves, crushed

1 small onion, cut into 8 pieces

225 g/8 oz green beans, halved

25 g/1 oz unsalted cashews

25 g/1 oz canned bamboo shoots, drained and rinsed

2 tsp dark soy sauce

2 tsp Chinese rice wine or dry sherry

125 ml/4 fl oz beef stock

2 tsp cornflour

4 tsp water

salt and pepper

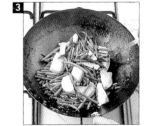

1 To make the marinade, mix together the cornflour, soy sauce and peanut oil.

2 Place the steak in a shallow glass bowl. Pour the marinade over the steak, turn to coat thoroughly, cover and leave to marinate in the refrigerator for at least 30 minutes.

3 To make the sauce, heat the oil in a preheated wok. Add the garlic, onion, beans, cashews and bamboo shoots and stir-fry for 2–3 minutes.

4 Remove the steak from the marinade, drain, add to the wok and stir-fry for 3–4 minutes.

5 Mix the soy sauce, Chinese rice wine or sherry and beef stock together. Blend the cornflour with the water and add to the soy sauce mixture, mixing to combine.

6 Stir the mixture into the wok and bring the sauce to the boil, stirring until thickened and clear. Reduce the heat and leave to simmer for 2–3 minutes. Season to taste and serve immediately.

Beef & Peanut Salad

This recipe looks stunning if you arrange the ingredients rather than toss them together.

NUTRITIONAL INFORMATION

Calories 194   Sugars 3g
Protein . . . . .21g   Fat 10g
Carbohydrate . . . .5g   Saturates 3g

 10 mins   🕐 10 mins

SERVES 4

INGREDIENTS

½ head Chinese leaves

1 large carrot

115 g/4 oz radishes

100 g/3½ oz baby corn cobs

1 tbsp groundnut oil

1 red chilli, seeded and chopped finely

1 clove garlic, chopped finely

350 g/12 oz lean beef (such as fillet, sirloin or rump), trimmed and shredded finely

1 tbsp dark soy sauce

25 g/1 oz fresh peanuts (optional)

red chilli, sliced, to garnish

DRESSING

1 tbsp smooth peanut butter

1 tsp caster sugar

2 tbsp light soy sauce

1 tbsp sherry vinegar

salt and pepper

VARIATION

If preferred, use chicken, turkey, lean pork or even strips of venison instead of beef in this recipe. Cut off all visible fat before you begin.

1 Finely shred the Chinese leaves and arrange on a platter.

2 Peel the carrot and cut into matchsticks. Wash, trim and quarter the radishes, and halve the baby corn cobs lengthways. Arrange these ingredients around the edge of the dish and set aside.

3 Heat the groundnut oil in a non-stick wok or large frying pan until really hot.

4 Add the red chilli, garlic and beef to the wok or frying pan and stir-fry for 5 minutes.

5 Add the dark soy sauce and stir-fry for a further 1–2 minutes until tender and cooked through.

6 Meanwhile, make the dressing. Place all of the ingredients in a small bowl and blend them together until smooth.

7 Place the hot cooked beef in the centre of the salad ingredients. Spoon over the dressing and sprinkle with a few peanuts, if using. Garnish with slices of red chilli and serve immediately.

Beef with Beansprouts

A quick-and-easy stir-fry for any day of the week, this simple beef recipe is a good one-pan main dish.

NUTRITIONAL INFORMATION

Calories 544	Sugars 8g
Protein 39g	Fat 21g
Carbohydrate . . .55g	Saturates 5g

5 mins   15 mins

SERVES 4

I N G R E D I E N T S

1 bunch spring onions

2 tbsp sunflower oil

1 garlic clove, crushed

1 tsp finely chopped fresh root ginger

500 g/1 lb 2 oz tender beef, cut into thin strips

1 large red pepper, seeded and sliced

1 small red chilli, seeded and chopped

350 g/12 oz fresh beansprouts

1 small lemon grass stalk, finely chopped

2 tbsp smooth peanut butter

4 tbsp coconut milk

1 tbsp rice vinegar

1 tbsp soy sauce

1 tsp soft light brown sugar

250 g/9 oz medium egg noodles

salt and pepper

1 Trim and thinly slice the spring onions, setting aside some slices to use as a garnish.

2 Heat the oil in a frying pan or wok over a high heat. Add the onions, garlic and ginger and then stir-fry for 2–3 minutes to soften. Add the beef and continue stir-frying for 4–5 minutes until browned evenly.

3 Add the pepper and stir-fry for a further 3–4 minutes. Add the chilli and beansprouts and stir-fry for 2 minutes. Mix together the lemon grass, peanut butter, coconut milk, vinegar, soy sauce and sugar, then stir this mixture into the wok.

4 Meanwhile, cook the egg noodles in boiling, lightly salted water for 4 minutes, or according to the packet directions. Drain and stir into the frying pan or wok, tossing to mix evenly.

5 Adjust seasoning with salt and pepper to taste. Sprinkle with the reserved spring onions and serve hot.

Fish & Seafood

Throughout the Far Eastern countries, fish and seafood play a major role in the diet of the native people; this is because these foods are both plentiful and very healthy. They are also very versatile: there are many different ways

of cooking fish and seafood in a wok – they may be steamed, deep-fried or stir-fried with a range of delicious spices and sauces.

Japan is famed for its *sushimi*, or raw fish, but this is just one of the wide range of fish dishes served. Fish and seafood are offered at every meal in Japan, many of them cooked in a wok.

When buying fish and seafood for the recipes in this chapter, freshness is imperative to flavour, so be sure to buy and use the fish that you have chosen as soon as possible, preferably on the same day.

Stir-Fried Cod with Mango

Fish and fruit are a classic combination, and in this recipe a tropical flavour is added which gives a great scented taste to the dish.

NUTRITIONAL INFORMATION

Calories	200	Sugars	........12g
Protein	........21g	Fat	...........7g
Carbohydrate	...14g	Saturates	.......1g

🍲 10 mins   🕐 15 mins

SERVES 4

I N G R E D I E N T S

175 g/6 oz carrots

2 tbsp vegetable oil

1 red onion, sliced

1 red pepper, seeded and sliced

1 green pepper, deseeded and sliced

450 g/1 lb skinless cod fillet

1 ripe mango

1 tsp cornflour

1 tbsp soy sauce

100 ml/3½ fl oz tropical fruit juice

1 tbsp lime juice

1 tbsp chopped fresh coriander, to garnish

1 Using a sharp knife, slice the carrots into thin sticks.

2 Heat the oil in a preheated wok and stir-fry the onion, carrots and peppers for 5 minutes.

3 Using a sharp knife, cut the cod into small cubes. Peel the mango, then carefully remove the flesh from the centre stone. Cut the flesh into thin slices.

4 Add the cod and mango to the wok and stir-fry for a further 4–5 minutes, or until the fish is cooked through. Be careful not to break the fish up.

5 Mix together the cornflour, soy sauce, fruit juice and lime juice. Pour the mixture into the wok and stir until the mixture bubbles and the juices thicken. Scatter with coriander and serve immediately.

 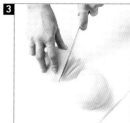 

VARIATION

You can use paw-paw as an alternative to the mango, if you prefer.

Braised Fish Fillets

Any white fish, such as lemon sole or plaice, is ideal for this delicious dish.

NUTRITIONAL INFORMATION

Calories 107   Sugars 2g
Protein . . . . .17g   Fat 2g
Carbohydrate . . . .6g   Saturates 0.3g

35 mins   10 mins

SERVES 4

INGREDIENTS

3–4 small Chinese dried mushrooms

300–350 g/10½–12 oz fish fillets

1 tsp salt

½ egg white, lightly beaten

1 tsp cornflour

600 ml/1 pint vegetable oil

1 tsp finely chopped fresh root ginger

2 spring onions, finely chopped

1 garlic clove, finely chopped

½ small green pepper, seeded
    and cut into small cubes

½ small carrot, thinly sliced

60 g/2 oz canned sliced bamboo shoots,
    rinsed and drained

½ tsp sugar

1 tbsp light soy sauce

1 tsp rice wine or dry sherry

1 tbsp chilli bean sauce

2–3 tbsp vegetable stock or water

a few drops of sesame oil

1 Soak the dried mushrooms in a bowl of warm water for 30 minutes. Drain thoroughly on kitchen paper, reserving the soaking water for stock or soup. Squeeze the mushrooms to extract all of the moisture, cut off and discard any hard stems and slice thinly.

2 Cut the fish into bite-sized pieces, then place in a shallow dish and mix with a pinch of salt, the egg white and cornflour, turning the fish to coat well.

3 Heat the oil in a preheated wok. Add the fish pieces to the wok and deep-fry for about 1 minute. Remove the fish pieces with a slotted spoon and leave to drain on kitchen paper.

4 Pour off the excess oil, leaving about 1 tablespoon in the wok. Add the ginger, spring onions and garlic to flavour the oil for a few seconds, then add the pepper, carrots and bamboo shoots and stir-fry for about 1 minute.

5 Add the sugar, soy sauce, wine, chilli bean sauce, stock or water, and the remaining salt and bring to the boil. Add the fish pieces, stirring to coat with the sauce, and braise for 1 minute. Sprinkle with sesame oil and serve.

Fish with Coconut & Basil

Fish curries are sensational and this is no exception. Red curry and coconut are fantastic flavours with the fried fish.

NUTRITIONAL INFORMATION

Calories 209   Sugars 10g
Protein . . . . .21g   Fat 8g
Carbohydrate . . .15g   Saturates 1g

 5 mins   15 mins

SERVES 4

I N G R E D I E N T S

2 tbsp vegetable oil

450 g/1 lb skinless cod fillet

25 g/1 oz seasoned flour

1 clove garlic, crushed

2 tbsp red curry paste

1 tbsp fish sauce

300 ml/10 fl oz coconut milk

175 g/6 oz cherry tomatoes, halved

20 fresh basil leaves

fragrant rice, to serve

1 Heat the vegetable oil in a large preheated wok.

2 Using a sharp knife, cut the fish into large cubes, removing any bones with a pair of clean tweezers.

3 Place the seasoned flour in a bowl. Add the cubes of fish and mix until well coated.

4 Add the coated fish to the wok and stir-fry over a high heat for 3–4 minutes, or until the fish just begins to brown at the edges.

5 In a small bowl, mix together the garlic, curry paste, fish sauce and coconut milk. Pour the mixture over the fish and bring to the boil.

6 Add the tomatoes to the mixture in the wok and leave to simmer for 5 minutes.

7 Roughly chop or tear the fresh basil leaves. Add the basil to the wok, stir carefully to combine, taking care not to break up the cubes of fish.

8 Transfer to serving plates and serve hot with fragrant rice.

COOK'S TIP

Take care not to overcook the dish once the tomatoes are added, otherwise they will break down and the skins will come away.

Szechuan White Fish

Szechuan pepper is quite hot and should be used sparingly to avoid making the dish unbearably spicy.

NUTRITIONAL INFORMATION

Calories 225   Sugars 3g
Protein . . . . .20g   Fat 8g
Carbohydrate . . .17g   Saturates 1g

5 mins   20 mins

SERVES 4

I N G R E D I E N T S

350 g/12 oz white fish fillets

1 small egg, beaten

3 tbsp plain flour

4 tbsp dry white wine

3 tbsp light soy sauce

vegetable oil, for frying

1 garlic clove, cut into slivers

1 tsp finely chopped fresh root ginger

1 onion, finely chopped

1 celery stick, chopped

1 fresh red chilli, chopped

3 spring onions, chopped

1 tsp rice wine vinegar

½ tsp ground Szechuan pepper

175 ml/6 fl oz fish stock

1 tsp caster sugar

1 tsp cornflour

2 tsp water

for 2–3 minutes, until golden brown. Remove with a slotted spoon, drain on kitchen paper, set aside and keep warm.

3 Pour all but 1 tablespoon of oil from the wok and return to the heat. Add the garlic, ginger, onion, celery, chilli and spring onions and stir-fry for 1–2 minutes. Stir in the remaining soy sauce and the vinegar.

4 Add the Szechuan pepper, fish stock and caster sugar to the wok. Mix the cornflour with the water to form a smooth paste and stir it into the stock. Bring to the boil and cook, stirring, for 1 minute, until the sauce thickens and clears.

5 Return the fish cubes to the wok and cook for 1–2 minutes. Serve immediately.

1 Cut the fish into 4-cm/1½-inch cubes. Beat together the egg, flour, wine and 1 tablespoon of soy sauce to make a batter. Dip the cubes of fish into the batter to coat well.

2 Heat the oil in a wok, reduce the heat slightly and cook the fish, in batches,

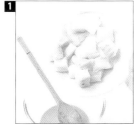

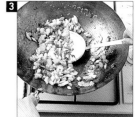

Crispy Fish

This is a very hot dish – not for the faint hearted! It may be made without the chilli flavourings, if preferred.

NUTRITIONAL INFORMATION

Calories 281   Sugars 3g
Protein . . . . .25g   Fat 12g
Carbohydrate . . .15g   Saturates 2g

30 mins   40 mins

SERVES 4

INGREDIENTS

450 g/1 lb white fish fillets

BATTER

60 g/2 oz plain flour

1 egg, separated

1 tbsp peanut oil

4 tbsp milk

vegetable oil, for deep-frying

SAUCE

1 fresh red chilli, chopped

2 garlic cloves, crushed

pinch of chilli powder

3 tbsp tomato purée

1 tbsp rice wine vinegar

2 tbsp dark soy sauce

2 tbsp Chinese rice wine

2 tbsp water

pinch of caster sugar

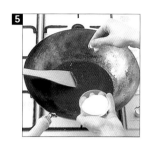
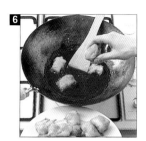

1 Cut the fish into 2.5-cm/1-inch cubes and set aside.

2 Sift the plain flour into a mixing bowl and make a well in the centre. Add the egg yolk and peanut oil to the mixing bowl and gradually stir in the milk, incorporating the flour to form a smooth batter. Leave to stand for about 20 minutes.

3 Whisk the egg white until it forms peaks and fold into the batter until thoroughly incorporated.

4 Heat the vegetable oil in a preheated wok or large frying pan. Dip the fish into the batter and fry, in batches, for 8–10 minutes, until cooked through. Remove the fish from the wok with a slotted spoon, set aside and keep warm until required.

5 Pour off all but 1 tablespoon of oil from the wok and return to the heat. Add the chilli, garlic, chilli powder, tomato purée, rice wine vinegar, soy sauce, Chinese rice wine, water and sugar and cook, stirring, for 3–4 minutes.

6 Return the fish to the wok and stir gently to coat it in the sauce. Cook for 2–3 minutes, until hot. Transfer to a serving dish and serve immediately.

Gingered Monkfish

This dish is a real treat and is perfect for special occasions. Monkfish has a tender flavour which is ideal with asparagus, chilli and ginger.

NUTRITIONAL INFORMATION

Calories 133   Sugars 0g
Protein . . . . .21g   Fat 5g
Carbohydrate . . . .1g   Saturates 1g

5 mins   10 mins

SERVES 4

INGREDIENTS

450 g/1 lb monkfish

1 tbsp grated fresh root ginger

2 tbsp sweet chilli sauce

1 tbsp corn oil

100 g/3½ oz fine asparagus

3 spring onions, sliced

1 tsp sesame oil

1 Using a sharp knife, slice the monkfish into thin flat rounds. Set aside until required.

2 Mix together the freshly grated root ginger and the sweet chilli sauce in a small bowl until thoroughly blended. Brush the ginger and chilli sauce mixture over the monkfish pieces, using a pastry brush.

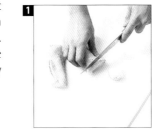  

3 Heat the corn oil in a large preheated wok or heavy-based frying pan.

4 Add the monkfish pieces, asparagus and chopped spring onions to the wok or frying pan and cook for about 5 minutes, stirring gently so the fish pieces do not break up.

5 Remove the wok or frying pan from the heat, drizzle the sesame oil over the stir-fry and toss well to combine.

6 Transfer the stir-fried gingered monkfish to warm serving plates and serve immediately.

COOK'S TIP

Monkfish is quite expensive, but it is well worth using as it has a wonderful flavour and texture. At a push you could use cubes of chunky cod fillet instead.

Trout with Pineapple

Pineapple is widely used in Chinese cooking. The tartness of fresh pineapple complements fish particularly well.

NUTRITIONAL INFORMATION

Calories 243   Sugars 4g
Protein . . . . .30g   Fat 11g
Carbohydrate . . . .6g   Saturates 2g

🍳 5 mins   🕐 15 mins

SERVES 4

INGREDIENTS

4 trout fillets, skinned

2 tbsp vegetable oil

2 garlic cloves, cut into slivers

4 slices fresh pineapple, peeled and diced

1 celery stick, sliced

1 tbsp light soy sauce

50 ml/2 fl oz fresh or unsweetened
   pineapple juice

150 ml/5 fl oz fish stock

1 tsp cornflour

2 tsp water

TO GARNISH

shredded celery leaves

fresh red chilli slices

1 Cut the trout fillets into strips. Heat 1 tablespoon of the vegetable oil in a preheated wok until almost smoking. Reduce the heat slightly, add the fish and sauté for 2 minutes. Remove from the wok.

2 Add the remaining oil to the wok, reduce the heat and add the garlic, diced pineapple and celery. Stir-fry for 1–2 minutes.

3 Add the soy sauce, pineapple juice and fish stock to the wok. Bring to the boil and cook, stirring, for 2–3 minutes, or until the sauce has reduced.

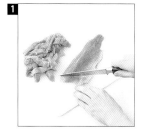

4 Blend the cornflour with the water to form a paste and stir it into the wok. Bring the sauce to the boil and cook, stirring constantly, until the sauce thickens and clears.

5 Return the fish to the wok, and cook, stirring gently, until heated through. Transfer to a warmed serving dish and serve, garnished with shredded celery leaves and red chilli slices.

VARIATION

Use canned pineapple instead of fresh pineapple if you wish, choosing slices in unsweetened, natural juice in preference to a syrup.

Stir-Fried Salmon with Leeks

Salmon is marinated in a deliciously rich, sweet sauce, stir-fried and served on a bed of crispy leeks.

NUTRITIONAL INFORMATION

Calories 360   Sugars 9g
Protein ....24g   Fat 25
Carbohydrate ....11g   Saturates 4g

35 mins   15 mins

SERVES 4

I N G R E D I E N T S

450 g/1 lb salmon fillet, skinned

2 tbsp sweet soy sauce

2 tbsp tomato ketchup

1 tsp rice wine vinegar

1 tbsp demerara sugar

1 clove garlic, crushed

4 tbsp corn oil

450 g/1 lb leeks, thinly shredded

finely chopped red chillies, to garnish

1 Using a sharp knife, cut the salmon into slices. Place the slices of salmon in a shallow non-metallic dish.

2 Mix together the soy sauce, tomato ketchup, rice wine vinegar, sugar and garlic.

3 Pour the mixture over the salmon, toss well and leave to marinate for about 30 minutes.

4 Meanwhile, heat 3 tablespoons of the corn oil in a large preheated wok.

5 Add the leeks to the wok and stir-fry over a medium-high heat for about 10 minutes, or until the leeks become crispy and tender.

6 Using a slotted spoon, carefully remove the leeks from the wok and transfer to warmed serving plates.

7 Add the remaining oil to the wok. Add the salmon and the marinade to the wok and cook for 2 minutes.

8 Remove the salmon from the wok and spoon over the leeks, garnish with finely chopped red chillies and serve immediately.

VARIATION

You can use a fillet of beef instead of the salmon, if you prefer.

Salmon with Pineapple

Presentation plays a major part in Chinese cooking and this dish demonstrates this perfectly with the wonderful combination of colours.

NUTRITIONAL INFORMATION

Calories 347	Sugars 12g	
Protein 24g	Fat 20g	
Carbohydrate ...16g	Saturates 3g	

10 mins   15 mins

SERVES 4

INGREDIENTS

2 tbsp sunflower oil

1 red onion, sliced

1 orange pepper, seeded and sliced

1 green pepper, seeded and sliced

100 g/3½ oz baby corn cobs

450 g/1 lb salmon fillet, skin removed

1 tbsp paprika

225 g/8 oz canned cubed pineapple, drained

100 g/3½ oz beansprouts

2 tbsp tomato ketchup

2 tbsp soy sauce

2 tbsp medium sherry

1 tsp cornflour

1 Cut each baby corn cob in half. Heat the oil in a large preheated wok. Add the onion, peppers and baby corn cobs to the wok and stir-fry for 5 minutes.

2 Rinse the salmon fillet under cold running water and pat dry with kitchen paper.

3 Cut the salmon flesh into thin strips and place in a large bowl. Sprinkle with the paprika and toss well to coat.

4 Add the salmon to the wok together with the pineapple and stir-fry for a further 2–3 minutes or until the fish is tender.

5 Add the beansprouts to the wok and toss well.

6 Mix together the tomato ketchup, soy sauce, sherry and cornflour. Add to the wok and cook until the juices start to thicken. Transfer to warm serving plates and serve immediately.

VARIATION

You can use trout fillets instead of the salmon as an alternative, if you prefer.

Five-Spice Salmon

Five-spice powder is a blend of star anise, fennel, cinnamon, cloves and Szechuan peppercorns that is often used in Chinese dishes.

NUTRITIONAL INFORMATION

Calories	267	Sugars	.........3g
Protein	........24g	Fat	..........17g
Carbohydrate	....4g	Saturates	......3g

15 mins   15 mins

SERVES 4

INGREDIENTS

4 salmon fillets, 125 g/4½ oz
    each, skinned

2 tsp Chinese five-spice powder

1 large leek

1 large carrot

115 g/4 oz mangetout

2.5-cm/1-inch piece fresh root ginger

2 tbsp ginger wine

2 tbsp light soy sauce

1 tbsp vegetable oil

salt and pepper

TO GARNISH

shredded leek

fresh root ginger, shredded

carrot, shredded

1 Wash the salmon and pat dry on kitchen paper. Rub the five-spice powder into both sides of the fish and season with salt and pepper. Set aside until required.

2 Trim the leek, slice it down the centre and rinse under cold water to remove any dirt. Finely shred the leek. Peel the carrot and cut it into very thin strips. Top and tail the mangetout and cut them into shreds. Peel the ginger and slice thinly into strips.

3 Place all of the vegetables into a large bowl and toss in the ginger wine and 1 tablespoon soy sauce.

4 Preheat the grill to medium. Place the salmon fillets on the rack and brush with the remaining soy sauce. Cook for 2–3 minutes on each side until cooked through.

5 While the salmon is cooking, heat the oil in a non-stick wok or large frying pan and stir-fry the vegetables for 5 minutes until just tender. Take care that you do not overcook the vegetables – they should still have bite. Transfer to serving plates. Drain the salmon on kitchen paper and serve on a bed of stir-fried vegetables. Garnish with shredded leek, ginger and carrot.

COOK'S TIP

Five-spice powder is strong and pungent and should be used sparingly.

Spicy Thai Seafood Stew

The fish in this fragrant, curry-like stew can be varied according to taste or availability, but do stick with those which stay firm when cooked.

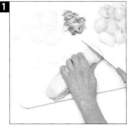

NUTRITIONAL INFORMATION

Calories	267	Sugars	.........7g
Protein	........42g	Fat	...........7g
Carbohydrate	....9g	Saturates	.......1g

🍲 5 mins   🕐 10 mins

SERVES 4

INGREDIENTS

200 g/7 oz squid, cleaned

500 g/1 lb 2 oz firm white fish fillet, preferably monkfish or halibut

1 tbsp sunflower oil

4 shallots, finely chopped

2 garlic cloves, finely chopped

2 tbsp green Thai curry paste

2 small lemon grass stalks, finely chopped

1 tsp shrimp paste

500 ml/18 fl oz coconut milk

200 g/7 oz raw tiger prawns, peeled and de-veined

12 fresh clams in shells, cleaned

8 basil leaves, finely shredded

extra basil leaves, to garnish

boiled rice, to serve

COOK'S TIP

If you prefer, fresh mussels in shells can be used instead of clams – add them in Step 4 and follow the recipe.

1 Cut the squid body cavities into thick rings, and the fish into bite-sized chunks.

2 Heat the oil in a large frying pan or wok and stir-fry the shallots, garlic and curry paste for 1–2 minutes. Add the lemon grass and shrimp paste, stir in the coconut milk and bring to the boil.

3 Reduce the heat until the liquid is simmering gently, then add the white fish, squid and prawns to the pan and simmer for 2 minutes.

4 Add the clams and simmer for a further minute until the clams open. Discard any clams that do not open.

5 Scatter the shredded basil leaves over the stew, and serve immediately, garnished with whole basil leaves and spooned over boiled rice.

Tuna & Vegetable Stir-Fry

Fresh tuna is a dark, meaty fish and is now widely available at fresh fish counters. It lends itself perfectly to the rich flavours in this recipe.

NUTRITIONAL INFORMATION

Calories 245   Sugars 11g
Protein ....30g   Fat 7g
Carbohydrate ...14g   Saturates 1g

 10 mins   10 mins

SERVES 4

INGREDIENTS

225 g/8 oz carrots

1 onion

175 g/6 oz baby corn cobs

2 tbsp corn oil

175 g/6 oz mangetout

450 g/1 lb fresh tuna

2 tbsp fish sauce

1 tbsp palm sugar

finely grated rind and juice of 1 orange

2 tbsp sherry

1 tsp cornflour

rice or noodles, to serve

1 Using a sharp knife, cut the carrots into thin sticks, slice the onion and halve the baby corn cobs.

2 Heat the corn oil in a large preheated wok or frying pan.

3 Add the onion, carrots, mangetout and baby corn cobs to the wok or frying pan and stir-fry for 5 minutes.

4 Using a sharp knife, thinly slice the fresh tuna.

5 Add the tuna slices to the wok or frying pan and stir-fry for about 2–3 minutes, or until the tuna turns opaque.

6 Mix together the fish sauce, palm sugar, orange zest and juice, sherry and cornflour.

7 Pour the mixture over the tuna and vegetables and cook for 2 minutes, or until the juices thicken. Serve the stir-fry with rice or noodles.

VARIATION

Try using swordfish steaks instead of the tuna. Swordfish steaks are now widely available and are similar in texture to tuna

Coconut Prawns

Fan-tail prawns make any meal a special occasion, especially when cooked in such a delicious crispy coating.

NUTRITIONAL INFORMATION

Calories . . . . . . .236 Sugars 1g
Protein . . . . .27g Fat 13g
Carbohydrate . . . .3g Saturates 7g

5 mins   10 mins

SERVES 4

I N G R E D I E N T S

50 g/1¾ oz desiccated coconut

25 g/1 oz fresh white breadcrumbs

1 tsp Chinese five-spice powder

½ tsp salt

finely grated rind of 1 lime

1 egg white

450 g/1 lb fan-tail prawns

sunflower or corn oil, for frying

lemon wedges, to garnish

soy or chilli sauce, to serve

1 Mix together the dessicated coconut, white breadcrumbs, Chinese five-spice powder, salt and finely grated lime rind in a bowl.

2 Lightly whisk the egg white in a separate bowl.

3 Rinse the prawns under cold running water, and pat dry with kitchen paper.

4 Dip the prawns into the egg white then into the coconut and breadcrumb mixture, so that they are evenly coated.

5 Heat about 5 cm/2 inches of sunflower or corn oil in a large preheated wok.

6 Add the prawns to the wok and stir-fry for about 5 minutes or until golden and crispy.

7 Remove the prawns with a slotted spoon and leave to drain on kitchen paper.

8 Transfer the coconut prawns to warm serving dishes and garnish with lemon wedges. Serve immediately with a soy or chilli sauce.

COOK'S TIP

Chinese five-spice powder is a mixture of star anise, fennel seeds, cloves, cinnamon bark and Szechuan pepper. It is very pungent, so should be used sparingly. It will keep indefinitely in an airtight container

Szechuan Prawns

Raw prawns should be used if possible, otherwise add the ready-cooked prawns at the beginning of step 3.

NUTRITIONAL INFORMATION

Calories . . . . .315 Sugars 1g
Protein . . . . .16g Fat 27g
Carbohydrate . . . .3g Saturates 3g

5 mins   10 mins

SERVES 4

I N G R E D I E N T S

250–300 g/9–10½ oz raw tiger prawns

pinch of salt

½ egg white, lightly beaten

1 tsp cornflour

600 ml/1 pint vegetable oil

fresh coriander leaves, to garnish

S A U C E

1 tsp finely chopped fresh root ginger

2 spring onions, finely chopped

1 garlic clove, finely chopped

3–4 small dried red chillies, seeded and chopped

1 tbsp light soy sauce

1 tsp rice wine or dry sherry

1 tbsp tomato purée

1 tbsp oyster sauce

2–3 tbsp vegetable stock or water

a few drops sesame oil

  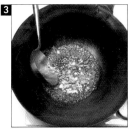

1 Peel the raw prawns, then mix with the salt, egg white and cornflour until the prawns are well coated.

2 Heat the oil in a preheated wok or large frying pan until it is smoking, then deep-fry the prawns in hot oil for about 1 minute. Remove with a slotted spoon and drain on kitchen paper.

3 Pour off the oil, leaving about 1 tablespoon in the wok. Add all the ingredients for the sauce, in the order listed, bring to the boil and stir until smooth and well blended.

4 Add the prawns to the sauce and stir until blended well.

5 Serve the prawns garnished with fresh coriander leaves.

Prawn Omelette

This really is a meal in minutes, combining many Chinese ingredients for a truly tasty dish.

NUTRITIONAL INFORMATION

Calories . . . . .270 Sugars 1g
Protein . . . . .30g Fat 15g
Carbohydrate . . . .3g Saturates 3g

 5 mins   10 mins

SERVES 4

I N G R E D I E N T S

2 tbsp sunflower oil

4 spring onions

350 g/12 oz peeled prawns

100 g/3½ oz beansprouts

1 tsp cornflour

1 tbsp light soy sauce

6 eggs

3 tbsp cold water

1 Heat the sunflower oil in a large preheated wok or frying pan.

2 Using a sharp knife, trim the spring onions and cut into slices.

3 Add the prawns, spring onions and bean sprouts to the wok and stir-fry for 2 minutes.

4 In a small bowl, mix together the cornflour and soy sauce until well combined.

5 In a separate bowl, beat the eggs with the water, using a metal fork, and then blend with the cornflour and soy mixture.

6 Add the egg mixture to the wok and cook for 5–6 minutes, or until the mixture sets.

7 Transfer the omelette to a warm serving plate and cut into quarters to serve.

COOK'S TIP

It is important to use fresh beansprouts for this dish as the canned ones don't have the crunchy texture necessary.

Prawns with Tomatoes

Basil and tomatoes are ideal flavourings for prawns spiced with cumin seeds and garlic.

NUTRITIONAL INFORMATION

Calories 237   Sugar 9g
Protein ....27g   Fat 10g
Carbohydrate ....11g   Saturates 1g

2 mins   20 mins

SERVES 4

I N G R E D I E N T S

2 tbsp corn oil

1 onion

2 cloves garlic, crushed

1 tsp cumin seeds

1 tbsp demerara sugar

400 g/14 oz canned chopped tomatoes

1 tbsp sundried tomato purée

1 tbsp chopped fresh basil

450 g/1 lb peeled king prawns

salt and pepper

1 Heat the corn oil in a large preheated wok.

2 Using a sharp knife, finely chop the onion.

3 Add the onion and garlic to the wok and stir-fry for 2–3 minutes, or until softened.

4 Stir in the cumin seeds and stir-fry for 1 minute.

5 Add the sugar, chopped tomatoes and sundried tomato purée to the wok. Bring the mixture to the boil, then reduce the heat and leave the sauce to simmer for 10 minutes.

6 Add the basil, prawns and salt and pepper to taste to the mixture in the wok. Increase the heat and cook for a further 2–3 minutes or until the prawns are completely cooked through.

COOK'S TIP

Always heat your wok before you add oil or other ingredients. This will prevent anything from sticking to it.

Prawns with Ginger

Crispy ginger is a wonderful garnish which offsets the spicy prawns both visually and in flavour.

NUTRITIONAL INFORMATION

Calories 229	Sugars 7g
Protein 29g	Fat 8g
Carbohydrate ...10g	Saturates 1g

🄖 🄖 🄖

🍲 10 mins   🕐 15 mins

SERVES 4

I N G R E D I E N T S

5-cm/2-inch piece fresh root ginger

oil, for frying

1 onion, diced

225 g/8 oz carrots, diced

100 g/3½ oz frozen peas

100 g/3½ oz beansprouts

450 g/1 lb peeled king prawns

1 tsp Chinese five-spice powder

1 tbsp tomato purée

1 tbsp soy sauce

1 Using a sharp knife, peel the ginger and slice it into very thin sticks.

2 Heat about 2.5 cm/1 inch of oil in a large preheated wok. Add the ginger and stir-fry for 1 minute or until the ginger is crispy. Remove the ginger with a slotted spoon and leave to drain on kitchen paper.

3 Drain all of the oil from the wok except for about 2 tablespoons. Add the onions and carrots to the wok and stir-fry for 5 minutes. Add the peas and beansprouts and stir-fry for 2 minutes.

4 Rinse the prawns under cold running water and pat dry with kitchen paper.

5 Combine the Chinese five-spice powder, tomato purée and soy sauce. Brush the mixture over the prawns.

6 Add the prawns to the wok and stir-fry for a further 2 minutes, or until the prawns are completely cooked through. Transfer the prawn mixture to a warm serving bowl and top with the reserved crispy ginger. Serve immediately.

VARIATION

Use slices of white fish instead of the prawns as an alternative, if you wish.

Prawns with Vegetables

In this recipe, a light Chinese omelette is shredded and tossed back into the dish before serving.

NUTRITIONAL INFORMATION

Calories 258   Sugars 7g
Protein . . . . .21g   Fat 15g
Carbohydrate . . .10g   Saturates 3g

10 mins   15 mins

SERVES 4

INGREDIENTS

225 g/8 oz courgettes

3 tbsp vegetable oil

2 eggs

2 tbsp cold water

225 g/8 oz carrots, grated

1 onion, sliced

150 g/5½ oz beansprouts

225 g/8 oz peeled prawns

2 tbsp soy sauce

pinch of Chinese five-spice powder

25 g/1 oz peanuts, chopped

2 tbsp fresh chopped coriander

1 Finely grate the courgettes.

2 Heat 1 tablespoon of the vegetable oil in a large preheated wok.

3 Beat the eggs with the water and pour the mixture into the wok and cook for 2–3 minutes or until the egg sets.

4 Remove the omelette from the wok and transfer to a clean board. Fold the omelette, cut it into thin strips and set aside until required.

5 Add the remaining oil to the wok. Add the carrots, onion and courgettes and stir-fry for 5 minutes.

6 Add the bean sprouts and prawns to the wok and cook for a further 2 minutes, or until the prawns are heated through.

7 Add the soy sauce, Chinese five-spice powder and peanuts to the wok, together with the strips of omelette and heat through. Garnish with chopped fresh coriander and serve.

COOK'S TIP

The water is mixed with the egg in step 3 for a lighter, less rubbery omelette.

Fried Prawns with Cashews

Cashew nuts are delicious as part of a stir-fry with almost any other ingredient. Use the unsalted variety in cooking.

NUTRITIONAL INFORMATION

Calories ....406 Sugar 3g
Protein ....31g Fat 25g
Carbohydrate ...13g Saturates 4g

5 mins   5 mins

SERVES 4

I N G R E D I E N T S

2 garlic cloves, crushed

1 tbsp cornflour

pinch of caster sugar

450 g/1 lb raw tiger prawns

4 tbsp vegetable oil

1 leek, sliced

125 g/4½ oz broccoli florets

1 orange pepper, seeded and diced

75 g/2¾ oz unsalted cashew nuts

S A U C E

175 ml/6 fl oz fish stock

1 tbsp cornflour

dash of chilli sauce

2 tsp sesame oil

1 tbsp Chinese rice wine

1 Mix together the garlic, cornflour and sugar in a bowl.

2 Peel and de-vein the prawns. Stir the prawns into the mixture to coat thoroughly.

3 Heat the vegetable oil in a preheated wok and add the prawn mixture. Stir-fry over a high heat for 20–30 seconds until the prawns turn pink. Remove the prawns from the wok with a slotted spoon, drain on kitchen paper and set aside until required.

4 Add the leek, broccoli and pepper to the wok and stir-fry for 2 minutes.

5 To make the sauce, place the fish stock, cornflour, chilli sauce to taste, the sesame oil and Chinese rice wine in a small bowl. Mix until thoroughly blended.

6 Add the sauce to the wok, together with the cashew nuts. Return the prawns to the wok and cook for 1 minute to heat through.

7 Transfer the prawn stir-fry to a warm serving dish and serve immediately.

Shrimp Fu Yong

The classic ingredients of this popular dish are eggs, carrots and shrimps. Add extra ingredients such as peas or crabmeat, if desired.

NUTRITIONAL INFORMATION

Calories	240	Sugars	.........1g
Protein	........22g	Fat	..........16g
Carbohydrate	....1g	Saturates	.......3g

 5 mins   10 mins

SERVES 4

I N G R E D I E N T S

2 tbsp vegetable oil

1 carrot, grated

5 eggs, beaten

225 g/8 oz raw shrimp, peeled

1 tbsp light soy sauce

pinch of Chinese five-spice powder

2 spring onions, chopped

2 tsp sesame seeds

1 tsp sesame oil

COOK'S TIP

If only cooked prawns are available, add them just before the end of cooking, but make sure they are fully incorporated into the fu yong. They require only heating through. Overcooking will make them chewy and tasteless.

1 Heat the vegetable oil in a preheated wok or frying pan, swirling it around until the oil is really hot.

2 Add the grated carrot and stir-fry for 1–2 minutes.

3 Push the carrot to one side of the wok or frying pan and add the beaten eggs. Cook, stirring gently, for 1–2 minutes.

4 Stir the shrimp, light soy sauce and five-spice powder into the mixture in the wok. Stir-fry the mixture for 2–3 minutes, or until the shrimps change colour and the mixture is almost dry.

5 Turn the shrimp fu yong out on to a warm plate and sprinkle the spring onions, sesame seeds and sesame oil on top. Serve immediately.

Cantonese Prawns

This prawn dish is very simple and is ideal for supper or lunch when time is short.

NUTRITIONAL INFORMATION

Calories 460   Sugar 3g
Protein . . . . .53g   Fat 24
Carbohydrate . . . .6g   Saturates 5g

 10 mins   20 mins

SERVES 4

I N G R E D I E N T S

5 tbsp vegetable oil

4 garlic cloves, crushed

675 g/1½lb raw prawns, shelled and
de-veined

4 tsp chopped fresh root ginger

175 g/6 oz lean pork, diced

1 leek, sliced

3 eggs, beaten

rice, to serve

S A U C E

2 tbsp Chinese rice wine or dry sherry

2 tbsp light soy sauce

2 tsp caster sugar

150 ml/5 fl oz fish stock

4½ tsp cornflour

3 tbsp water

T O   G A R N I S H

shredded leek

red pepper matchsticks

1 Heat 2 tablespoons of the vegetable oil in a preheated wok.

2 Add the garlic to the wok and stir-fry for 30 seconds.

3 Add the prawns to the wok and stir-fry for 5 minutes, or until they

change colour. Remove the prawns from the wok or frying pan with a slotted spoon, set aside and keep warm.

4 Add the remaining oil to the wok and heat, swirling the oil around the base of the wok until it is really hot.

5 Add the ginger, diced pork and leek to the wok and stir-fry over a medium heat for 4–5 minutes, or until the pork is lightly coloured and sealed.

6 To make the sauce, add the rice wine or sherry, soy sauce, caster sugar and fish stock to the wok and stir to blend.

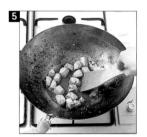

7 In a small bowl, blend the cornflour with the water to form a smooth paste and stir it into the wok. Cook, stirring, until the sauce thickens and clears.

8 Return the prawns to the wok and add the beaten eggs. Cook for 5–6 minutes, gently stirring occasionally, until the eggs set.

9 Transfer to a warm serving dish, garnish with shredded leek and pepper matchsticks and serve immediately with rice.

Scallop Pancakes

Scallops, like most shellfish, require very little cooking, and this original dish is a perfect example of how to use shellfish to its full potential.

NUTRITIONAL INFORMATION

Calories 240	Sugars 1g	
Protein 29g	Fat 9g	
Carbohydrate 11g	Saturates 1g	

5 mins   30 mins

SERVES 4

INGREDIENTS

100 g/3½ oz fine green beans

1 red chilli

450 g/1 lb scallops, without roe

1 egg

3 spring onions, sliced

50 g/1¾ oz cup rice flour

1 tbsp fish sauce

oil, for frying

salt

sweet chilli dip, to serve

1 Using a sharp knife, trim the green beans and slice them very thinly.

2 Using a sharp knife, deseed and very finely chop the red chilli.

3 Bring a small saucepan of lightly salted water to the boil. Add the green beans to the pan and cook for 3–4 minutes or until just softened.

4 Roughly chop the scallops and place them in a large bowl. Add the cooked beans to the scallops.

5 Mix the egg with the spring onions, rice flour, fish sauce and chilli until well combined. Add to the scallops and mix well.

6 Heat about 2.5 cm/1 inch of oil in a large preheated wok. Add a ladleful of the mixture to the wok and cook for 5 minutes until golden and set.

7 Remove the pancake from the wok and leave to drain on kitchen paper. Keep warm while cooking the remaining pancake mixture. Serve the pancakes hot with a sweet chilli dip.

VARIATION

You could use prawns or shelled clams instead of the scallops, if you prefer.

Seared Scallops

Scallops have a terrific, subtle flavour which is complemented in this dish by the buttery sauce.

NUTRITIONAL INFORMATION

Calories 272   Sugars 0g
Protein ....28g   Fat 17g
Carbohydrate ....2g   Saturates 8g

🕑 5 mins   🕐 10 mins

SERVES 4

I N G R E D I E N T S

450 g/1 lb fresh scallops, without roe, or the same amount of frozen scallops, defrosted thoroughly

6 spring onions

2 tbsp vegetable oil

1 green chilli, seeded and sliced

3 tbsp sweet soy sauce

2 tbsp butter, cubed

1 Rinse the scallops thoroughly under cold running water, drain and pat the scallops dry with kitchen paper.

2 Using a sharp knife, slice each scallop in half horizontally.

COOK'S TIP

If you buy scallops on the shell, slide a knife underneath the membrane to loosen it and cut off the tough muscle that holds the scallop to the shell. Discard the black stomach sac and intestinal vein.

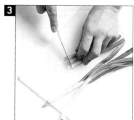

3 Using a sharp knife, trim and slice the spring onions.

4 Heat the vegetable oil in a large preheated wok or heavy-based frying pan, swirling the oil around the base of the wok until it is really hot.

5 Add the sliced green chilli, spring onions and scallops to the wok and stir-fry over a high heat for 4–5 minutes, or until the scallops are just cooked through. If using frozen scallops, be sure not to overcook them as they will easily disintegrate.

6 Add the soy sauce and butter to the scallop stir-fry and heat through until the butter melts.

7 Transfer to warm serving bowls and serve hot.

Scallops in Ginger Sauce

Scallops are both attractive and delicious. Cooked with ginger and orange, this dish is perfect served with plain rice.

NUTRITIONAL INFORMATION

Calories 216   Sugars 4g
Protein . . . . .30g   Fat 8g
Carbohydrate . . . .8g   Saturates 1g

🧊 5 mins   🕐 10 mins

SERVES 4

I N G R E D I E N T S

2 tbsp vegetable oil

450 g/1 lb scallops, cleaned and halved

2 tsp finely chopped fresh root ginger

3 garlic cloves, crushed

2 leeks, shredded

75 g/2¾ oz cup shelled peas

125 g/4½ oz canned bamboo shoots, drained and rinsed

2 tbsp light soy sauce

2 tbsp unsweetened orange juice

1 tsp caster sugar

orange rind, to garnish

1 Heat the vegetable oil in a preheated wok or large frying pan. Add the scallops and stir-fry for 1–2 minutes. Remove the scallops from the wok with a slotted spoon, keep warm and set aside until required.

2 Add the ginger and garlic to the wok and stir-fry for 30 seconds. Stir in the leeks and peas and cook, stirring, for a further 2 minutes.

3 Add the bamboo shoots and return the scallops to the wok. Stir gently to mix without breaking up the scallops.

4 Stir in the soy sauce, orange juice and caster sugar and cook for 1–2 minutes.

5 Transfer the stir-fry to a serving dish, garnish with the orange zest and serve immediately.

COOK'S TIP

The edible parts of a scallop are the round white muscle and the orange and white coral or roe. The frilly skirt surrounding the muscle – the gills and mantle – may be used for making shellfish stock. All other parts should be discarded.

Mussels with Lettuce

Mussels require careful preparation but very little cooking. They are available fresh or in vacuum packs when out of season.

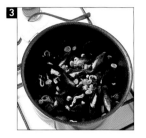

NUTRITIONAL INFORMATION

Calories 205   Sugars 0.3g
Protein . . . . .31g   Fat 9g
Carbohydrate . . . .1g   Saturates 4g

 15 mins   5 mins

SERVES 4

INGREDIENTS

1 kg/2 lb 4 oz mussels in their shells, scrubbed

2 stalks lemon grass

1 Iceberg lettuce

2 tbsp lemon juice

100 ml/3½ fl oz water

2 tbsp butter

finely grated rind of 1 lemon

2 tbsp oyster sauce

1 Place the scrubbed mussels in a large saucepan.

2 Using a sharp knife, thinly slice the lemon grass and shred the lettuce.

3 Add the lemon grass, lemon juice and water to the pan of mussels, cover with a tight-fitting lid and cook for 5 minutes or until the mussels have opened. Discard any mussels that do not open.

4 Carefully remove the cooked mussels from their shells, using a fork and set aside until required.

5 Heat the butter in a large preheated wok or frying pan. Add the lettuce and finely grated lemon rind to the wok or frying pan and stir-fry for 2 minutes, or until the lettuce begins to wilt.

6 Add the oyster sauce to the mixture in the wok and heat through, stirring well until the sauce is thoroughly incorporated in the mixture.

7 Transfer the mixture in the wok to a warm serving dish and serve immediately.

COOK'S TIP

When using fresh mussels, be sure to discard any opened mussels before scrubbing and any unopened mussels after cooking.

Mussels in Black Bean Sauce

This dish looks so impressive, the combination of colours making it look almost too good to eat!

NUTRITIONAL INFORMATION

Calories 174   Sugars 4g
Protein ....19g   Fat 8g
Carbohydrate ....6g   Saturates 1g

5 mins   10 mins

SERVES 4

INGREDIENTS

350 g/12 oz leeks

350 g/12 oz cooked, green-lipped mussels

1 tsp cumin seeds

2 tbsp vegetable oil

2 cloves garlic, crushed

1 red pepper, seeded and sliced

50 g/1¾ oz canned bamboo shoots, drained

175 g/6 oz baby spinach

160 g/5¾ oz jar black bean sauce

1 Using a sharp knife, trim the leeks and shred them.

2 Place the cooked green-lipped mussels in a large bowl, sprinkle with the cumin seeds and toss well to coat all over. Set aside until required.

3 Heat the vegetable oil in a preheated wok, swirling the oil around the base of the wok until it is really hot.

4 Add the shredded leeks, garlic and sliced red pepper to the wok and stir-fry for 5 minutes, or until the vegetables are tender.

5 Add the bamboo shoots, baby spinach leaves and cooked green-lipped mussels to the wok and stir-fry for about 2 minutes.

6 Pour the black bean sauce over the ingredients in the wok, toss well to coat all the ingredients in the sauce and leave to simmer for a few seconds, stirring occasionally.

7 Transfer the stir-fry to warm serving bowls and serve immediately.

COOK'S TIP

If the green-lipped mussels are not available they can be bought shelled in cans and jars from most large supermarkets.

Oysters with Tofu

Oysters are often eaten raw, but are delicious when quickly cooked as in this recipe, and mixed with salt and citrus flavours.

NUTRITIONAL INFORMATION

Calories 175   Sugars 2g
Protein . . . . .18g   Fat 10g
Carbohydrate . . . .3g   Saturates 1g

5 mins   10 mins

SERVES 4

I N G R E D I E N T S

225 g/8 oz leeks

350 g/12 oz tofu

2 tbsp sunflower oil

350 g/12 oz shelled oysters

2 tbsp fresh lemon juice

1 tsp cornflour

2 tbsp light soy sauce

100 ml/3½ fl oz fish stock

2 tbsp chopped fresh coriander

1 tsp finely grated lemon rind

1 Using a sharp knife, trim and slice the leeks.

2 Cut the tofu into bite-sized pieces.

3 Heat the sunflower oil in a large preheated wok or frying pan. Add the leeks to the wok and stir-fry for about 2 minutes.

4 Add the tofu and oysters to the wok or frying pan and stir-fry for 1–2 minutes.

5 Mix together the lemon juice, cornflour, light soy sauce and fish stock in a small bowl, stirring until well blended.

6 Pour the cornflour mixture into the wok and cook, stirring occasionally, until the juices start to thicken.

7 Transfer to serving bowls and scatter the coriander and lemon rind on top. Serve immediately.

VARIATION

Shelled clams or mussels could be used instead of the oysters, if you prefer.

Crab Claws with Chilli

Crab claws are frequently used in Chinese cooking, and look sensational. They are perfect with this delicious chilli sauce.

NUTRITIONAL INFORMATION

Calories 154   Sugar 3g
Protein ....16g   Fat 7g
Carbohydrate ....8g   Saturates 1g

  5 mins   10 mins

SERVES 4

I N G R E D I E N T S

700 g/1 lb 9 oz crab claws

1 tbsp corn oil

2 cloves garlic, crushed

1 tbsp grated fresh root ginger

3 red chillies, seeded and finely chopped

2 tbsp sweet chilli sauce

3 tbsp tomato ketchup

300 ml/10 fl oz cooled fish stock

1 tbsp cornflour

salt and pepper

1 tbsp fresh chives, snipped

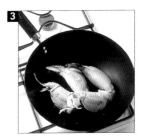

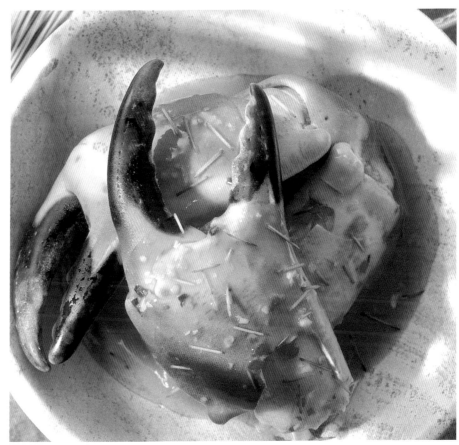

1 Gently crack the crab claws with a nut cracker. This process will allow the flavours of the chilli, garlic and ginger to fully penetrate the crab meat.

2 Heat the corn oil in a large preheated wok.

3 Add the crab claws to the wok and stir-fry for about 5 minutes.

4 Add the garlic, ginger and chillies to the wok and stir-fry for 1 minute, tossing the crab claws to coat all over.

5 Mix together the sweet chilli sauce, tomato ketchup, fish stock and cornflour in a small bowl. Add this mixture to the wok and cook, stirring occasionally, until the sauce starts to thicken.

6 Season the mixture in the wok with salt and pepper to taste.

7 Transfer the crab claws and chilli sauce to warm serving dishes, garnish with snipped fresh chives and serve.

COOK'S TIP

If crab claws are not easily available, use a whole crab, cut into eight pieces, instead.

Vegetables

Vegetables play an important role in wok and stir-fry cooking in the Far East and are used extensively in all meals. It is perfectly possible to enjoy a meal from a selection of the following recipes contained in this chapter without meat or fish. Baby corn cobs, Chinese leaves and green beans, young spinach leaves and pak choi can all bring a unique flavour and freshness to a stir-fried dish.

Native Far Eastern people enjoy their vegetables crisp, so cooking times in this chapter reflect this factor in order to bring out the flavours and textures of the ingredients used.

When selecting vegetables for cooking, importance is attached to the freshness of the ingredients used. Always buy firm, crisp vegetables, and cook them as soon as possible. Another point to remember is to wash the vegetables just before cutting and to cook them as soon as they have been cut so that the vitamin content is not lost through evaporation.

Honey-Fried Chinese Leaves

Chinese leaves are rather similar to lettuce in that the leaves are delicate with a sweet flavour.

NUTRITIONAL INFORMATION

Calories	121	Sugars	.........6g
Protein	.........5g	Fat	...........7g
Carbohydrate	...10g	Saturates	.......1g

5 mins   10 mins

SERVES 4

INGREDIENTS

450 g/1 lb Chinese leaves

1 tbsp peanut oil

1 tsp grated fresh root ginger

2 garlic cloves, crushed

1 fresh red chilli, sliced

1 tbsp Chinese rice wine or dry sherry

4½ tsp light soy sauce

1 tbsp clear honey

125 ml/4 fl oz orange juice

1 tbsp sesame oil

2 tsp sesame seeds

orange rind, to garnish

COOK'S TIP

Single-flower honey has a better, more individual flavour than blended honey. Acacia honey is typically Chinese, but you could also try clover, lemon blossom, lime flower or orange blossom.

1 Separate the Chinese leaves and shred them finely, using a sharp knife.

2 Heat the peanut oil in a preheated wok. Add the ginger, garlic and chilli to the wok and stir-fry the mixture for about 30 seconds.

3 Add the Chinese leaves, Chinese rice wine or sherry, soy sauce, honey and orange juice to the wok. Reduce the heat

and leave to simmer for 5 minutes.

4 Add the sesame oil to the wok, sprinkle the sesame seeds on top and mix to combine.

5 Transfer to a warm serving dish, garnish with the orange rind and serve immediately.

Green Stir-Fry

The basis of this recipe is pak choi, also known as bok choy or Chinese greens. If unavailable, use Swiss chard or Savoy cabbage instead.

NUTRITIONAL INFORMATION

Calories 107   Sugars 6g
Protein . . . . .4g   Fat 8g
Carbohydrate . . . .6g   Saturates 1g

5 mins   10 mins

SERVES 4

I N G R E D I E N T S

2 tbsp peanut oil

2 garlic cloves, crushed

½ tsp ground star anise

1 tsp salt

350 g/12 oz pak choi, shredded

225 g/8 oz baby spinach

25 g/1 oz mangetout

1 celery stick, sliced

1 green pepper, seeded and sliced

50 ml/2 fl oz vegetable stock

1 tsp sesame oil

1 Heat the peanut oil in a preheated wok or large frying pan, swirling the oil around the base of the wok until it is really hot.

2 Add the crushed garlic to the wok or frying pan and stir-fry for about 30 seconds.

3 Stir in the ground star anise, salt, shredded pak choi, spinach, mangetout, celery and green pepper and stir-fry for 3–4 minutes.

4 Add the vegetable stock, cover the wok and cook for 3–4 minutes.

5 Remove the lid from the wok and stir in the sesame oil. Mix thoroughly to combine all the ingredients.

6 Transfer the green vegetable stir-fry to a warm serving dish and serve.

COOK'S TIP

Star anise is an important ingredient in Chinese cuisine. The attractive star-shaped pods are often used whole to add a decorative garnish to dishes. The flavour is similar to liquorice, but with spicy undertones, and is quite strong.

Crispy Cabbage & Almonds

This dish is better known as crispy seaweed. It does not actually contain seaweed, but consists of spring greens or pak choi.

NUTRITIONAL INFORMATION

Calories	431	Sugars	........17g
Protein	.........9g	Fat	..........37g
Carbohydrate	...17g	Saturates	.......4g

 10 mins   10 mins

SERVES 4

INGREDIENTS

1.25 kg/2 lb 12 oz pak choi or
    spring greens

750 ml/1¼ pints vegetable oil

75 g/2¾ oz blanched almonds

1 tsp salt

1 tbsp light brown sugar

pinch of ground cinnamon

1 Separate the leaves from the pak choi or spring greens and rinse them well. Drain thoroughly and pat dry with kitchen paper.

2 Shred the greens into thin strips, using a sharp knife.

3 Heat the vegetable oil in a preheated wok or large, heavy-based frying pan until the oil is almost smoking.

4 Reduce the heat and add the pak choi or spring greens. Cook for 2–3 minutes, or until the greens begin to float in the oil and are crisp.

5 Remove the greens from the oil with a slotted spoon and leave to drain thoroughly on kitchen paper.

6 Add the blanched almonds to the oil in the wok and cook for 30 seconds. Remove the almonds from the oil with a slotted spoon and drain thoroughly on kitchen paper.

7 Mix together the salt, light brown sugar and ground cinnamon and sprinkle on to the greens.

8 Toss the almonds into the greens.

9 Transfer the greens and almonds to a warm serving dish and serve immediately.

COOK'S TIP

Ensure that the greens are completely dry before adding them to the oil, otherwise it will spit. The greens will not become crisp if they are wet when placed in the oil.

Creamy Green Vegetables

This dish is very quick to make. A dash of cream is added to the sauce, but this may be omitted, if preferred.

NUTRITIONAL INFORMATION

Calories 111   Sugars 2g
Protein . . . . .5g   Fat 8g
Carbohydrate . . . .7g   Saturates 2g

5 mins   20 mins

SERVES 4

INGREDIENTS

450 g/1 lb Chinese leaves, shredded

2 tbsp peanut oil

2 leeks, shredded

4 garlic cloves, crushed

300 ml/10 fl oz vegetable stock

1 tbsp light soy sauce

2 tsp cornflour

4 tsp water

2 tbsp single cream or natural yogurt

1 tbsp chopped coriander

1 Blanch the Chinese leaves in boiling water for 30 seconds. Drain, rinse under cold running water, then drain thoroughly again.

2 Heat the oil in a preheated wok and add the Chinese leaves, leeks and garlic. Stir-fry for 2–3 minutes.

3 Add the stock and soy sauce to the wok, reduce the heat to low, cover and simmer for 10 minutes.

4 Remove the vegetables from the wok with a slotted spoon and set aside. Bring the stock to the boil and boil vigorously until reduced by about half.

5 Blend the cornflour with the water and stir into the wok. Bring to the boil, and cook, stirring constantly, until thickened and clear.

6 Reduce the heat and stir in the vegetables and cream or yogurt. Cook over a low heat for 1 minute.

7 Transfer to a serving dish, sprinkle over the chopped coriander and serve immediately.

COOK'S TIP

Do not boil the sauce once the cream or yogurt has been added, as it will separate.

Stir-Fried Chilli Cucumber

Warm cucumbers are absolutely delicious, especially when combined with the heat of chilli and the flavour of ginger.

NUTRITIONAL INFORMATION

Calories ....67 Sugars 4g
Protein ....1g Fat 5g
Carbohydrate ....5g Saturates 1g

30 mins   5 mins

SERVES 4

INGREDIENTS

2 medium cucumbers

2 tsp salt

1 tbsp vegetable oil

2 garlic cloves, crushed

1 tsp grated fresh root ginger

2 fresh red chillies, chopped

2 spring onions, chopped

1 tsp yellow bean sauce

1 tbsp clear honey

125 ml/4 fl oz water

1 tsp sesame oil

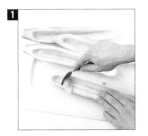

1 Peel the cucumbers and cut in half lengthways. Scrape the seeds from the centre with a teaspoon or melon baller and discard.

2 Cut the cucumber into strips and place on a plate. Sprinkle the salt over the cucumber strips and set aside for 20 minutes. Rinse well under cold running water and pat dry with kitchen paper.

3 Heat the vegetable oil in a preheated wok or large frying pan until it is almost smoking. Lower the heat slightly and add the garlic, ginger, chillies and spring onions and stir-fry for 30 seconds.

4 Add the cucumbers to the wok, together with the yellow bean sauce and honey and stir-fry for 30 seconds.

5 Add the water and cook over a high heat until most of the water has evaporated.

6 Sprinkle the sesame oil over the stir-fry. Transfer to a warm serving dish and serve immediately.

COOK'S TIP

The cucumber is sprinkled with salt and left to stand in order to draw out the excess water, thus preventing a soggy meal!

Garlic Spinach

This has to be one of the simplest recipes, yet it is so tasty. Spinach is fried with garlic and lemon grass and tossed in soy sauce and sugar.

NUTRITIONAL INFORMATION

Calories 118   Sugars 6g
Protein . . . . .7g   Fat 7g
Carbohydrate . . . .7g   Saturates 1g

 5 mins   10 mins

SERVES 4

INGREDIENTS

2 garlic cloves

1 tsp lemon grass

900 g/2 lb fresh spinach

2 tbsp peanut oil

salt

1 tbsp dark soy sauce

2 tsp brown sugar

1 Peel the garlic cloves and crush them in a pestle and mortar. Set aside until required.

2 Using a sharp knife, finely chop the lemon grass. Set aside until required.

3 Carefully remove the stems from the spinach. Rinse the spinach leaves and drain them thoroughly, patting them dry with kitchen paper.

4 Heat the peanut oil in a preheated wok or large frying pan until it is almost smoking.

5 Reduce the heat slightly, add the garlic and lemon grass and stir-fry for 30 seconds.

6 Add the spinach leaves and a pinch of salt to the wok or frying pan and stir-fry for 2–3 minutes, or until the spinach

leaves have just wilted.

7 Stir the dark soy sauce and brown sugar into the mixture in the wok or frying pan and cook for a further 3–4 minutes.

8 Transfer the garlic spinach to a warm serving dish and serve as an accompaniment to a main dish.

COOK'S TIP

Lemon grass is available fresh, dried and canned or bottled. Dried lemon grass must be soaked for 2 hours before using. The stems are hard and are usually used whole and removed from the dish before serving. The roots can be crushed or finely chopped.

Green Bean Stir-Fry

These beans are simply cooked in a spicy, hot sauce for a tasty and very easy recipe.

NUTRITIONAL INFORMATION

Calories 86   Sugars 4g
Protein . . . . .2g   Fat 6g
Carbohydrates . . . .6g   Saturates 1g

 5 mins   5 mins

SERVES 4

INGREDIENTS

450 g/1 lb thin green beans

2 fresh red chillies

2 tbsp peanut oil

½ tsp ground star anise

1 garlic clove, crushed

2 tbsp light soy sauce

2 tsp clear honey

½ tsp sesame oil

1 Using a sharp knife, cut the green beans in half.

2 Slice the fresh chillies, removing the seeds first if you prefer a milder dish.

3 Heat the oil in a preheated wok or large frying pan until it is almost smoking.

4 Lower the heat slightly, add the halved green beans to the wok and stir-fry for 1 minute.

5 Add the sliced red chillies, star anise and garlic to the wok and stir-fry for a further 30 seconds.

6 Mix together the soy sauce, honey and sesame oil in a small bowl.

7 Stir the sauce mixture into the wok. Cook for 2 minutes, tossing the beans to ensure that they are thoroughly coated in the sauce.

8 Transfer the mixture in the wok or pan to a warm serving dish and serve immediately.

VARIATION

This recipe is surprisingly delicious made with Brussels sprouts instead of green beans. Trim the sprouts, then shred them finely. Stir-fry the sprouts in hot oil for 2 minutes, then proceed with the recipe from step 4.

Gingered Broccoli

Ginger and broccoli are a perfect combination of flavours and make an exceptionally tasty side dish.

NUTRITIONAL INFORMATION

Calories	118	Sugars	.........3g
Protein	.........8g	Fat	...........7g
Carbohydrate	....6g	Saturates	.......1g

5 mins   15 mins

SERVES 4

INGREDIENTS

5-cm/2-inch piece fresh root ginger

2 tbsp peanut oil

1 garlic clove, crushed

675 g/1½ lb broccoli florets

1 leek, sliced

75 g/2¾ oz water chestnuts, halved

½ tsp caster sugar

125 ml/4 fl oz vegetable stock

1 tsp dark soy sauce

1 tsp cornflour

2 tsp water

1 Using a sharp knife, finely chop the ginger. (Alternatively, cut the ginger into larger strips, to be discarded later, for a slightly milder ginger flavour.)

2 Heat the peanut oil in a preheated wok. Add the garlic and ginger and stir-fry for 30 seconds.

3 Add the broccoli, leek and water chestnuts and stir-fry for a further 3–4 minutes.

4 Add the caster sugar, vegetable stock and dark soy sauce to the wok, reduce the heat and simmer for 4–5 minutes, or until the broccoli is almost cooked.

5 Blend the cornflour with the water to form a smooth paste and stir it into the wok. Bring to the boil and cook, stirring constantly, for 1 minute or until thickened.

6 If using larger strips of ginger, remove from the wok and discard.

7 Transfer the vegetables to a serving dish and serve immediately.

VARIATION

Use spinach instead of the broccoli, if you prefer. Trim the woody ends and cut the remainder into 5-cm/2-inch lengths, keeping the stalks and leaves separate. Add the stalks with the leek in step 3 and add the leaves 2 minutes later. Reduce the cooking time in step 4 to 3–4 minutes.

Vegetarian & Vegan

As vegetables are so plentiful and diverse in the Far East, they play a major role in the diet. Other ingredients, such as tofu and quorn, are also added to the vegetarian diet, which is both a healthy and an economical choice. Tofu is

produced from the soya bean, which is grown in abundance in these countries. The cake variety of tofu is frequently used in stir-frying for texture and it is perfect for absorbing all of the component flavours of the dish. It is also an ideal ingredient for the vegan cook.

The wok is perfect for cooking vegetables as it cooks them very quickly, which helps to retain their nutrients and crispness. This produces a range of colourful and flavoursome recipes, which display the wonderful versatility of vegetables.

Spiced Aubergine

This is a spicy and sweet dish, flavoured with mango chutney and heated up with chillies for a really wonderful combination of flavours.

NUTRITIONAL INFORMATION

Calories 208	Sugars 17g
Protein 1g	Fat 15g
Carbohydrate ...17g	Saturates 2g

 5 mins 25 mins

SERVES 4

INGREDIENTS

3 tbsp groundnut oil

2 onions, sliced

2 cloves garlic, chopped

2 aubergines, diced

2 red chillies, seeded and very finely chopped

2 tbsp demerara sugar

6 spring onions, sliced

3 tbsp mango chutney

oil, for deep-frying

2 cloves garlic, sliced, to garnish

1 Heat the groundnut oil in a large preheated wok or heavy-based frying pan, swirling the oil around the base of the wok until it is really hot.

2 Add the onions and chopped garlic to the wok, stirring well.

3 Add the diced aubergine and chillies to the wok and stir-fry for 5 minutes.

4 Add the demerara sugar, spring onions and mango chutney to the wok, stirring well.

5 Reduce the heat, cover and leave to simmer, stirring from time to time, for 15 minutes until the aubergine is tender.

6 Transfer the stir-fry to serving bowls and keep warm.

7 Heat the oil for deep-frying in the wok and quickly stir-fry the slices of garlic, until they brown slightly. Garnish the stir-fry with the deep-fried garlic and serve immediately.

COOK'S TIP

The hotness of chillies varies enormously so always use with caution, but as a general guide the smaller they are the hotter they will be. The seeds are the hottest part and so are usually discarded.

Spicy Aubergines

Try to obtain the smaller Chinese aubergines for this dish, as they have a slightly sweeter taste.

NUTRITIONAL INFORMATION

Calories . . . . .120 Sugars 7g
Protein . . . . .2g Fat 9g
Carbohydrate . . . .9g Saturates 1g

35 mins   20 mins

SERVES 4

INGREDIENTS

450 g/1 lb aubergines, rinsed

2 tsp salt

3 tbsp vegetable oil

2 garlic cloves, crushed

2 tsp chopped fresh root ginger

1 onion, halved and sliced

1 fresh red chilli, sliced

2 tbsp dark soy sauce

1 tbsp hoisin sauce

½ tsp chilli sauce

1 tbsp dark brown sugar

1 tbsp wine vinegar

1 tsp ground Szechuan pepper

300 ml/10 fl oz vegetable stock

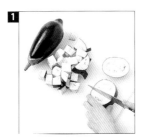  

1 Cut the aubergines into cubes if you are using the larger variety, or cut the smaller type in half. Place in a colander and sprinkle with the salt. Let stand for 30 minutes. Rinse under cold running water and pat dry with kitchen paper.

2 Heat the oil in a preheated wok and add the garlic, ginger, onion and fresh chilli. Stir-fry for 30 seconds and add the aubergines. Continue to cook for 1–2 minutes.

3 Add the soy sauce, hoisin sauce, chilli sauce, sugar, wine vinegar, Szechuan pepper and vegetable stock to the wok, reduce the heat and leave to simmer, uncovered, for 10 minutes, or until the aubergines are cooked.

4 Increase the heat and boil to reduce the sauce until thickened enough to coat the aubergines. Serve immediately.

COOK'S TIP

Sprinkling the aubergines with salt and letting them stand removes the bitter juices, which would otherwise taint the flavour of the dish.

Carrot & Orange Stir-Fry

Carrots and oranges have long been combined in Oriental cooking, the orange juice bringing out the sweetness of the carrots.

NUTRITIONAL INFORMATION

Calories 341   Sugars 26g
Protein . . . . .10g   Fat 21g
Carbohydrate . . .28g   Saturates 4g

 10 mins   10 mins

SERVES 4

INGREDIENTS

2 tbsp sunflower oil

450 g/1 lb carrots, grated

225 g/8 oz leeks, shredded

2 oranges, peeled and segmented

2 tbsp tomato ketchup

1 tbsp demerara

2 tbsp light soy sauce

100 g/3½ oz chopped
    peanuts

VARIATION

You could use pineapple instead of orange, if you prefer. If using canned pineapple, make sure that it is in natural juice not syrup, as syrup will spoil the fresh taste of this dish.

1 Heat the sunflower oil in a large preheated wok.

2 Add the grated carrot and leeks to the wok and stir-fry for 2–3 minutes, or until the vegetables have just softened.

3 Add the orange segments to the wok and heat through gently, ensuring that you do not break up the orange segments as you stir the mixture.

4 Mix the tomato ketchup, demerara sugar and soy sauce together in a small bowl.

5 Add the tomato and sugar mixture to the wok and stir-fry for a further 2 minutes.

6 Transfer the stir-fry to warm serving bowls and scatter with the chopped peanuts. Serve immediately.

Deep-Fried Chilli Corn Balls

These small corn balls have a wonderful hot and sweet flavour, offset by the pungent coriander.

NUTRITIONAL INFORMATION

Calories 248   Sugars 6g
Protein ....6g   Fat 12
Carbohydrate ...30g   Saturates 5g

15 mins   30 mins

SERVES 4

INGREDIENTS

6 spring onions, sliced

3 tbsp fresh coriander, chopped

225 g/8 oz canned sweetcorn kernels

1 tsp mild chilli powder

1 tbsp sweet chilli sauce

25 g/1 oz desiccated coconut

1 egg

75 g/2¾ oz polenta

oil, for deep-frying

extra sweet chilli sauce, to serve

1 In a large bowl, mix together the spring onions, coriander, sweetcorn, chilli powder, chilli sauce, coconut, egg and polenta until well blended.

2 Cover the bowl with clingfilm and leave to stand for about 10 minutes.

3 Heat the oil for deep-frying in a large preheated wok or frying pan to 180°C/350°F or until a cube of bread browns in 30 seconds.

4 Carefully drop spoonfuls of the chilli and polenta mixture into the hot oil. Deep-fry the chilli corn balls, in batches, for 4–5 minutes or until crispy and a deep golden brown colour.

5 Remove the chilli corn balls with a slotted spoon, transfer to absorbent kitchen paper and leave to drain thoroughly.

6 Transfer the chilli corn balls to serving plates and serve with an extra sweet chilli sauce for dipping.

COOK'S TIP

For safe deep-frying in a round-bottomed wok, place it on a wok rack so that it rests securely. Only half-fill the wok with oil. Never leave the wok unattended over a high heat.

Butternut Squash Stir-Fry

Butternut squash is as its name suggests, deliciously buttery and nutty in flavour. If the squash is not in season, use sweet potatoes instead.

NUTRITIONAL INFORMATION

Calories 301	Sugars 4g
Protein 9g	Fat 22g
Carbohydrate . . .19g	Saturates 4g

5 mins   25 mins

SERVES 4

INGREDIENTS

1 kg/2 lb 4 oz butternut squash, peeled

3 tbsp groundnut oil

1 onion, sliced

2 cloves garlic, crushed

1 tsp coriander seeds

1 tsp cumin seeds

2 tbsp chopped coriander

150 ml/5 fl oz coconut milk

100 ml/3½ fl oz water

100 g/3½ oz salted cashew nuts

TO GARNISH

freshly grated lime rind

fresh coriander

lime wedges

1 Using a sharp knife, slice the butternut squash into small, bite-sized cubes.

2 Heat the groundnut oil in a large preheated wok.

3 Add the butternut squash, onion and garlic to the wok and stir-fry for 5 minutes.

4 Stir in the coriander seeds, cumin seeds and fresh coriander and stir-fry for 1 minute.

5 Add the coconut milk and water to the wok and bring to the boil. Cover the wok and leave to simmer for 10–15 minutes, or until the squash is tender.

6 Add the cashew nuts and stir to combine.

7 Transfer to warm serving dishes and garnish with freshly grated lime rind, fresh coriander and lime wedges. Serve hot and immediately.

COOK'S TIP

If you do not have coconut milk, grate some creamed coconut into the dish with the water in step 5.

Leeks with Yellow Bean Sauce

This is a simple side dish which is ideal with other main meal vegetarian dishes.

NUTRITIONAL INFORMATION

Calories 131   Sugars 3g
Protein . . . . .6g   Fat 9g
Carbohydrate . . . .7g   Saturates 2g

5 mins   10 mins

SERVES 4

I N G R E D I E N T S

450 g/1 lb leeks

175 g/6 oz baby corn cobs

6 spring onions

3 tbsp groundnut oil

225 g/8 oz Chinese leaves, shredded

4 tbsp yellow bean sauce

1 Using a sharp knife, slice the leeks, halve the baby corn cobs and thinly slice the spring onions.

2 Heat the groundnut oil in a large preheated wok or frying pan until smoking.

3 Add the leeks, shredded Chinese leaves and baby corn cobs to the wok or frying pan.

4 Stir-fry the vegetables over a high heat for about 5 minutes or until the edges of the vegetables are slightly brown.

5 Add the spring onions to the wok or frying pan, stirring to combine.

6 Add the yellow bean sauce to the wok or frying pan.

7 Stir-fry the mixture in the wok for a further 2 minutes, or until heated through and the vegetables are thoroughly coated in the sauce.

8 Transfer the vegetables and sauce to warm serving dishes and serve immediately.

COOK'S TIP

Yellow bean sauce adds an authentic Chinese flavour to stir-fries. It is made from crushed salted soya beans mixed with flour and spices to make a thick paste. It is mild in flavour and is excellent with a range of vegetables.

Deep-Fried Courgettes

These courgette fritters are irresistible and could be served as a starter or snack with a chilli dip.

NUTRITIONAL INFORMATION

Calories 117   Sugars 2g
Protein . . . . .3g   Fat 6g
Carbohydrate . . .14g   Saturates 1g

🥄 5 mins   🕐 20 mins

SERVES 4

I N G R E D I E N T S

450 g/1 lb courgettes

1 egg white

50 g/1¾ oz cornflour

1 tsp salt

1 tsp Chinese five-spice powder

oil, for deep-frying

chilli dip, to serve

1 Using a sharp knife, slice the courgettes into rings or chunky sticks.

2 Place the egg white in a small mixing bowl. Lightly whip the egg white until foamy, using a fork.

3 Mix the cornflour, salt and Chinese five-spice powder together and sprinkle on to a large plate.

4 Heat the oil for deep-frying in a large preheated wok or frying pan with a heavy base.

5 Dip each piece of courgette into the beaten egg white then coat in the cornflour and five-spice mixture.

6 Deep-fry the courgettes, in batches, for about 5 minutes or until pale golden and crispy. Repeat this process with all the remaining courgettes.

7 Remove the courgettes with a slotted spoon and leave to drain on kitchen paper while deep-frying the remainder.

8 Transfer the courgettes to serving plates and serve immediately with a chilli dip.

VARIATION

Alter the seasoning by using chilli powder or curry powder instead of the Chinese five-spice powder, if you prefer.

Aspagarus Parcels

These small parcels are ideal as part of a main meal and irresistible as a quick snack with extra plum sauce for dipping.

NUTRITIONAL INFORMATION

Calories ....194 Sugars 2g
Protein ....3g Fat 16g
Carbohydrate ....11g Saturates 4g

5 mins   25 mins

SERVES 4

INGREDIENTS

100 g/3½ oz fine tip asparagus

1 red pepper, seeded and thinly sliced

50 g/1¾ oz beansprouts

2 tbsp plum sauce

1 egg yolk

8 sheets filo pastry

oil, for deep-frying

1 Place the asparagus, pepper and beansprouts in a large mixing bowl.

2 Add the plum sauce to the vegetables and mix until well-combined.

3 Beat the egg yolk and set aside until required.

4 Lay the sheets of filo pastry out on to a clean work surface.

5 Place a little of the asparagus and red pepper filling at the top end of each filo pastry sheet. Brush the edges of the filo pastry with a little of the beaten egg yolk.

6 Roll up the filo pastry, tucking in the ends and enclosing the filling like a spring roll. Repeat with the remaining filo sheets.

7 Heat the oil for deep-frying in a large preheated wok. Carefully cook the parcels, 2 at a time, in the hot oil for 4–5 minutes or until crispy.

8 Remove the parcels with a slotted spoon and leave them to drain on kitchen paper.

9 Transfer the parcels to warm serving plates and serve immediately.

COOK'S TIP

Be sure to use fine-tipped asparagus as it is more tender than the larger stems.

Broccoli & Black Bean Sauce

Broccoli works well with the black bean sauce in this recipe, while the almonds add extra crunch and flavour.

NUTRITIONAL INFORMATION

Calories 139   Sugars 3g
Protein . . . . .7g   Fat 10g
Carbohydrate . . . .5g   Saturates 1g

5 mins   15 mins

SERVES 4

INGREDIENTS

450 g/1 lb broccoli florets

2 tbsp sunflower oil

1 onion, sliced

2 cloves garlic, thinly sliced

25 g/1 oz flaked almonds

1 head Chinese leaves, shredded

4 tbsp black bean sauce

1 Bring a large saucepan of water to the boil.

2 Add the broccoli florets to the pan and cook for 1 minute. Drain the broccoli thoroughly.

3 Meanwhile, heat the sunflower oil in a large preheated wok.

4 Add the onion and garlic slices to the wok and stir-fry until just beginning to brown.

5 Add the drained broccoli florets and the flaked almonds to the mixture in the wok and stir-fry for a further 2–3 minutes.

6 Add the shredded Chinese leaves to the wok and stir-fry for a further 2 minutes, stirring the leaves briskly around the wok.

7 Stir the black bean sauce into the vegetables in the wok, tossing to coat the vegetables thoroughly in the sauce and cook until the juices are just beginning to bubble.

8 Transfer the vegetables to warm serving bowls and serve immediately.

VARIATION

Use unsalted cashew nuts instead of the almonds, if preferred.

Cabbage & Walnut Stir-Fry

This is a really quick, one-pan dish using white and red cabbage for colour and flavour.

NUTRITIONAL INFORMATION

Calories 422   Sugars 9g
Protein ....13g   Fat 37g
Carbohydrate ...10g   Saturates 5g

10 mins   10 mins

SERVES 4

INGREDIENTS

350 g/12 oz white cabbage

350 g/12 oz red cabbage

4 tbsp peanut oil

1 tbsp walnut oil

2 garlic cloves, crushed

8 spring onions, trimmed

225 g/8 oz firm tofu, cubed

2 tbsp lemon juice

100 g/3½ oz walnut halves

2 tsp Dijon mustard

2 tsp poppy seeds

salt and pepper

1 Using a sharp knife, shred the white and red cabbages thinly and set aside until required.

2 Heat the peanut and walnut oils in a preheated wok. Add the garlic, cabbage, spring onions and tofu and cook for 5 minutes, stirring.

3 Add the lemon juice, walnuts and mustard, season with salt and pepper and cook for a further 5 minutes or until the cabbage is tender.

4 Transfer the stir-fry to a warm serving bowl, sprinkle with poppy seeds and serve immediately.

VARIATION

Sesame seeds could be used instead of the poppy seeds and drizzle 1 teaspoon of sesame oil over the dish just before serving, if you wish.

Stir-Fried Japanese Noodles

This quick dish is an ideal lunchtime meal, packed with mixed mushrooms in a sweet sauce.

NUTRITIONAL INFORMATION

Calories ... 379   Sugars ... 8g
Protein ... 12g   Fat ... 13g
Carbohydrate ... 53g   Saturates ... 3g

  15 mins   15 mins

SERVES 4

INGREDIENTS

250 g/9 oz Japanese egg noodles

2 tbsp sunflower oil

1 red onion, sliced

1 clove garlic, crushed

450 g/1 lb mixed mushrooms (shiitake, oyster, brown cap)

350 g/12 oz pak choi (or Chinese leaves)

2 tbsp sweet sherry

6 tbsp oyster sauce

4 spring onions, sliced

1 tbsp toasted sesame seeds

1 Place the Japanese egg noodles in a large bowl. Pour over enough boiling water to cover and leave to soak for 10 minutes.

2 Heat the sunflower oil in a large preheated wok.

3 Add the red onion and garlic to the wok and stir-fry for 2–3 minutes, or until softened.

4 Add the mushrooms to the wok and stir-fry for about 5 minutes, or until the mushrooms have softened.

5 Drain the egg noodles thoroughly.

6 Add the the pak choi (or Chinese leaves), noodles, sweet sherry and oyster sauce to the wok. Toss all of the ingredients together and stir-fry for 2–3 minutes or until the liquid is just bubbling.

7 Transfer the mushroom noodles to warm serving bowls and scatter with sliced spring onions and toasted sesame seeds. Serve immediately.

COOK'S TIP

The variety of mushrooms in supermarkets has greatly improved and a good mixture should be easily obtainable. If not, use the more common button and flat mushrooms.

Tofu with Peppers

Tofu is perfect for marinating as it readily absorbs flavours for a great-tasting main dish.

NUTRITIONAL INFORMATION

Calories ....267 Sugars 2g
Protein ....9g Fat 23g
Carbohydrate ....5g Saturates 3g

 25 mins   15 mins

SERVES 4

INGREDIENTS

350 g/12 oz tofu

2 cloves garlic, crushed

4 tbsp soy sauce

1 tbsp sweet chilli sauce

6 tbsp sunflower oil

1 onion, sliced

1 green pepper, seeded and diced

1 tbsp sesame oil

1 Using a sharp knife, cut the tofu into bite-sized pieces. Place the tofu in a shallow, non-metallic dish.

2 Mix together the garlic, soy sauce and sweet chilli sauce and drizzle over the tofu. Toss well to coat and leave to marinate for about 20 minutes.

3 Meanwhile, heat the sunflower oil in a large preheated wok.

4 Add the onion to the wok and stir-fry over a high heat until brown and crispy. Remove the onion with a slotted spoon and leave to drain on kitchen paper.

5 Add the tofu to the hot oil and stir-fry for about 5 minutes.

6 Remove all but 1 tablespoon of the sunflower oil from the wok. Add the pepper to the wok and stir-fry for 2–3 minutes, or until softened.

7 Return the tofu and onions to the wok and heat through, stirring occasionally.

8 Drizzle with sesame oil. Transfer to serving plates and serve immediately.

COOK'S TIP

If you are in a real hurry, buy ready-marinated tofu from your supermarket.

Quorn & Vegetable Stir-Fry

Quorn, like tofu, absorbs all of the flavours in a dish, making it ideal for this recipe which is packed with classic Chinese flavourings.

NUTRITIONAL INFORMATION

Calories 167   Sugars 8g
Protein . . . . .12g   Fat 9g
Carbohydrate . . .10g   Saturates 1g

30 mins   10 mins

SERVES 4

I N G R E D I E N T S

1 tbsp grated fresh root ginger

1 tsp ground ginger

1 tbsp tomato purée

2 tbsp sunflower oil

1 clove garlic, crushed

2 tbsp soy sauce

350 g/12 oz Quorn (or soya cubes)

225 g/8 oz carrots, sliced

100 g/3½ oz green beans, sliced

4 celery sticks, sliced

1 red pepper, seeded and sliced

boiled rice, to serve

COOK'S TIP

Ginger root will keep for several weeks in a cool, dry place. Ginger root can also be kept frozen – break off lumps as needed.

1 Place the grated fresh root ginger, ground ginger, tomato purée, 1 tablespoon of the sunflower oil, garlic, soy sauce and Quorn (or soya cubes) in a large bowl. Mix well to combine, stirring carefully so that you don't break up the Quorn or soya cubes. Cover and leave to marinate for 20 minutes.

2 Heat the remaining sunflower oil in a large preheated wok.

3 Add the marinated Quorn mixture to the wok and stir-fry for about 2 minutes.

4 Add the carrots, green beans, celery and red pepper to the wok and stir-fry for a further 5 minutes.

5 Transfer the stir-fry to warm serving dishes and serve immediately with freshly cooked boiled rice.

Tofu Casserole

Tofu is ideal for absorbing all the other flavours in this dish. If marinated tofu is used, it will add a flavour of its own.

NUTRITIONAL INFORMATION

Calories ....228 Sugars 3g
Protein ....16g Fat 15g
Carbohydrate ....7g Saturates 2g

🧊 5 mins   🕐 15 mins

SERVES 4

INGREDIENTS

450 g/1 lb tofu

2 tbsp peanut oil

8 spring onions, cut into batons

2 celery sticks, sliced

125 g/4½ oz broccoli florets

125 g/4½ oz courgettes, sliced

2 garlic cloves, thinly sliced

450 g/1 lb baby spinach

rice, to serve

SAUCE

425 ml/15 fl oz vegetable stock

2 tbsp light soy sauce

3 tbsp hoisin sauce

½ tsp chilli powder

1 tbsp sesame oil

1 Cut the tofu into 2.5-cm/1-inch cubes and set aside until required.

2 Heat the peanut oil in a preheated wok or large frying pan.

3 Add the spring onions, celery, broccoli, courgettes, garlic, spinach and tofu to the wok or frying pan and stir-fry for 3–4 minutes.

4 To make the sauce, mix together the vegetable stock, soy sauce, hoisin sauce, chilli powder and sesame oil in a flameproof casserole and bring to the boil.

5 Add the stir-fried vegetables and tofu to the saucepan, reduce the heat, cover and simmer for 10 minutes.

6 Transfer the tofu and vegetables to a warm serving dish and serve with rice.

VARIATION

This recipe has a green vegetable theme, but you can alter the colour and flavour by adding your favourite vegetables. Add 75 g/2¾ oz fresh or canned and drained straw mushrooms with the vegetables in step 2.

Sweet & Sour Tofu

Sweet-and-sour sauce was one of the first Chinese sauces introduced to Western diets, and remains one of the most popular.

NUTRITIONAL INFORMATION

Calories 205	Sugars 12g
Protein 11g	Fat 11g
Carbohydrate ...17g	Saturates 1g

 5 mins   🕐 10 mins

SERVES 4

I N G R E D I E N T S

2 celery sticks

1 carrot

1 green pepper, seeded

75 g/2¾ oz mangetout

2 tbsp vegetable oil

2 garlic cloves, crushed

8 baby corn cobs

125 g/4½ oz beansprouts

450 g/1 lb tofu, cubed

rice or noodles, to serve

S A U C E

2 tbsp light brown sugar

2 tbsp wine vinegar

225 ml/8 fl oz vegetable stock

1 tsp tomato purée

1 tbsp cornflour

1 Using a sharp knife, thinly slice the celery, cut the carrot into thin strips, dice the pepper and cut the mangetout in half diagonally.

2 Heat the vegetable oil in a preheated wok until it is almost smoking. Reduce the heat slightly, add the crushed garlic, celery, carrot, pepper, mangetout and corn cobs and stir-fry for 3–4 minutes.

3 Add the bean sprouts and tofu to the wok and cook for 2 minutes, stirring well.

4 To make the sauce, combine the sugar, wine vinegar, stock, tomato purée and cornflour, stirring well to mix. Stir into the wok, bring to the boil and cook, stirring, until the sauce thickens and clears. Continue to cook for 1 minute. Serve with rice or noodles.

COOK'S TIP

Be careful not to break up the tofu cubes when stirring.

Tofu with Mushrooms & Peas

Chinese mushrooms are available from Chinese supermarkets
and health food shops and add a unique flavour to Oriental dishes.

NUTRITIONAL INFORMATION

Calories . . . . .218 Sugars 1g
Protein . . . . .12g Fat 14g
Carbohydrate . . .13g Saturates 2g

15 mins   15 mins

SERVES 4

I N G R E D I E N T S

25 g/1 oz dried Chinese mushrooms

450 g/1 lb tofu

4 tbsp cornflour

oil, for deep-frying

2 cloves garlic, finely chopped

2 tsp fresh grated root ginger

100 g/3½ oz frozen or fresh peas

1 Place the Chinese mushrooms in a large bowl. Pour in enough boiling water to cover and leave to stand for about 10 minutes.

2 Meanwhile, cut the tofu into bite-sized cubes, using a sharp knife.

3 Place the cornflour in a large bowl.

4 Add the tofu to the bowl and toss in the cornflour until evenly coated.

5 Heat the oil for deep-frying in a large preheated wok.

6 Add the cubes of tofu to the wok and deep-fry, in batches, for 2–3 minutes or until golden and crispy. Remove the tofu with a slotted spoon and leave to drain on kitchen paper.

7 Drain off all but 2 tablespoons of oil from the wok. Add the garlic, ginger and Chinese mushrooms to the wok and stir-fry for 2–3 minutes.

8 Return the cooked tofu to the wok and add the peas. Heat through for 1 minute then serve hot.

COOK'S TIP

Chinese dried mushrooms add flavour and a distinctive aroma. Sold dried in packets, they can be expensive but only a few are needed per dish and they store indefinitely. If they are unavailable, use open-cap mushrooms instead.

Sherry & Soy Vegetables

This is a simple, yet tasty side dish which is just as delicious as a snack or main course.

NUTRITIONAL INFORMATION

Calories 374   Sugars 10g
Protein . . . . .14g   Fat 25g
Carbohydrate . . .20g   Saturates 5g

 10 mins   🕐 15 mins

SERVES 4

INGREDIENTS

2 tbsp sunflower oil

1 red onion, sliced

175 g/6 oz carrots, thinly sliced

175 g/6 oz courgettes, sliced diagonally

1 red pepper, seeded and sliced

1 small head Chinese leaves, shredded

150 g/5½ oz beansprouts

225 g/8 oz canned bamboo shoots, drained

150 g/5½ oz toasted cashew nuts

SAUCE

3 tbsp medium sherry

3 tbsp light soy sauce

1 tsp ground ginger

1 clove garlic, crushed

1 tsp cornflour

1 tbsp tomato purée

1 Heat the sunflower oil in a large preheated wok.

2 Add the red onion and stir-fry for 2–3 minutes or until softened.

3 Add the carrots, courgettes and pepper slices to the wok and stir-fry for a further 5 minutes.

4 Add the Chinese leaves, beansprouts and bamboo shoots and heat through for 2–3 minutes, or until the leaves begin to wilt. Stir in the cashews.

5 Combine the sherry, soy sauce, ginger, garlic, cornflour and tomato purée. Pour over the vegetables and toss well. Leave to simmer for 2–3 minutes or until the juices start to thicken. Serve immediately.

VARIATION

Use any mixture of fresh vegetables that you have to hand in this very versatile dish.

Chinese Vegetable Rice

This tasty rice can either be served as a meal or as an accompaniment to other vegetable recipes.

NUTRITIONAL INFORMATION

Calories 228   Sugars 5g
Protein ....5g   Fat 7g
Carbohydrate ...37g   Saturates 1g

5 mins   25 mins

SERVES 4

INGREDIENTS

350 g/12 oz long-grain white rice

1 tsp turmeric

2 tbsp sunflower oil

225 g/8 oz courgettes, sliced

1 red pepper, seeded and sliced

1 green pepper, seeded and sliced

1 green chilli, seeded and finely chopped

1 carrot, roughly grated

150 g/5½ oz beansprouts

6 spring onions, sliced, plus extra to garnish (optional)

2 tbsp soy sauce

salt

1 Place the rice and turmeric in a pan of lightly salted water and bring to the boil. Reduce the heat and leave to simmer until the rice is just tender. Drain the rice thoroughly and press out any excess water with a sheet of kitchen paper. Set aside until required.

2 Heat the sunflower oil in a large preheated wok.

3 Add the courgettes to the wok and stir-fry for about 2 minutes.

4 Add the peppers and chilli to the wok and stir-fry for 2–3 minutes.

5 Add the cooked rice to the mixture in the wok, a little at a time, tossing well after each addition.

6 Add the carrots, beansprouts and spring onions to the wok and stir-fry for a further 2 minutes.

7 Drizzle with soy sauce and serve at once, garnished with extra spring onions, if desired.

COOK'S TIP

For real luxury, add a few saffron strands infused in boiling water instead of the turmeric.

Vegetables with Hoisin

This spicy vegetable stir-fry has rice added to it and it can be served as a meal in itself.

NUTRITIONAL INFORMATION

Calories 120   Sugars 6g
Protein ....4g   Fat 6g
Carbohydrate ...12g   Saturates 1g

20 mins   10 mins

SERVES 4

INGREDIENTS

1 red onion

100 g/3½ oz carrots

1 yellow pepper

2 tbsp sunflower oil

50 g/1¾ oz cooked brown rice

175 g/6 oz mangetout

175 g/6 oz beansprouts

4 tbsp hoisin sauce

1 tbsp snipped fresh chives

1 Using a sharp knife, thinly slice the red onion.

2 Thinly slice the carrots.

3 Seed and dice the yellow pepper.

4 Heat the sunflower oil in a large preheated wok or a frying pan with a heavy base.

5 Add the red onion slices, carrots and yellow pepper to the wok and stir-fry for about 3 minutes.

6 Add the cooked brown rice, mangetout and beansprouts to the mixture in the wok and stir-fry for a further 2 minutes. Stir briskly to ensure that the ingredients are well mixed and the rice grains are separated.

7 Stir the hoisin sauce into the vegetables and mix until well combined and completely heated through.

8 Transfer the vegetable stir-fry to warm serving dishes and scatter with the snipped fresh chives. Serve immediately.

COOK'S TIP

Hoisin sauce is a dark brown, reddish sauce made from soy beans, garlic, chilli and various other spices, and is commonly used in Chinese cookery. It may also be used as a dipping sauce.

Vegetable Stir-Fry

A range of delicious flavours are captured in this simple recipe, which is ideal if you are in a hurry.

NUTRITIONAL INFORMATION

Calories 138	Sugars 5g
Protein 3g	Fat 12g
Carbohydrate 5g	Saturates 2g

5 mins   25 mins

SERVES 4

INGREDIENTS

3 tbsp vegetable oil

8 baby onions, halved

1 aubergine, cubed

225 g/8 oz courgettes, sliced

225 g/8 oz open-cap mushrooms, halved

2 cloves garlic, crushed

400 g/14 oz canned chopped tomatoes

2 tbsp sun-dried tomato paste

2 tbsp soy sauce

1 tsp sesame oil

1 tbsp Chinese rice wine or dry sherry

freshly ground black pepper

fresh basil leaves, to garnish

1 Heat the vegetable oil in a large preheated wok or frying pan.

2 Add the baby onions and aubergine to the wok or frying pan and stir-fry for 5 minutes, or until the vegetables are golden and just beginning to soften.

3 Add the sliced courgettes, mushrooms, garlic, chopped tomatoes and sun-dried tomato paste to the wok and stir-fry for about 5 minutes. Reduce the heat and leave to simmer for 10 minutes, or until the vegetables are tender.

4 Add the soy sauce, sesame oil and rice wine or sherry to the wok, bring back to the boil and cook for 1 minute.

5 Season the vegetable stir-fry with freshly ground black pepper and scatter with fresh basil leaves. Serve immediately.

COOK'S TIP

Basil has a very strong flavour which is perfect with vegetables and Chinese flavourings. Instead of using basil simply as a garnish in this dish, try adding a handful of fresh basil leaves to the stir-fry in step 4.

Peppers with Chestnuts

This is a crisp and colourful recipe, topped with crisp, shredded leeks for both flavour and colour.

NUTRITIONAL INFORMATION

Calories ....192 Sugars 5g
Protein ....3g Fat 14g
Carbohydrate ...13g Saturates 13g

5 mins   15 mins

SERVES 4

INGREDIENTS

225 g/8 oz leeks

oil, for deep-frying

3 tbsp groundnut oil

1 yellow pepper, seeded and diced

1 green pepper, seeded and diced

1 red pepper, seeded and diced

200 g/7 oz canned water chestnuts, drained and sliced

2 cloves garlic, crushed

3 tbsp light soy sauce

1 To make the garnish, finely slice the leeks into thin strips, using a sharp knife.

2 Heat the oil for deep-frying in a wok or large, heavy-based frying pan.

3 Add the sliced leeks to the wok or frying pan and cook for 2–3 minutes, or until crispy. Set aside until they are required.

4 Heat the 3 tablespoons of groundnut oil in the wok or frying pan.

5 Add the yellow, green and red peppers to the wok and stir-fry over a high heat for about 5 minutes, or until they are just beginning to brown at the edges and to soften.

6 Add the sliced water chestnuts, garlic and light soy sauce to the wok and stir-fry all of the vegetables for a further 2–3 minutes.

7 Spoon the pepper stir-fry on to warm serving plates, garnish with the crispy leeks and serve.

COOK'S TIP

Add 1 tbsp of hoisin sauce with the soy sauce in step 6 for extra flavour and spice.

Vegetable Stir-Fry with Eggs

Known as Gado Gado in China, this is a true classic which never fades from popularity. A delicious warm salad with a peanut sauce.

NUTRITIONAL INFORMATION

Calories	269	Sugars	........12g
Protein	........12g	Fat	..........19g
Carbohydrate	...14g	Saturates	.......3g

10 mins   15 mins

SERVES 4

I N G R E D I E N T S

2 eggs

225 g/8 oz carrots

350 g/12 oz white cabbage

2 tbsp vegetable oil

1 red pepper, seeded and thinly sliced

150 g/5½ oz beansprouts

1 tbsp tomato ketchup

2 tbsp soy sauce

75 g/2¾ oz salted peanuts, chopped

1 Bring a small saucepan of water to the boil. Add the eggs to the pan and cook for about 7 minutes. Remove the eggs from the pan and leave to cool under cold running water for 1 minute. Peel the shell from the eggs and then cut the eggs into quarters.

2 Peel and coarsely grate the carrots.

3 Remove any outer leaves from the white cabbage and cut out the stem, then shred the leaves very finely, either with a sharp knife or by using the fine slicing blade on a food processor.

4 Heat the vegetable oil in a large preheated wok or large frying pan.

5 Add the carrots, white cabbage and pepper to the wok and stir-fry for 3 minutes.

6 Add the beansprouts to the wok and stir-fry for 2 minutes.

7 Combine the tomato ketchup and soy sauce in a small bowl and add to the wok or frying pan.

8 Add the chopped peanuts to the wok and stir-fry for 1 minute.

9 Transfer the stir-fry to warm serving plates and garnish with the hard-boiled egg quarters. Serve immediately.

COOK'S TIP

The eggs are cooled in cold water immediately after cooking in order to prevent the egg yolk blackening around the edges.

Vegetable Chop Suey

Make sure that the vegetables are all cut into pieces of a similar size in this recipe, so that they cook within the same amount of time.

NUTRITIONAL INFORMATION

Calories ....155 Sugars 6g
Protein ....4g Fat 12g
Carbohydrate ....9g Saturates 2g

5 mins   5 mins

SERVES 4

INGREDIENTS

1 yellow pepper, seeded

1 red pepper, seeded

1 carrot

1 courgette

1 fennel bulb

1 onion

60 g/2 oz mangetout

2 tbsp peanut oil

3 garlic cloves, crushed

1 tsp grated fresh root ginger

125 g/4½ oz beansprouts

2 tsp light brown sugar

2 tbsp light soy sauce

125 ml/4 fl oz vegetable stock

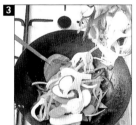

1 Cut the peppers, carrot, courgette and fennel into thin slices. Cut the onion into quarters and then cut each quarter in half. Slice the mangetout diagonally to create the maximum surface area.

2 Heat the oil in a preheated wok, add the garlic and ginger and stir-fry for 30 seconds. Add the onion and stir-fry for a further 30 seconds.

3 Add the peppers, carrot, courgette, fennel and mangetout to the wok and stir-fry for 2 minutes.

4 Add the beansprouts to the wok and stir in the sugar, soy sauce and stock. Reduce the heat to low and simmer for 1–2 minutes, until the vegetables are tender and coated in the sauce.

5 Transfer the vegetables and sauce to a serving dish and serve immediately.

VARIATION

Use any combination of colourful vegetables that you have to hand to make this versatile dish.

Vegetable Sesame Stir-Fry

Sesame seeds add a delicious flavour to any recipe and are particularly good with vegetables in this soy and rice wine or sherry sauce.

NUTRITIONAL INFORMATION

Calories 118   Sugars 2g
Protein . . . . .3g   Fat 9g
Carbohydrate . . . .5g   Saturates 1g

🍲 5 mins   ⏱ 10 mins

SERVES 4

I N G R E D I E N T S

2 tbsp vegetable oil

3 garlic cloves, crushed

1 tbsp sesame seeds,
    plus extra to garnish

2 celery sticks, sliced

2 baby corn cobs, sliced

60 g/2 oz button mushrooms

1 leek, sliced

1 courgette, sliced

1 small red pepper, sliced

1 fresh green chilli, sliced

60 g/2 oz Chinese leaves, shredded

rice or noodles, to serve

S A U C E

½ tsp Chinese curry powder

2 tbsp light soy sauce

1 tbsp Chinese rice wine or dry sherry

1 tsp sesame oil

1 tsp cornflour

4 tbsp water

1 Heat the vegetable oil in a preheated wok or heavy-based frying pan, swirling the oil around the base of the wok until it is almost smoking.

2 Lower the heat slightly, add the garlic and sesame seeds and stir-fry for 30 seconds.

3 Add the celery, baby corn cobs, mushrooms, leek, courgette, pepper, chilli and Chinese leaves and stir-fry for 4–5 minutes, until the vegetables are just beginning to soften.

4 To make the sauce, mix together the Chinese curry powder, light soy sauce, Chinese rice wine or dry sherry, sesame oil, cornflour and water.

5 Stir the sauce mixture into the wok until well combined with the other ingredients.

6 Bring to the boil and cook, stirring constantly, until the sauce thickens and clears.

7 Cook for 1 minute, spoon into a warm serving dish and garnish with sesame seeds. Serve the vegetable sesame stir-fry immediately with rice or noodles.

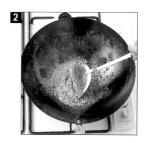

Eight Jewel Vegetables

This recipe, as the title suggests, is a colourful mixture of eight vegetables, cooked in a black bean and soy sauce.

NUTRITIONAL INFORMATION

Calories 110   Sugars 3g
Protein . . . . .4g   Fat 8g
Carbohydrate . . . .7g   Saturates 1g

5 mins   10 mins

SERVES 4

I N G R E D I E N T S

2 tbsp peanut oil

6 spring onions, sliced

3 garlic cloves, crushed

1 green pepper, seeded and diced

1 red pepper, seeded and diced

1 fresh red chilli, sliced

2 tbsp chopped water chestnuts

1 courgette, chopped

125 g/4½ oz oyster mushrooms

3 tbsp black bean sauce

2 tsp Chinese rice wine or dry sherry

4 tbsp dark soy sauce

1 tsp dark brown sugar

2 tbsp water

1 tsp sesame oil

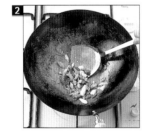  

1 Heat the peanut oil in a preheated wok or large frying pan until it is almost smoking.

2 Lower the heat slightly, add the spring onions and garlic and stir-fry for about 30 seconds.

3 Add the red and green peppers, fresh red chilli, water chestnuts and courgette to the wok or frying pan and stir-fry for 2–3 minutes, or until the

vegetables are just beginning to soften.

4 Add the oyster mushrooms, black bean sauce, Chinese rice wine or dry sherry, dark soy sauce, dark brown sugar and water to the wok and stir-fry for a further 4 minutes.

5 Sprinkle the stir-fry with sesame oil and serve immediately.

COOK'S TIP

Eight jewels or treasures form a traditional part of the Chinese New Year celebrations, which start in the last week of the old year. The Kitchen God, an important figure, is sent to give a report to heaven, returning on New Year's Eve in time for the feasting.

Spicy Fried Tofu Triangles

Marinated tofu is ideal in this recipe for added flavour, although the spicy coating is very tasty with plain tofu.

NUTRITIONAL INFORMATION

Calories 224   Sugars 17g
Protein . . . . .10g   Fat 13g
Carbohydrate . . .18g   Saturates 2g

1¼ hours   10 mins

SERVES 4

I N G R E D I E N T S

1 tbsp sea salt

4½ tsp Chinese five-spice powder

3 tbsp light brown sugar

2 garlic cloves, crushed

1 tsp grated fresh root ginger

450 g/1 lb firm tofu

vegetable oil, for deep-frying

2 leeks, shredded and halved

shredded leek, to garnish

1 Mix together the salt, Chinese five-spice powder, sugar, garlic and ginger in a bowl and transfer to a plate.

2 Cut the tofu cakes in half diagonally to form two triangles. Cut each triangle in half and then in half again to form 16 triangles.

3 Roll the tofu triangles in the spice mixture, turning to coat thoroughly. Set aside for 1 hour.

4 Heat the vegetable oil for deep-frying in a wok until it is almost smoking.

5 Reduce the heat slightly, add the tofu triangles and fry for 5 minutes, until golden brown. Remove the tofu from the wok with a slotted spoon, set aside and keep warm until required.

6 Add the leeks to the wok and stir-fry for 1 minute. Remove from the wok and drain on kitchen paper.

7 Arrange the leeks on a warm serving plate and place the fried tofu on top. Garnish with the fresh shredded leek and serve immediately.

COOK'S TIP

Fry the tofu in batches and keep each batch warm until all of the tofu has been fried and is ready to serve.

Chinese Vegetable Casserole

This mixed vegetable casserole is very versatile and is delicious with any combination of vegetables of your choice.

NUTRITIONAL INFORMATION

Calories 218   Sugars 4g
Protein . . . . .7g   Fat 14g
Carbohydrate . . .12g   Saturates 2g

 5 mins   30 mins

SERVES 4

I N G R E D I E N T S

4 tbsp vegetable oil

2 carrots, sliced

1 courgette, sliced

4 baby corn cobs, halved lengthways

125 g/4½ oz cauliflower florets

1 leek, sliced

125 g/4½ oz water chestnuts, halved

225 g/8 oz tofu, cubed

300 ml/10 fl oz vegetable stock

1 tsp salt

2 tsp dark brown sugar

2 tsp dark soy sauce

2 tbsp dry sherry

1 tbsp cornflour

2 tbsp water

1 tbsp chopped fresh coriander, to garnish

COOK'S TIP

If there is too much liquid remaining, boil vigorously for 1 minute before adding the cornflour to reduce it slightly.

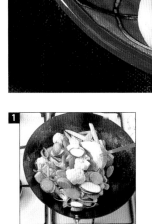

1 Heat the oil in a preheated wok until it is almost smoking. Lower the heat slightly, add the carrots, courgette, corn cobs, cauliflower and leek to the wok and stir-fry for 2–3 minutes.

2 Stir in the water chestnuts, tofu, stock, salt, sugar, soy sauce and sherry and bring to the boil. Reduce the heat, cover and simmer for 20 minutes.

3 Blend the cornflour with the water to form a smooth paste.

4 Stir the cornflour mixture into the wok. Bring the sauce to the boil and cook, stirring constantly until it thickens and clears.

5 Transfer the casserole to a warm serving dish, sprinkle with chopped coriander and serve immediately.

Cantonese Garden Vegetables

This dish tastes as fresh as it looks. Try to get hold of baby vegetables as they look and taste so much better in this dish.

NUTRITIONAL INFORMATION

Calories ....130 Sugars 8g
Protein ....6g Fat 8g
Carbohydrate ....8g Saturates 1g

5 mins   10 mins

SERVES 4

INGREDIENTS

2 tbsp peanut oil

1 tsp Chinese five-spice powder

75 g/2¾ oz baby carrots, halved

2 celery sticks, sliced

2 baby leeks, sliced

50 g/1¾ oz mangetout

4 baby courgettes, halved lengthways

8 baby corn cobs

225 g/8 oz firm marinated tofu, cubed

4 tbsp fresh orange juice

1 tbsp clear honey

cooked rice or noodles, to serve

TO GARNISH

celery leaves

orange rind

VARIATION

Lemon juice would be just as delicious as the orange juice in this recipe, but use 3 tablespoons instead of 4 tablespoons.

1 Heat the peanut oil in a preheated wok or large frying pan until almost smoking.

2 Add the Chinese five-spice powder, carrots, celery, leeks, mangetout, courgettes and corn cobs and stir-fry for 3–4 minutes.

3 Add the tofu to the wok or frying pan and cook for a further 2 minutes, stirring gently so the tofu does not break up into smaller pieces.

4 Stir the fresh orange juice and clear honey into the wok or frying pan, reduce the heat and cook for 1–2 minutes.

5 Transfer the stir-fry to a serving dish, garnish with celery leaves and orange rind and serve with rice or noodles.

Rice & Noodles

Rice and noodles are staples in the Far East, as they are cheap, plentiful, nutritious and delicious. They are extremely versatile ingredients and are therefore always served as part of a meal. Many rice and noodle dishes are

served as accompaniments and others as main dishes combined with meat, vegetables and fish, all flavoured with fragrant spices and seasonings.

Plain rice is served to punctuate a large meal and help settle the stomach between rich, spicy courses. Noodles vary from country to country and are eaten in various forms. Thin egg noodles are made from wheat flour, water and egg and are probably the most common in the Western diet. Available fresh or dried, they require very little cooking and are ideal for quick and easy meals.

Fried Rice with Spicy Beans

This rice is really colourful with the addition of sweetcorn and red kidney beans. It may be served as a main vegetarian dish or as a side dish.

NUTRITIONAL INFORMATION

Calories 374	Sugars 6g	
Protein 9g	Fat 9g	
Carbohydrate ...64g	Saturates 1g	

2 mins   25 mins

SERVES 4

INGREDIENTS

3 tbsp sunflower oil

1 onion, finely chopped

225 g/8 oz long-grain white rice

1 green pepper, seeded and diced

1 tsp chilli powder

600 ml/1 pint boiling water

100 g/3½ oz canned sweetcorn kernels

225 g/8 oz canned red kidney beans

2 tbsp chopped fresh coriander

1 Heat the sunflower oil in a large preheated wok.

2 Add the finely chopped onion to the wok and stir-fry for about 2 minutes or until the onion has softened.

3 Add the long-grain rice, diced pepper and chilli powder to the wok and stir-fry for 1 minute.

4 Pour the boiling water into the wok. Bring back to the boil, then reduce the heat and leave the mixture to simmer for 15 minutes.

5 Add the sweetcorn, kidney beans and coriander to the wok and heat through, stirring occasionally.

6 Transfer to a serving bowl and serve hot, scattered with extra coriander, if wished.

VARIATION

For extra heat, add 1 chopped red chilli as well as the chilli powder in step 3.

Fragrant Coconut Rice

This fragrant, sweet rice is delicious served with meat, vegetable or fish dishes as part of a Chinese menu.

NUTRITIONAL INFORMATION

Calories 306	Sugars 2g	
Protein 5g	Fat 6g	
Carbohydrate ...61g	Saturates 4g	

 5 mins   15 mins

SERVES 4

INGREDIENTS

275 g/9½ oz long-grain white rice

600 ml/1 pint water

½ tsp salt

100 ml/3½ fl oz coconut milk

25 g/1 oz desiccated coconut

1 Rinse the rice thoroughly under cold running water until the water runs completely clear.

2 Drain the rice thoroughly in a sieve set over a large bowl. This is to remove some of the starch and to prevent the grains from sticking together.

3 Place the rice in a wok with the water.

4 Add the salt and coconut milk to the wok and bring to the boil.

5 Cover the wok with a lid or a lid made of foil, curved into a domed shape and resting on the sides of the wok. Reduce the heat and leave to simmer for 10 minutes.

6 Remove the lid from the wok and fluff up the rice with a fork – all of the liquid should be absorbed and the rice grains should be tender. If not, add more water and continue to simmer for a few more minutes until all the liquid has been absorbed.

7 Spoon the rice into a warm serving bowl and scatter with the desiccated coconut. Serve immediately.

COOK'S TIP

Coconut milk is not the liquid found inside coconuts – that is called coconut water. Coconut milk is made from the white coconut flesh soaked in water and milk and then squeezed to extract all of the flavour. You can make your own or buy it in cans.

Egg Fried Rice

In this classic Chinese dish, boiled rice is fried with peas, spring onions and egg and flavoured with soy sauce.

NUTRITIONAL INFORMATION

Calories 203   Sugars 1g
Protein ....9g   Fat 11g
Carbohydrate ...19g   Saturates 2g

20 mins   10 mins

SERVES 4

INGREDIENTS

150 g/5½ oz long-grain rice

3 eggs, beaten

2 tbsp vegetable oil

2 garlic cloves, crushed

4 spring onions, chopped

125 g/4½ oz cooked peas

1 tbsp light soy sauce

pinch of salt

shredded spring onion, to garnish

1 Cook the rice in a pan of boiling water for 10–12 minutes, until almost cooked, but not soft. Drain well, rinse under cold water and drain again.

2 Place the beaten eggs in a saucepan and cook over a gentle heat, stirring until softly scrambled.

3 Heat the vegetable oil in a preheated wok or large frying pan, swirling the oil around the base of the wok until it is really hot.

4 Add the crushed garlic, spring onions and peas and sauté, stirring occasionally, for 1–2 minutes. Stir the rice into the wok, mixing to combine.

5 Add the eggs, light soy sauce and a pinch of salt to the wok or frying pan and stir to mix the egg in thoroughly.

6 Transfer the egg fried rice to serving dishes and serve garnished with the shredded spring onion.

COOK'S TIP

The rice is rinsed under cold water to wash out the starch and prevent it from sticking together.

Stir-Fried Rice with Egg

Many Thai rice dishes are made from leftover rice that has been cooked for an earlier meal. Any leftover vegetables or meat can be used too.

NUTRITIONAL INFORMATION

Calories 334   Sugars 49g
Protein . . . . .7g   Fat 9g
Carbohydrate . . .60g   Saturates 1g

5–10 mins   5 mins

SERVES 4

INGREDIENTS

2 tbsp groundnut oil

1 egg, beaten with 1 tsp water

1 garlic clove, finely chopped

1 small onion, finely chopped

1 tbsp Thai red curry paste

250 g/9 oz long-grain rice, cooked

55 g/2 oz cooked peas

1 tbsp Thai fish sauce

2 tbsp tomato ketchup

2 tbsp chopped fresh coriander

TO GARNISH

red chillies

cucumber slices

1 To make chilli flowers for the garnish, hold the stem of each chilli with your fingertips and use a small sharp, pointed knife to cut a slit down the length from near the stem end to the tip. Turn the chilli about a quarter turn and make another cut. Repeat to make a total of 4 cuts, then scrape out the seeds. Cut each 'petal' again in half, or into quarters, to make 8–16 petals. Place the chilli in iced water.

2 Heat about 1 teaspoon of the oil in a wok. Pour in the egg mixture, swirling it to coat the pan evenly and make a thin layer. When set and golden, remove the egg from the pan and roll up. Keep to one side.

3 Add the remaining oil to the pan and stir-fry the garlic and onion for 1 minute. Add the curry paste, then stir in the rice and peas.

4 Stir in the fish sauce and ketchup. Remove the pan from the heat and pile the rice on to a serving dish.

5 Slice the egg roll into spiral strips, without unrolling, and use to garnish the rice. Add the cucumber slices and chilli flowers. Serve hot.

Vegetable Fried Rice

This dish can be served as part of a substantial meal for a number of people or as a vegetarian meal in itself for four.

NUTRITIONAL INFORMATION

Calories ....175 Sugars 3g
Protein ....3g Fat 10g
Carbohydrate ...20g Saturates 2g

10 mins   20 mins

SERVES 4

INGREDIENTS

125 g/4½ oz long-grain white rice

3 tbsp peanut oil

2 garlic cloves, crushed

½ tsp Chinese five-spice powder

60 g/2 oz green beans

1 green pepper, seeded and chopped

4 baby corn cobs, sliced

25 g/1 oz bamboo shoots, chopped

3 tomatoes, skinned, seeded and
  chopped

60 g/2 oz cooked peas

1 tsp sesame oil

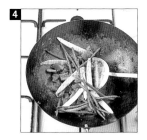  

1 Bring a large saucepan of water to the boil.

2 Add the long-grain white rice to the saucepan and cook for about 15 minutes. Drain the rice well, rinse under cold running water and drain thoroughly again.

3 Heat the peanut oil in a preheated wok or large frying pan. Add the garlic and Chinese five-spice and stir-fry for 30 seconds.

4 Add the green beans, chopped green pepper and sliced corn cobs and stir-fry the ingredients in the wok for 2 minutes.

5 Stir the bamboo shoots, tomatoes, peas and rice into the mixture in the wok and stir-fry for 1 further minute.

6 Sprinkle with sesame oil and transfer to serving dishes. Serve immediately.

VARIATION

Use a selection of vegetables of your choice in this recipe, cutting them to a similar size in order to ensure that they cook in the same amount of time.

Green Fried Rice

Spinach is used in this recipe to give the rice a wonderful green colouring. Tossed with the carrot strips, it is a really appealing dish.

NUTRITIONAL INFORMATION

Calories ....139 Sugars 2g
Protein ....3g Fat 7g
Carbohydrate ...18g Saturates 1g

 5 mins   20 mins

SERVES 4

I N G R E D I E N T S

150 g/5½ oz long-grain rice

2 tbsp vegetable oil

2 garlic cloves, crushed

1 tsp grated fresh root ginger

1 carrot, cut into matchsticks

1 courgette, diced

225 g/8 oz baby spinach

2 tsp light soy sauce

2 tsp light brown sugar

1 Cook the rice in a saucepan of boiling water for about 15 minutes. Drain the rice well, rinse under cold running water and then rinse the rice thoroughly again. Set aside until required.

2 Heat the vegetable oil in a preheated wok or a large frying pan with a heavy base.

3 Add the crushed garlic and grated fresh root ginger to the wok or frying pan and stir-fry for about 30 seconds.

4 Add the carrot matchsticks and diced courgette to the mixture in the wok and stir-fry for about 2 minutes, so the vegetables still retain their crunch.

5 Add the baby spinach and stir-fry for 1 minute, until wilted.

6 Add the rice, soy sauce and sugar to the wok and mix together well.

7 Transfer the green-fried rice to serving dishes and serve immediately.

COOK'S TIP

Light soy sauce has more flavour than the sweeter, dark soy sauce, which gives the food a rich, reddish colour.

Special Fried Rice

This dish is a popular choice in Chinese restaurants. Ham and prawns are mixed with vegetables in a soy-flavoured rice.

NUTRITIONAL INFORMATION

Calories 301   Sugars 1g
Protein . . . . .26g   Fat 13g
Carbohydrate . . .21g   Saturates 3g

 5 mins   30 mins

SERVES 4

INGREDIENTS

150 g/5½ oz long-grain rice

2 tbsp vegetable oil

2 eggs, beaten

2 garlic cloves, crushed

1 tsp grated fresh root ginger

3 spring onions, sliced

75 g/2¾ oz cooked peas

150 g/5½ oz beansprouts

225 g/8 oz shredded ham

150 g/5½ oz peeled, cooked prawns

2 tbsp light soy sauce

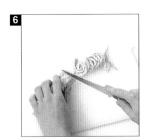

1 Cook the rice in a saucepan of boiling water for about 15 minutes. Drain well, rinse under cold water and drain thoroughly again.

2 Heat 1 tablespoon of the vegetable oil in a preheated wok.

3 Add the beaten eggs and a further 1 teaspoon of oil. Tilt the wok so that the egg covers the base to make a thin pancake.

4 Cook until lightly browned on the underside, then flip the pancake over and cook on the other side for 1 minute. Remove from the wok and leave to cool.

5 Heat the remaining oil in the wok and stir-fry the garlic and ginger for 30 seconds. Add the spring onions, peas, beansprouts, ham and prawns. Stir-fry for 2 minutes.

6 Stir in the soy sauce and rice and cook for a further 2 minutes. Transfer the rice to serving dishes. Roll up the pancake, slice it very thinly and use to garnish the rice. Serve immediately.

COOK'S TIP

As this recipe contains meat and fish, it is ideal served with simpler vegetable dishes.

Crab Congee

This is a typical Chinese breakfast dish although it is probably best served as a lunch or supper dish at a Western table!

NUTRITIONAL INFORMATION

Calories 327   Sugars 0.1g
Protein . . . . .18g   Fat 7g
Carbohydrate . . .50g   Saturates 2g

5 mins   1¼ hrs

SERVES 4

I N G R E D I E N T S

225 g/8 oz short-grain rice

1.5 litres/2½ pints fish stock

½ tsp salt

100 g/3½ oz Chinese sausage,
    thinly sliced

225 g/8 oz white crab meat

6 spring onions, sliced

2 tbsp chopped fresh coriander

freshly ground black pepper, to serve

1 Place the short-grain rice in a large preheated wok or frying pan.

2 Add the fish stock to the wok or frying pan and bring to the boil.

3 Reduce the heat, then simmer gently for 1 hour, stirring the mixture from time to time.

4 Add the salt, sliced Chinese sausage, white crab meat, sliced spring onions and chopped fresh coriander to the wok and heat through for about 5 minutes.

5 Add a little more water to the wok if the congee 'porridge' is too thick, stirring well.

6 Transfer the crab congee to warm serving bowls, sprinkle with freshly ground black pepper and serve immediately.

COOK'S TIP

Always buy the freshest possible crab meat; fresh is best, although frozen or canned will work for this recipe. In the West, crabs are almost always sold ready-cooked. The crab should feel heavy for its size, and when it is shaken, there should be no sound of water inside.

Crab Fried Rice

Canned crabmeat is used in this recipe for convenience, but fresh white crabmeat could be used - quite deliciously - in its place.

NUTRITIONAL INFORMATION

Calories 225   Sugars 1g
Protein . . . . .12g   Fat 11g
Carbohydrate . . .20g   Saturates 2g

5 mins   25 mins

SERVES 4

INGREDIENTS

150 g/5½ oz long-grain rice

2 tbsp peanut oil

125 g/4½ oz canned white crabmeat, drained

1 leek, sliced

150 g/5½ oz beansprouts

2 eggs, beaten

1 tbsp light soy sauce

2 tsp lime juice

1 tsp sesame oil

salt

sliced lime, to garnish

1 Cook the rice in a saucepan of boiling salted water for 15 minutes. Drain well, rinse under cold running water and drain again thoroughly.

2 Heat the peanut oil in a preheated wok until it is really hot.

3 Add the crabmeat, leek and beansprouts to the wok and stir-fry for 2–3 minutes. Remove the mixture from the wok with a slotted spoon and set aside until required.

4 Add the eggs to the wok and cook, stirring occasionally, for 2–3 minutes, until they begin to set.

5 Stir the rice and the crabmeat, leek and beansprout mixture into the eggs in the wok.

6 Add the soy sauce and lime juice to the mixture in the wok. Cook for 1 minute, stirring to combine, and sprinkle with the sesame oil.

7 Transfer the crab fried rice to a serving dish, garnish with the sliced lime and serve immediately.

VARIATION

Cooked lobster may be used instead of the crab for a really special dish.

Rice with Seafood

This soup-like main course rice dish is packed with fresh seafood and is typically Thai in flavour.

NUTRITIONAL INFORMATION

Calories 370   Sugars 0g
Protein . . . . .27g   Fat 8g
Carbohydrate . . .52g   Saturates 1g

 5–10 mins   20 mins

SERVES 4

INGREDIENTS

12 mussels in their shells, cleaned

2 litres/3½ pints fish stock

2 tbsp vegetable oil

1 garlic clove, crushed

1 tsp grated fresh root ginger

1 red bird-eye chilli, chopped

2 spring onions, chopped

225 g/8 oz long-grain rice

2 small squid, cleaned and sliced

100 g/3½ oz firm white fish fillet, such as halibut or monkfish, cut into chunks

100 g/3½ oz raw prawns, peeled

2 tbsp Thai fish sauce

3 tbsp shredded fresh coriander

1 Discard any mussels with damaged shells or open ones that do not close when firmly tapped. Heat 4 tablespoons of the stock in a large pan. Add the mussels, cover and shake the pan until the mussels open. Remove from the heat and discard any which do not open.

2 Heat the oil in a large frying pan or wok and fry the garlic, ginger, chilli and spring onions for 30 seconds. Add the stock and bring to the boil.

3 Stir in the rice, then add the squid, fish fillet and prawns. Lower the heat and simmer gently for 15 minutes, or until the rice is cooked. Add the fish sauce and mussels.

4 Ladle into wide bowls and sprinkle with coriander, before serving.

COOK'S TIP

You could use leftover cooked rice for this dish. Just simmer the seafood gently until cooked, then stir in the rice at the end.

Rice with Five-Spice Chicken

This dish has a wonderful colour obtained from the turmeric, and a great spicy flavour, making it very appealing all round.

NUTRITIONAL INFORMATION

Calories 412   Sugars 1g
Protein . . . . .23g   Fat 13g
Carbohydrate . . .53g   Saturates 2g

5 mins   20 mins

SERVES 4

I N G R E D I E N T S

1 tbsp Chinese five-spice powder

2 tbsp cornflour

350 g/12 oz boneless, skinless chicken breasts, cubed

3 tbsp groundnut oil

1 onion, diced

225 g/8 oz long-grain white rice

½ tsp turmeric

600 ml/1 pint chicken stock

2 tbsp snipped fresh chives

1 Place the Chinese five-spice powder and cornflour in a large bowl. Add the chicken pieces and toss to coat all over.

2 Heat 2 tablespoons of the groundnut oil in a large preheated wok. Add the chicken pieces to the wok and stir-fry for 5 minutes. Using a slotted spoon, remove the chicken and set aside.

3 Add the remaining groundnut oil to the wok.

4 Add the onion to the wok and stir-fry for 1 minute.

5 Add the rice, turmeric and chicken stock to the wok and gently bring to the boil.

6 Return the chicken pieces to the wok, reduce the heat and leave to simmer for 10 minutes, or until the liquid has been absorbed and the rice is tender.

7 Add the snipped fresh chives, stir to mix and serve hot.

COOK'S TIP

Be careful when using turmeric as it can stain the hands and clothes a distinctive shade of yellow.

Chinese Chicken Rice

This is a really colourful main meal or side dish which tastes just as good as it looks.

NUTRITIONAL INFORMATION

Calories 324   Sugars 4g
Protein . . . . .24g   Fat 10g
Carbohydrate . . .37g   Saturates 2g

5 mins   25 mins

SERVES 4

INGREDIENTS

350 g/12 oz long-grain white rice

1 tsp turmeric

2 tbsp sunflower oil

350 g/12 oz skinless, boneless chicken breasts or thighs, sliced

1 red pepper, seeded and sliced

1 green pepper, seeded and sliced

1 green chilli, seeded and finely chopped

1 carrot, roughly grated

150 g/5½ oz beansprouts

6 spring onions, sliced, plus extra to garnish

2 tbsp soy sauce

salt

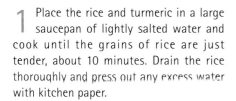

1 Place the rice and turmeric in a large saucepan of lightly salted water and cook until the grains of rice are just tender, about 10 minutes. Drain the rice thoroughly and press out any excess water with kitchen paper.

2 Heat the sunflower oil in a large preheated wok or frying pan.

3 Add the strips of chicken to the wok or frying pan and stir-fry over a high heat until the chicken is just beginning to turn a golden colour.

4 Add the sliced peppers and green chilli to the wok and stir-fry for 2–3 minutes.

5 Add the cooked rice to the wok, a little at a time, tossing well after each addition until well combined and the grains of rice are separated.

6 Add the carrot, beansprouts and spring onions to the wok and stir-fry for a further 2 minutes.

7 Drizzle with the soy sauce and toss to combine.

8 Transfer the Chinese chicken rice to a warm serving dish, garnish with extra spring onions, if wished, and serve at once.

Chicken & Rice Casserole

This is a quick-cooking, spicy casserole of rice, chicken, vegetables and chilli in a soy and ginger flavoured liquor.

NUTRITIONAL INFORMATION

Calories 502   Sugars 2g
Protein ....55g   Fat 9g
Carbohydrate ...52g   Saturates 3g

35 mins   50 mins

SERVES 4

INGREDIENTS

150 g/5½ oz long-grain rice

1 tbsp dry sherry

2 tbsp light soy sauce

2 tbsp dark soy sauce

2 tsp dark brown sugar

1 tsp salt

1 tsp sesame oil

900 g/2 lb skinless, boneless
    chicken meat, diced

900 ml/1½ pints chicken stock

2 open-cap mushrooms, sliced

60 g/2 oz water chestnuts, halved

75 g/2¾ oz broccoli florets

1 yellow pepper, sliced

4 tsp grated fresh root ginger

whole chives, to garnish

VARIATION

This dish would work
equally well with beef or pork.
Chinese dried mushrooms may be
used instead of the open-cap
mushrooms, if rehydrated before
adding to the dish.

1 Cook the rice in a saucepan of boiling water for about 15 minutes. Drain well, rinse under cold water and drain again thoroughly.

2 Mix together the sherry, soy sauces, sugar, salt and sesame oil.

3 Stir the chicken into the soy mixture, turning to coat the chicken well. Leave to marinate for about 30 minutes.

4 Bring the stock to the boil in a saucepan or preheated wok. Add the chicken with the marinade, mushrooms, water chestnuts, broccoli, pepper and ginger.

5 Stir in the rice, reduce the heat, cover and cook for 25-30 minutes, until the chicken and vegetables are cooked through. Transfer to serving plates, garnish with chives and serve.

Chicken Chow Mein

This classic dish requires no introduction as it is already a favourite amongst most Chinese food enthusiasts.

NUTRITIONAL INFORMATION

Calories 230   Sugars 2g
Protein . . . . .19g   Fat 11g
Carbohydrate . . .14g   Saturates 2g

   5 mins   20 mins

SERVES 4

INGREDIENTS

250 g/9 oz packet medium egg
  noodles

2 tbsp sunflower oil

275 g/9½ oz cooked chicken breasts,
  shredded

1 clove garlic, finely chopped

1 red pepper, seeded and thinly sliced

100 g/3½ oz shiitake mushrooms,
  sliced

6 spring onions, sliced

100 g/3½ oz beansprouts

3 tbsp soy sauce

1 tbsp sesame oil

1 Place the egg noodles in a large bowl or dish and break them up slightly. Pour over enough boiling water to cover the noodles and leave to stand.

2 Heat the sunflower oil in a large preheated wok. Add the shredded chicken, finely chopped garlic, pepper slices, mushrooms, spring onions and beansprouts to the wok and stir-fry for about 5 minutes.

3 Drain the noodles thoroughly. Add the noodles to the wok, toss well and stir-fry for a further 5 minutes.

4 Drizzle the soy sauce and sesame oil over the chow mein and toss until well combined.

5 Transfer the chicken chow mein to warm serving bowls and serve immediately.

VARIATION

You can make the chow mein with a selection of vegetables for a vegetarian dish, if you prefer.

Sweet Chilli Pork Fried Rice

This is a variation of egg fried rice which may be served as an accompaniment to a main meal dish.

NUTRITIONAL INFORMATION

Calories ....366 Sugars 5g
Protein ....29g Fat 16g
Carbohydrate ...28g Saturates 4g

25 mins   20 mins

SERVES 4

I N G R E D I E N T S

450 g/1 lb pork fillet

2 tbsp sunflower oil

2 tbsp sweet chilli sauce, plus extra to serve

1 onion, sliced

175 g/6 oz carrots, cut into matchsticks

175 g/6 oz courgettes, cut into matchsticks

100 g/3½ oz canned bamboo shoots, drained

275 g/9½ oz cooked long-grain rice

1 egg, beaten

1 tbsp chopped fresh parsley

1 Using a sharp knife, cut the pork fillet into thin slices.

2 Heat the sunflower oil in a large preheated wok or frying pan.

3 Add the pork to the wok and stir-fry for 5 minutes.

4 Add the chilli sauce to the wok and allow to bubble, stirring, for 2–3 minutes or until syrupy.

5 Add the onion, carrots, courgettes and bamboo shoots to the wok and stir-fry for a further 3 minutes.

6 Add the cooked rice and stir-fry for 2–3 minutes, or until the rice is heated through.

7 Drizzle the beaten egg over the top of the fried rice and cook, tossing the ingredients in the wok with two spoons, until the egg sets.

8 Scatter with chopped fresh parsley and serve immediately, with extra sweet chilli sauce, if desired.

COOK'S TIP

For a really quick dish, add frozen mixed vegetables to the rice instead of the freshly prepared vegetables.

Fried Rice with Pork

This dish is a meal in itself, containing pieces of pork, fried with rice, peas, tomatoes and mushrooms.

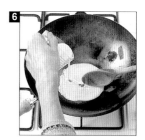

NUTRITIONAL INFORMATION

Calories . . . . . . .285 Sugars 2g
Protein . . . . .18g Fat 16g
Carbohydrate . . .19g Saturates 4g

 10 mins   30 mins

SERVES 4

I N G R E D I E N T S

150 g/5½ oz long-grain rice

3 tbsp peanut oil

1 large onion, cut into 8 pieces

225 g/8 oz pork fillet, thinly sliced

2 open-cap mushrooms, sliced

2 garlic cloves, crushed

1 tbsp light soy sauce

1 tsp light brown sugar

2 tomatoes, skinned, seeded and chopped

60 g/2 oz cooked peas

2 eggs, beaten

1 Cook the rice in a saucepan of boiling water for about 15 minutes, until tender, but not soft. Drain well, rinse under cold running water and drain again thoroughly.

2 Heat the peanut oil in a preheated wok. Add the sliced onion and pork and stir-fry for 3–4 minutes, until just beginning to colour.

3 Add the mushrooms and garlic to the wok and stir-fry for 1 minute.

4 Add the soy sauce and sugar to the mixture in the wok and stir-fry for a further 2 minutes.

5 Stir in the rice, tomatoes and peas, mixing well. Transfer the mixture to a warmed dish.

6 Stir the eggs into the wok and cook, stirring with a wooden spoon, for 2–3 minutes, until beginning to set.

7 Return the rice mixture to the wok and mix well. Transfer to serving dishes and serve immediately.

COOK'S TIP

You can cook the rice in advance and chill or freeze it until required.

Rice with Seven-Spice Beef

Beef fillet is used in this recipe as it is very suitable for quick cooking and has a wonderful flavour.

NUTRITIONAL INFORMATION

Calories 171   Sugars 8g
Protein . . . . .28g   Fat 15g
Carbohydrate . . .60g   Saturates 6g

5 mins   30 mins

SERVES 4

INGREDIENTS

225 g/8 oz long-grain white rice

600 ml/1 pint water

350 g/12 oz beef fillet

2 tbsp soy sauce

2 tbsp tomato ketchup

1 tbsp seven-spice seasoning

2 tbsp groundnut oil

1 onion, diced

225 g/8 oz carrots, diced

100 g/3½o frozen peas

2 eggs, beaten

2 tbsp cold water

1 Rinse the rice under cold running water, then drain thoroughly. Place the rice in a saucepan with the water, bring to the boil, cover and leave to simmer for 12 minutes. Turn the cooked rice out on to a tray and leave to cool.

2 Using a sharp knife, thinly slice the beef fillet.

3 Mix together the soy sauce, tomato ketchup and seven-spice seasoning. Spoon over the beef and toss well to coat.

4 Heat the oil in a preheated wok. Add the beef and stir-fry for 3–4 minutes.

5 Add the onion, carrots and peas to the wok and stir-fry for a further 2–3 minutes. Add the cooked rice to the wok and stir to combine.

6 Beat the eggs with 2 tablespoons of cold water. Drizzle the egg mixture over the rice and stir-fry for 3–4 minutes, or until the rice is heated through and the egg has set. Transfer to a warm serving bowl and serve immediately.

VARIATION

You can use pork fillet or chicken instead of the beef, if you prefer.

Stir-Fried Rice with Sausage

This is a very quick rice dish as it uses pre-cooked rice. It is therefore ideal when time is short or for a quick lunch-time dish.

NUTRITIONAL INFORMATION

Calories ....383 Sugars 9g
Protein ....19g Fat 17g
Carbohydrate ...42g Saturates 4g

5 mins   20 mins

SERVES 4

INGREDIENTS

350 g/12 oz Chinese sausage

2 tbsp sunflower oil

2 tbsp soy sauce

1 onion, sliced

175 g/6 oz carrots, cut into matchsticks

175 g/6 oz peas

100 g/3½ oz canned pineapple cubes, drained

275 g/9½ oz cooked long-grain rice

1 egg, beaten

1 tbsp chopped fresh parsley

1 Using a sharp knife, thinly slice the Chinese sausage.

2 Heat the sunflower oil in a large preheated wok. Add the sausage to the wok and stir-fry for 5 minutes.

3 Stir in the soy sauce and allow to bubble for about 2–3 minutes, or until syrupy.

4 Add the onion, carrots, peas and pineapple to the wok and stir-fry for a further 3 minutes.

5 Add the cooked rice to the wok and stir-fry the mixture for about 2–3 minutes, or until the rice is completely heated through.

6 Drizzle the beaten egg over the top of the rice and cook, tossing the ingredients in the wok, until the egg sets.

7 Transfer the stir-fried rice to a large, warm serving bowl and scatter with plenty of chopped fresh parsley. Serve immediately.

COOK'S TIP

Cook extra rice and freeze it in preparation for some of the other rice dishes included in this book, as it saves time and enables you to prepare a meal in minutes. Be sure to cool any leftover cooked rice quickly before freezing to avoid food poisoning.

Chinese Risotto

Risotto is a creamy Italian dish made with risotto rice.
This Chinese version is simply delicious!

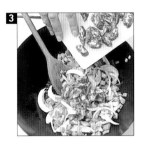

NUTRITIONAL INFORMATION

Calories 436	Sugars 7g	
Protein 13g	Fat 14g	
Carbohydrate ...70g	Saturates 4g	

 5 mins 25 mins

SERVES 4

INGREDIENTS

2 tbsp groundnut oil

1 onion, sliced

2 cloves garlic, crushed

1 tsp Chinese five-spice powder

225 g/8 oz Chinese sausage, sliced

225 g/8 oz carrots, diced

1 green pepper, seeded and diced

275 g/9½ oz risotto rice

900 ml/1½ pints vegetable or chicken stock

1 tbsp fresh chives

1 Heat the groundnut oil in a large preheated wok or a frying pan with a heavy base.

2 Add the onion slices, crushed garlic and Chinese five-spice powder to the wok or frying pan and stir-fry for 1 minute.

3 Add the Chinese sausage, carrots and green pepper to the wok and stir to combine.

4 Stir in the risotto rice and cook for 1 minute.

5 Gradually add the vegetable or chicken stock, a little at a time, stirring constantly until the liquid has been completely absorbed and the rice grains are tender.

6 Snip the chives with a pair of clean kitchen scissors and stir into the wok with the last of the stock.

7 Transfer the Chinese risotto to warm serving bowls and serve immediately.

COOK'S TIP

Chinese sausage is highly flavoured and is made from chopped pork fat, pork meat and spices. Use a spicy Portuguese sausage if Chinese sausage is unavailable.

Crispy Rice Noodles

This is a version of a favourite Thai dish, 'mee krob', one of those exciting dishes which varies from one day to the next.

NUTRITIONAL INFORMATION

Calories 490   Sugars 11g
Protein . . . . .24g   Fat . . . .,16g
Carbohydrate . . .63g   Saturates 2g

5 mins   15 mins

SERVES 4

I N G R E D I E N T S

vegetable oil for deep frying, plus 1½ tbsp
    for shallow frying

200 g/7 oz rice vermicelli noodles

1 onion, finely chopped

4 garlic cloves, finely chopped

1 boneless, skinless chicken breast,
    finely chopped

2 red bird-eye chillies, seeded and sliced

4 tbsp dried black mushrooms, soaked
    and thinly sliced

3 tbsp dried prawns

4 spring onions, sliced

3 tbsp lime juice

2 tbsp soy sauce

2 tbsp Thai fish sauce

2 tbsp rice vinegar

2 tbsp soft light brown sugar

2 eggs, beaten

3 tbsp chopped fresh coriander

spring onion curls, to garnish

1 Heat the oil in a large frying pan or wok until very hot and deep-fry the noodles quickly, occasionally turning them, until puffed up, crisp and pale golden brown. Lift on to paper towels and drain well.

2 Heat 1 tablespoon of oil and fry the onion and garlic for 1 minute. Add the chicken and stir-fry for 3 minutes. Add the chillies, mushrooms, dried prawns and spring onions.

3 Mix together the lime juice, soy sauce, fish sauce, rice vinegar and sugar, then stir into the pan and cook for a further minute. Remove the pan from the heat.

4 Heat the remaining oil in a wide pan and pour in the eggs to coat the base of the pan evenly, making a thin omelette. Cook until set and golden, then turn it over and cook the other side. Turn out and roll up, then slice into long ribbon strips.

5 Toss together the fried noodles, stir-fried ingredients, coriander and omelette strips. Garnish with spring onion curls and serve at once.

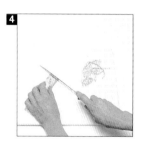

Spicy Japanese Noodles

These noodles are highly spiced with chilli and flavoured with sesame seeds for a nutty taste which is a true delight.

NUTRITIONAL INFORMATION

Calories 381   Sugars 12g
Protein . . . . .11g   Fat 13g
Carbohydrate . . .59g   Saturates 2g

🧄 5 mins   🕐 15 mins

SERVES 4

I N G R E D I E N T S

450 g/1 lb fresh Japanese noodles

1 tbsp sesame oil

1 tbsp sesame seeds

1 tbsp sunflower oil

1 red onion, sliced

100 g/3½ oz mangetout

175 g/6 oz carrots, thinly sliced

350 g/12 oz white cabbage, shredded

3 tbsp sweet chilli sauce

2 spring onions, sliced, to garnish

1 Bring a large saucepan of water to the boil. Add the Japanese noodles to the pan and cook for 2–3 minutes. Drain the noodles thoroughly.

2 Toss the noodles with the sesame oil and sesame seeds.

3 Heat the sunflower oil in a large preheated wok.

4 Add the onion slices, mangetout, carrot slices and shredded cabbage to the wok and stir-fry for about 5 minutes.

5 Add the sweet chilli sauce to the wok and cook, stirring occasionally, for a further 2 minutes.

6 Add the sesame noodles to the wok, toss well to combine and heat through for a further 2–3 minutes. (You may wish to serve the noodles separately, so transfer them to the serving bowls.)

7 Transfer the Japanese noodles and spicy vegetables to warm serving bowls and garnish with sliced spring onions. Serve immediately.

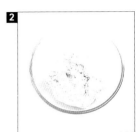

COOK'S TIP

If fresh Japanese noodles are difficult to get hold of, use dried rice noodles or thin egg noodles instead.

Rice Noodles with Beans

These rice noodles and vegetables are tossed in a crunchy peanut and chilli sauce for a quick satay-flavoured recipe.

NUTRITIONAL INFORMATION

Calories 259   Sugars 9g
Protein . . . . .28g   Fat 8g
Carbohydrate . . .20g   Saturates 1g

12 mins   8 mins

SERVES 4

INGREDIENTS

275 g/10 oz flat rice noodles

3 tbsp groundnut oil

2 cloves garlic, crushed

2 shallots, sliced

225 g/8 oz green beans, sliced

100 g/3¾ oz cherry tomatoes, halved

1 tsp chilli flakes

4 tbsp crunchy peanut butter

150 ml/5 fl oz coconut milk

1 tbsp tomato purée

sliced spring onions, to garnish

1 Place the rice noodles in a large bowl and pour over enough boiling water to cover. Leave to stand for 10 minutes.

2 Heat the groundnut oil in a large preheated wok. Add the garlic and shallots and stir-fry for 1 minute.

3 Drain the rice sticks thoroughly.

4 Add the green beans and drained noodles to the wok and stir-fry for 5 minutes.

5 Add the cherry tomatoes to the wok and mix well.

6 Mix together the chilli flakes, peanut butter, coconut milk and tomato purée.

7 Pour the chilli mixture over the noodles, toss well to combine and heat through.

8 Transfer to warm serving dishes and garnish with spring onion slices. Serve immediately.

VARIATION

Add slices of chicken or beef to the recipe and stir-fry with the beans and noodles in step 4 for a more substantial main meal.

Hot & Sour Noodles

This simple, fast-food dish is sold from street food stalls in Thailand, with many and varied additions of meat and vegetables.

NUTRITIONAL INFORMATION

Calories 337   Sugars 1g
Protein ....10g   Fat 11g
Carbohydrate ...53g   Saturates 1g

🍲 5 mins   🕐 8 mins

SERVES 4

I N G R E D I E N T S

250 g/9 oz dried medium egg noodles

1 tbsp sesame oil

1 tbsp chilli oil

1 garlic clove, crushed

2 spring onions, finely chopped

55 g/2 oz button mushrooms, sliced

40 g/1½ oz dried Chinese black
mushrooms, soaked, drained and sliced

2 tbsp lime juice

3 tbsp light soy sauce

1 tsp sugar

shredded Chinese leaves, to serve

T O   G A R N I S H

2 tbsp shredded fresh coriander

2 tbsp chopped, toasted peanuts

COOK'S TIP

Thai chilli oil is very hot, so if you want a milder flavour, use vegetable oil for the initial cooking instead, then add a final dribble of chilli oil just for seasoning.

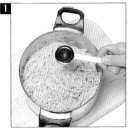  

1 Cook the noodles in a large pan of boiling water for 3–4 minutes, or according to the package directions. Drain well, return to the pan, toss with the sesame oil and set aside.

2 Heat the chilli oil in a large frying pan or wok and quickly stir-fry the garlic, onions and button mushrooms to soften them.

3 Add the black mushrooms, lime juice, soy sauce and sugar and continue stir-frying until boiling. Add the noodles and toss to mix.

4 Serve spooned over Chinese leaves, garnished with coriander and peanuts.

Fried Vegetable Noodles

In this recipe, noodles are first boiled and then deep-fried for a crisply textured dish, and tossed with fried vegetables.

NUTRITIONAL INFORMATION

Calories ....229 Sugars 4g
Protein ....5g Fat 15g
Carbohydrate ...20g Saturates 2g

5 mins   25 mins

SERVES 4

INGREDIENTS

350 g/12 oz dried egg noodles

2 tbsp peanut oil

2 garlic cloves, crushed

½ tsp ground star anise

1 carrot, cut into matchsticks

1 green pepper, cut into matchsticks

1 onion, quartered and sliced

125 g/4½ oz broccoli florets

75 g/2¾ oz bamboo shoots

1 celery stick, sliced

1 tbsp light soy sauce

150 ml/5 fl oz vegetable stock

oil, for deep-frying

1 tsp cornflour

2 tsp water

1 Cook the noodles in a saucepan of boiling water for 1–2 minutes. Drain well and rinse under cold running water. Leave the noodles to drain thoroughly in a colander until required.

2 Heat the peanut oil in a preheated wok until smoking. Reduce the heat, add the crushed garlic and ground star anise and stir-fry for 30 seconds. Add the remaining vegetables and stir-fry for 1–2 minutes.

3 Add the soy sauce and vegetable stock to the wok and cook over a low heat for 5 minutes.

4 Heat the oil for deep-frying in a separate wok to 180°C/350°F, or until a cube of bread browns in 30 seconds.

5 Using a fork, twist the drained noodles and form them into rounds. Deep-fry them in batches until crisp, turning once. Leave them to drain on kitchen paper.

6 Blend the cornflour with the water to form a paste and stir into the vegetables. Bring to the boil, stirring until the sauce is thickened and clear.

7 Arrange the noodles on a warm serving plate, spoon the vegetables on top and serve immediately.

Noodle & Mango Salad

Fruit combines well with the peanut dressing, peppers and chilli in this delicious hot salad.

NUTRITIONAL INFORMATION

Calories	368	Sugars	........11g
Protein	........11g	Fat	..........26g
Carbohydrate	...24g	Saturates	.......5g

15 mins   5 mins

SERVES 4

I N G R E D I E N T S

250 g/9 oz thread egg noodles

2 tbsp groundnut oil

4 shallots, sliced

2 cloves garlic, crushed

1 red chilli, seeded and sliced

1 red pepper, seeded and sliced

1 green pepper, seeded and sliced

1 ripe mango, sliced into thin strips

25 g/1 oz salted peanuts, chopped

D R E S S I N G

4 tbsp peanut butter

100 ml/3½ fl oz coconut milk

1 tbsp tomato purée

1 Place the egg noodles in a large dish or bowl. Pour over enough boiling water to cover the noodles and leave to stand for 10 minutes.

COOK'S TIP

If preferred, gently heat the peanut dressing before pouring over the noodle salad.

2 Heat the groundnut oil in a large preheated wok or frying pan.

3 Add the shallots, crushed garlic, chilli and pepper slices to the wok or frying pan and stir-fry for 2–3 minutes.

4 Drain the egg noodles thoroughly in a colander. Add the drained noodles and mango slices to the wok or frying pan and heat through for about 2 minutes.

5 Transfer the noodle and mango salad to warmed serving dishes and scatter with chopped peanuts.

6 To make the dressing, mix together the peanut butter, coconut milk and tomato purée then spoon over the noodle salad. Serve immediately.

Yellow Bean Noodles

Cellophane or thread noodles are excellent re-heated, unlike other noodles which must be served as soon as they are ready.

NUTRITIONAL INFORMATION

Calories 212   Sugars 0.5g
Protein . . . . .28g   Fat 7g
Carbohydrate . . .10g   Saturates 2g

5 mins   30 mins

SERVES 4

I N G R E D I E N T S

175 g/6 oz cellophane noodles

1 tbsp peanut oil

1 leek, sliced

2 garlic cloves, crushed

450 g/1 lb minced chicken

425 ml/15 fl oz chicken stock

1 tsp chilli sauce

2 tbsp yellow bean sauce

4 tbsp light soy sauce

1 tsp sesame oil

chopped fresh chives, to garnish

1 Place the cellophane noodles in a bowl, pour over boiling water and soak for 15 minutes.

COOK'S TIP

Cellophane noodles are available from many supermarkets and all Chinese supermarkets.

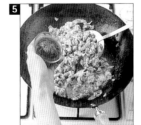

2 Drain the noodles thoroughly and cut into short lengths with a pair of kitchen scissors.

3 Heat the oil in a wok or frying pan and stir-fry the leek and garlic for 30 seconds.

4 Add the chicken to the wok and stir-fry for 4–5 minutes, until the chicken is completely cooked through.

5 Add the chicken stock, chilli sauce, yellow bean sauce and soy sauce to the wok and cook for 3–4 minutes.

6 Add the drained noodles and sesame oil to the wok and cook, tossing to mix well, for 4–5 minutes.

7 Spoon the mixture into warm serving bowls, sprinkle with chopped chives and serve immediately.

Noodles with Cod & Mango

Fish and fruit are tossed with a trio of peppers in this spicy dish served with noodles for a quick, healthy meal.

NUTRITIONAL INFORMATION

Calories 274	Sugars 11g
Protein 25g	Fat 8g
Carbohydrate ...26g	Saturates 1g

10 mins   25 mins

SERVES 4

INGREDIENTS

250 g/9 oz packet egg noodles

450 g/1 lb skinless cod fillet

1 tbsp paprika

2 tbsp sunflower oil

1 red onion, sliced

1 orange pepper, seeded and sliced

1 green pepper, seeded and sliced

100 g/3½ oz baby corn cobs, halved

1 mango, sliced

100 g/3½ oz beansprouts

2 tbsp tomato ketchup

2 tbsp soy sauce

2 tbsp medium sherry

1 tsp cornflour

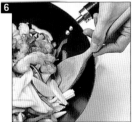

1 Place the egg noodles in a large bowl and cover with boiling water. Leave to stand for about 10 minutes.

2 Rinse the cod fillet and pat dry with kitchen paper. Cut the cod flesh into thin strips.

3 Place the cod strips in a large bowl. Add the paprika and toss well to coat the fish.

4 Heat the sunflower oil in a large preheated wok.

5 Add the onion, peppers and baby corn cobs to the wok and stir-fry for about 5 minutes.

6 Add the cod to the wok together with the sliced mango and stir-fry for a further 2-3 minutes or until the fish is tender.

7 Add the beansprouts to the wok and toss well to combine.

8 Mix together the tomato ketchup, soy sauce, sherry and cornflour. Add the mixture to the wok and cook, stirring occasionally, until the juices thicken.

9 Drain the noodles thoroughly and transfer to warm serving bowls. Transfer the cod and mango stir-fry to separate serving bowls and serve immediately.

Sweet & Sour Noodles

This delicious dish combines sweet and sour flavours with the addition of egg, rice noodles, king prawns and vegetables for a real treat.

NUTRITIONAL INFORMATION

Calories 352   Sugars 14g
Protein . . . . .23g   Fat 17g
Carbohydrate . . .29g   Saturates 3g

10 mins   10 mins

SERVES 4

INGREDIENTS

3 tbsp fish sauce

2 tbsp distilled white vinegar

2 tbsp caster or palm sugar

2 tbsp tomato purée

2 tbsp sunflower oil

3 cloves garlic, crushed

350 g/12 oz rice noodles, soaked in boiling water for 5 minutes

8 spring onions, sliced

175 g/6 oz carrot, grated

150 g/5½ oz beansprouts

2 eggs, beaten

225 g/8 oz peeled king prawns

50 g/1¾ oz chopped peanuts

1 tsp chilli flakes, to garnish

1 Mix together the fish sauce, vinegar, sugar and tomato purée.

2 Heat the sunflower oil in a large preheated wok.

3 Add the garlic to the wok and stir-fry for 30 seconds.

4 Drain the noodles thoroughly and add them to the wok together with the fish sauce and tomato purée mixture. Mix well to combine.

5 Add the spring onions, carrot and beansprouts to the wok and stir-fry for 2–3 minutes.

6 Move the stir-fry mixture to one side of the wok, add the beaten eggs to the empty part of the wok and cook until the egg sets. Add the noodles, prawns and peanuts to the wok and mix well. Transfer to warm serving dishes and garnish with chilli flakes. Serve hot.

COOK'S TIP

Chilli flakes may be found in the spice section of large supermarkets.

Chilli Prawn Noodles

This is a simple dish to prepare and is packed with flavour, making it an ideal choice for special occasions.

NUTRITIONAL INFORMATION

Calories ....259 Sugars 9g
Protein ....28g Fat 8g
Carbohydrate ...20g Saturates 1g

10 mins   5 mins

SERVES 4

I N G R E D I E N T S

250 g/9 oz thin glass noodles

2 tbsp sunflower oil

1 onion, sliced

2 red chillies, seeded and very finely chopped

4 lime leaves, thinly shredded

1 tbsp fresh coriander

2 tbsp palm or caster sugar

2 tbsp fish sauce

450 g/1 lb raw tiger prawns, peeled

1 Place the noodles in a large bowl. Pour over enough boiling water to cover the noodles and leave to stand for 5 minutes. Drain thoroughly and set aside until required.

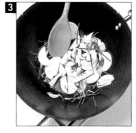  

COOK'S TIP

If you cannot buy raw tiger prawns, use cooked prawns instead and cook them with the noodles for 1 minute only, just to heat through.

2 Heat the sunflower oil in a large preheated wok or frying pan until it is really hot.

3 Add the onion, red chillies and lime leaves to the wok and stir-fry for 1 minute.

4 Add the coriander, palm or caster sugar, fish sauce and prawns to the wok or frying pan and stir-fry for a further 2 minutes or until the prawns turn pink.

5 Add the drained noodles to the wok, toss to mix well, and stir-fry for 1–2 minutes or until heated through.

6 Transfer the noodles and prawns to warm serving bowls and serve immediately.

Special Noodles

This dish combines meat, vegetables, prawns and noodles in a curried coconut sauce. Serve as a main meal or as an accompaniment.

NUTRITIONAL INFORMATION

Calories 409   Sugars 12g
Protein . . . . .24g   Fat 23g
Carbohydrate . . .28g   Saturates 8g

5 mins   25 mins

SERVES 4

I N G R E D I E N T S

250 g/9 oz thin rice noodles

4 tbsp groundnut oil

2 cloves garlic, crushed

2 red chillies, seeded and very
   finely chopped

1 tsp grated fresh root ginger

2 tbsp Madras curry paste

2 tbsp rice wine vinegar

1 tbsp caster sugar

225 g/8 oz cooked ham, finely
   shredded

100 g/3½ oz canned water chestnuts, sliced

100 g/3½ oz mushrooms, sliced

100 g/3½ oz peas

1 red pepper, seeded and thinly sliced

100 g/3½ oz peeled prawns

2 large eggs

4 tbsp coconut milk

25 g/1 oz desiccated coconut

2 tbsp chopped fresh coriander

1 Place the rice noodles in a large bowl, cover with boiling water and leave to soak for about 10 minutes. Drain the noodles thoroughly, then toss with 2 tablespoons of groundnut oil.

2 Heat the remaining groundnut oil in a large preheated wok until the oil is really hot.

3 Add the garlic, chillies, ginger, curry paste, rice wine vinegar and caster sugar to the wok and stir-fry for 1 minute.

4 Add the ham, water chestnuts, mushrooms, peas and red pepper to the wok and stir-fry for 5 minutes.

5 Add the noodles and prawns to the wok and stir-fry for 2 minutes.

6 In a small bowl, beat together the eggs and coconut milk. Drizzle over the mixture in the wok and stir-fry until the egg sets.

7 Add the desiccated coconut and chopped fresh coriander to the wok and toss to combine. Transfer the noodles to warm serving dishes and serve immediately.

Cellophane Noodles & Prawns

Tiger prawns are cooked with orange juice, peppers, soy sauce and vinegar and served on a bed of cellophane noodles.

NUTRITIONAL INFORMATION

Calories 118   Sugar 4g
Protein . . . . .7g   Fat 4g
Carbohydrate . . .15g   Saturates 1g

 10 mins   25 mins

SERVES 4

I N G R E D I E N T S

175 g/6 oz cellophane noodles

1 tbsp vegetable oil

1 garlic clove, crushed

2 tsp grated fresh root ginger

24 raw tiger prawns, peeled and de-veined

1 red pepper, seeded and thinly sliced

1 green pepper, seeded and thinly sliced

1 onion, chopped

2 tbsp light soy sauce

juice of 1 orange

2 tsp wine vinegar

pinch of brown sugar

150 ml/5 fl oz fish stock

1 tbsp cornflour

2 tsp water

orange slices, to garnish

1 Cook the noodles in a pan of boiling water for 1 minute. Drain well, rinse under cold water and then drain again.

2 Heat the oil in a wok and stir-fry the garlic and ginger for 30 seconds.

3 Add the prawns and stir-fry for 2 minutes. Remove with a slotted spoon and keep warm.

4 Add the peppers and onion to the wok and stir-fry for 2 minutes. Stir in the soy sauce, orange juice, vinegar, sugar and stock. Return the prawns to the wok and cook for 8–10 minutes, until cooked through.

5 Blend the cornflour with the water and stir into the wok. Bring to the boil, add the noodles and cook for 1–2 minutes. Garnish and serve.

VARIATION

Lime or lemon juice and slices may be used instead of the orange. Use 3–5½ tsp of these juices.

Sesame Noodles with Prawns

Delicately scented with sesame and coriander, these noodles make an unusual lunch or supper dish.

NUTRITIONAL INFORMATION

Calories	430	Sugars	........2g
Protein	........23g	Fat	.........15g
Carbohydrate	...56g	Saturates	.......3g

5 mins   10 mins

SERVES 4

I N G R E D I E N T S

1 garlic clove, chopped

1 spring onion, chopped

1 small red chilli, seeded and sliced

1 tbsp chopped, fresh coriander

300 g/10½ oz fine egg noodles

2 tbsp vegetable oil

2 tsp sesame oil

1 tsp shrimp paste

225 g/8 oz raw prawns, peeled

2 tbsp lime juice

2 tbsp Thai fish sauce

1 tsp sesame seeds, toasted

1 Place the garlic, onion, chilli and coriander into a pestle and mortar and grind to a smooth paste.

2 Drop the noodles into a pan of boiling water and bring back to the boil, then simmer for 4 minutes, or according to the packet instructions.

3 Meanwhile, heat the oils in a pan and stir in the shrimp paste and ground coriander mixture. Stir over a medium heat for 1 minute.

4 Stir in the prawns and stir-fry for 2 minutes. Stir in the lime juice and fish sauce and cook for a further minute.

5 Drain the noodles and toss them into the wok. Sprinkle with the sesame seeds and serve.

COOK'S TIP

The roots of coriander are widely used in Thai cooking, so if you can buy fresh coriander with the root attached, the whole plant can be used in this dish for maximum flavour. If not, just use the stems and leaves.

Oyster Sauce Noodles

Chicken and noodles are cooked and then tossed in an oyster sauce and egg mixture in this delicious recipe.

NUTRITIONAL INFORMATION

Calories 278   Sugars 2g
Protein ....30g   Fat 12g
Carbohydrate ...13g   Saturates 3g

5 mins   25 mins

SERVES 4

INGREDIENTS

250 g/9 oz egg noodles

450 g/1 lb chicken thighs

2 tbsp groundnut oil

100 g/3½ oz carrots, sliced

3 tbsp oyster sauce

2 eggs

3 tbsp cold water

1 Place the egg noodles in a large bowl or dish. Pour enough boiling water over the noodles to cover and leave to stand for 10 minutes.

2 Meanwhile, remove the skin from the chicken thighs. Cut the chicken flesh into small pieces, using a sharp knife.

VARIATION

Flavour the eggs with soy sauce or hoisin sauce as an alternative to the oyster sauce, if you prefer.

 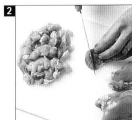 

3 Heat the groundnut oil in a large preheated wok or frying pan, swirling the oil around the base of the wok until it is really hot.

4 Add the pieces of chicken and the carrot slices to the wok and stir-fry for about 5 minutes.

5 Drain the noodles thoroughly. Add the noodles to the wok and stir-fry for a further 2–3 minutes or until the noodles are heated through.

6 Beat together the oyster sauce, eggs and the water. Drizzle the mixture over the noodles and stir-fry for a further 2–3 minutes or until the eggs set.

7 Transfer the mixture in the wok to warm serving bowls and serve hot.

Chicken Noodles

Rice noodles are used in this recipe. They are available in large supermarkets or specialist Chinese supermarkets.

NUTRITIONAL INFORMATION

Calories . . . . . . .169 Sugars 2g
Protein . . . . .14g Fat 7g
Carbohydrate . . .12g Saturates 2g

🧊 5 mins   ⏱ 15 mins

SERVES 4

I N G R E D I E N T S

225 g/8 oz rice noodles

2 tbsp peanut oil

225 g/8 oz skinless, boneless chicken
   breast, sliced

2 garlic cloves, crushed

1 tsp grated fresh root ginger

1 tsp Chinese curry powder

1 red pepper, seeded and
   thinly sliced

75 g/2¾ oz mangetout, shredded

1 tbsp light soy sauce

2 tsp Chinese rice wine

2 tbsp chicken stock

1 tsp sesame oil

1 tbsp chopped fresh coriander

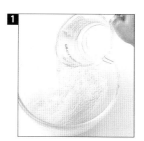

1 Soak the rice noodles for 4 minutes in warm water. Drain thoroughly and set aside until required.

2 Heat the peanut oil in a preheated wok or large heavy-based frying pan and stir-fry the chicken slices for 2–3 minutes.

3 Add the garlic, ginger and Chinese curry powder and stir-fry for a further 30 seconds. Add the red pepper and mangetout to the mixture in the wok and stir-fry for 2–3 minutes.

4 Add the noodles, soy sauce, Chinese rice wine and chicken stock to the wok and mix well, stirring occasionally, for 1 minute.

5 Sprinkle the sesame oil and chopped coriander over the noodles. Transfer to serving plates and serve.

VARIATION

You can use pork or duck in this recipe instead of the chicken, if you prefer.

Singapore Noodles

This is a special and well-known dish, which is a delicious meal in itself, packed with chicken, prawns and vegetables.

NUTRITIONAL INFORMATION

Calories 627   Sugars 3g
Protein . . . . .44g   Fat 32g
Carbohydrate . . .44g   Saturates 4g

5 mins   20 mins

SERVES 4

I N G R E D I E N T S

225 g/8 oz dried egg noodles

6 tbsp vegetable oil

4 eggs, beaten

3 garlic cloves, crushed

1½ tsp chilli powder

225 g/8 oz skinless, boneless chicken, cut into thin strips

3 celery sticks, sliced

1 green pepper, seeded and sliced

4 spring onions, sliced

25 g/1 oz water chestnuts, quartered

2 fresh red chillies, sliced

300 g/10 oz peeled, cooked prawns

175 g/6 oz beansprouts

2 tsp sesame oil

1 Soak the noodles in boiling water for 4 minutes, or until soft. Leave to drain on kitchen paper.

2 Heat 2 tablespoons of the oil in a preheated wok. Add the eggs and stir until set. Remove the cooked eggs from the wok, set aside and keep warm.

3 Add the remaining oil to the wok. Add the garlic and chilli powder and stir-fry for 30 seconds.

4 Add the chicken and stir-fry for 4–5 minutes, until just beginning to brown.

5 Stir in the celery, pepper, spring onions, water chestnuts and chillies and cook for a further 8 minutes, or until the chicken is cooked through.

6 Add the prawns and the reserved noodles to the wok, together with the beansprouts, and toss to mix well.

7 Break the cooked egg with a fork and sprinkle over the noodles, together with the sesame oil. Serve immediately.

COOK'S TIP

When mixing pre-cooked ingredients into the dish, such as the egg and noodles, ensure that they are heated right through and are hot when ready to serve.

Chicken on Crispy Noodles

Blanched noodles are fried in the wok until crisp and brown, and then topped with a shredded chicken sauce for a delightfully tasty dish.

NUTRITIONAL INFORMATION

Calories 376   Sugars 2g
Protein . . . . .15g   Fat 27g
Carbohydrate . . .17g   Saturates 4g

 35 mins   25 mins

SERVES 4

I N G R E D I E N T S

225 g/8 oz skinless, boneless chicken breasts, shredded

1 egg white

5 tsp cornflour

225 g/8 oz thin egg noodles

300 ml/10 fl oz vegetable oil

600 ml/1 pint chicken stock

2 tbsp dry sherry

2 tbsp oyster sauce

1 tbsp light soy sauce

1 tbsp hoisin sauce

1 red pepper, seeded and very thinly sliced

2 tbsp water

3 spring onions, chopped

1 Mix together the chicken, egg white and 2 teaspoons of the cornflour in a bowl. Leave to stand for at least 30 minutes.

2 Blanch the noodles in boiling water for 2 minutes, then drain thoroughly.

3 Heat the vegetable oil in a preheated wok. Add the noodles, spreading them to cover the base of the wok. Cook over a low heat for about 5 minutes, until the noodles are browned on the underside.

Flip the noodles over and brown on the other side. Remove from the wok when crisp and browned, place on a serving plate and keep warm. Drain the oil from the wok.

4 Add 300 ml/½ pint of the chicken stock to the wok. Remove from the heat and add the chicken, stirring well so that it does not stick. Return to the heat and cook for 2 minutes. Drain, discarding the stock.

5 Wipe the wok with kitchen paper and return to the heat. Add the sherry, sauces, pepper and the remaining stock and bring to the boil. Blend the remaining cornflour with the water and stir it into the mixture.

6 Return the chicken to the wok and cook over a low heat for 2 minutes. Place the chicken on top of the noodles and sprinkle with spring onions.

Chilli Pork Noodles

This is quite a spicy dish, with a delicious peanut flavour. Increase or reduce the amount of chilli to your liking.

NUTRITIONAL INFORMATION

Calories 421   Sugars 3g
Protein . . . . .27g   Fat 26g
Carbohydrate . . .20g   Saturates 6g

35 mins   10 mins

SERVES 4

INGREDIENTS

350 g/12 oz minced pork

1 tbsp light soy sauce

1 tbsp dry sherry

350 g/12 oz egg noodles

2 tsp sesame oil

2 tbsp vegetable oil

2 garlic cloves, crushed

2 tsp grated fresh root ginger

2 fresh red chillies, sliced

1 red pepper, seeded and finely sliced

25 g/1 oz unsalted peanuts

3 tbsp peanut butter

3 tbsp dark soy sauce

dash of chilli oil

300 ml/10 fl oz pork stock

1 Mix together the pork, light soy sauce and dry sherry in a large bowl. Cover and leave to marinate for 30 minutes.

2 Meanwhile, cook the noodles in a saucepan of boiling water for 4 minutes. Drain well, rinse in cold water and drain again. Toss the noodles in the sesame oil.

3 Heat the vegetable oil in a preheated wok and stir-fry the garlic, ginger, chillies and pepper for 30 seconds.

4 Add the pork to the mixture in the wok, together with the marinade. Continue cooking for about 1 minute, until the pork is sealed.

5 Add the peanuts, peanut butter, soy sauce, chilli oil and stock and cook for 2–3 minutes.

6 Toss the noodles in the mixture and serve at once.

VARIATION

Minced chicken or lamb would also be excellent in this recipe instead of the pork.

Pad Thai Noodles

The combination of ingredients in this classic noodle dish varies, but it commonly contains a mixture of pork and prawns or other seafood.

NUTRITIONAL INFORMATION

Calories	477	Sugars	.........6g
Protein	........26g	Fat	...........14g
Carbohydrate	...60g	Saturates	.......3g

10 mins   5 mins

SERVES 4

I N G R E D I E N T S

250 g/9 oz rice stick noodles

3 tbsp groundnut oil

3 garlic cloves, finely chopped

125 g/4½ oz pork fillet, chopped into 5-mm/¼-inch pieces

200 g/7 oz prawns, peeled

1 tbsp sugar

3 tbsp Thai fish sauce

1 tbsp tomato ketchup

1 tbsp lime juice

2 eggs, beaten

125 g/4½ oz beansprouts

TO GARNISH

1 tsp dried red chilli flakes

2 spring onions, thickly sliced

2 tbsp chopped fresh coriander

1 Soak the rice noodles in hot water for about 10 minutes, or according to the packet instructions. Drain well and put to one side.

2 Heat the oil in a large frying pan or wok and fry the garlic over a high heat for 30 seconds. Add the pork and stir-fry for 2–3 minutes until browned.

3 Stir in the prawns, then add the sugar, fish sauce, ketchup and lime juice, and continue stir-frying for a further 30 seconds.

4 Stir in the eggs and stir-fry until lightly set. Stir in the noodles, then add the beansprouts and stir-fry for a further 30 seconds to cook lightly.

5 Turn out on to a serving dish and scatter with chilli flakes, spring onions and coriander.

COOK'S TIP

Drain the rice noodles before adding to the pan, as excess moisture will spoil the texture of the dish.

Mushroom & Pork Noodles

This dish benefits from the use of coloured oyster mushrooms. If these are unavailable, plain grey mushrooms will suffice.

NUTRITIONAL INFORMATION

Calories 286   Sugars 3g
Protein . . . . .23g   Fat 13g
Carbohydrate . . .21g   Saturates 3g

 10 mins   20 mins

SERVES 4

I N G R E D I E N T S

450 g/1 lb thin egg noodles

2 tbsp peanut oil

350 g/12 oz pork fillet, sliced

2 garlic cloves, crushed

1 onion, cut into 8 pieces

225 g/8 oz oyster mushrooms

4 tomatoes, skinned, seeded and thinly
  sliced

2 tbsp light soy sauce

50 ml/2 fl oz pork stock

1 tbsp chopped fresh coriander

1 Cook the noodles in a saucepan of boiling water for 2–3 minutes. Drain well, rinse under cold running water and drain thoroughly again.

2 Heat 1 tablespoon of the oil in a preheated wok or frying pan.

3 Add the noodles to the wok or frying pan and stir-fry for about 2 minutes.

4 Using a slotted spoon, remove the noodles from the wok, drain well and set aside until required.

5 Heat the remaining peanut oil in the wok. Add the pork slices and stir-fry for 4–5 minutes.

6 Stir in the crushed garlic and chopped onion and stir-fry for a further 2–3 minutes.

7 Add the oyster mushrooms, tomatoes, light soy sauce, pork stock and drained noodles. Stir well and cook for 1–2 minutes.

8 Sprinkle with chopped coriander and serve immediately.

COOK'S TIP

For crisper noodles, add 2 tablespoons of oil to the wok and fry the noodles for 5–6 minutes, spreading them thinly in the wok and turning half-way through cooking.

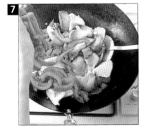

Twice-Cooked Lamb

Here lamb is first boiled and then fried with soy sauce, oyster sauce and spinach and finally tossed with noodles for a richly flavoured dish.

NUTRITIONAL INFORMATION

Calories 315	Sugars 5g
Protein 27g	Fat 16g
Carbohydrate . . .16g	Saturates 6g

🕒 5 mins   🕓 30 mins

SERVES 4

I N G R E D I E N T S

250 g/9 oz packet egg noodles

450 g/1 lb lamb loin fillet, thinly sliced

2 tbsp soy sauce

2 tbsp sunflower oil

2 cloves garlic, crushed

1 tbsp caster sugar

2 tbsp oyster sauce

175 g/6 oz baby spinach

1 Place the egg noodles in a large bowl and cover with boiling water. Leave to soak for about 10 minutes.

2 Bring a large saucepan of water to the boil. Add the lamb and cook for 5 minutes. Drain thoroughly.

3 Place the slices of lamb in a bowl and mix with the soy sauce and 1 tablespoon of the sunflower oil.

4 Heat the remaining sunflower oil in a large preheated wok, swirling the oil around until it is really hot.

5 Add the marinated lamb and crushed garlic to the wok and stir-fry for about 5 minutes or until the meat is just beginning to brown.

6 Add the caster sugar and oyster sauce to the wok and stir well to combine.

7 Drain the noodles thoroughly. Add the noodles to the wok and stir-fry for a further 5 minutes.

8 Add the spinach to the wok and cook for 1 minute or until the leaves just wilt. Transfer the lamb and noodles to serving bowls and serve hot.

COOK'S TIP

If using dried noodles, follow the instructions on the packet as they require less soaking.

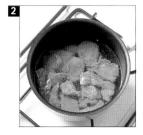

Lamb with Noodles

Lamb is quick fried, coated in a soy sauce and served on a bed of transparent noodles for a richly flavoured dish.

NUTRITIONAL INFORMATION

Calories ....285 Sugars 1g
Protein ....27g Fat 16g
Carbohydrate ...10g Saturates 6g

5 mins   15 mins

SERVES 4

INGREDIENTS

150 g/5½ oz cellophane noodles

2 tbsp peanut oil

450 g/1 lb lean lamb, thinly sliced

2 garlic cloves, crushed

2 leeks, sliced

3 tbsp dark soy sauce

250 ml/9 fl oz lamb stock

dash of chilli sauce

red chilli strips, to garnish

1 Bring a large saucepan of water to the boil. Add the cellophane noodles and cook for 1 minute. Drain the noodles well, place in a sieve, rinse under cold running water and drain thoroughly again. Set aside until required.

2 Heat the peanut oil in a preheated wok or frying pan, swirling the oil around until it is really hot.

3 Add the lamb to the wok or frying pan and stir-fry for about 2 minutes.

4 Add the crushed garlic and sliced leeks to the wok and stir-fry for a further 2 minutes.

5 Stir in the dark soy sauce, lamb stock and chilli sauce and cook for 3–4

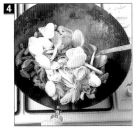  

minutes, stirring frequently, until the meat is cooked through.

6 Add the drained cellophane noodles to the wok or frying pan and cook for about 1 minute, stirring, until heated through.

7 Transfer the lamb and cellophane noodles to serving plates, garnish with red chilli strips and serve.

COOK'S TIP

Transparent noodles are available in Chinese supermarkets. Use egg noodles instead if transparent noodles are unavailable, and cook them according to the instructions on the packet.

Beef with Crispy Noodles

Crispy noodles are terrific and may also be served on their own as a side dish, sprinkled with sugar and salt.

NUTRITIONAL INFORMATION

Calories	244	Sugars	.........9g
Protein	........20g	Fat	..........10g
Carbohydrate	...19g	Saturates	.......2g

 5 mins   30 mins

SERVES 4

INGREDIENTS

225 g/8 oz medium egg noodles

350 g/12 oz beef fillet

2 tbsp sunflower oil

1 tsp ground ginger

1 clove garlic, crushed

1 red chilli, seeded and very finely chopped

100 g/3½ oz carrots, cut into matchsticks

6 spring onions, sliced

2 tbsp lime marmalade

2 tbsp soy sauce

oil, for frying

1 Place the noodles in a large dish or bowl. Pour over enough boiling water to cover the noodles and leave to stand for about 10 minutes while you stir-fry the rest of the ingredients.

2 Using a sharp knife, thinly slice the beef fillet.

3 Heat the sunflower oil in a large preheated wok or frying pan.

4 Add the beef and ground ginger to the wok or frying pan and stir-fry for about 5 minutes.

5 Add the crushed garlic, chopped red chilli, carrots and spring onions to the wok and stir-fry for a further 2–3 minutes.

6 Add the lime marmalade and soy sauce to the wok and allow to bubble for 2 minutes. Remove the chilli beef and ginger mixture, set aside and keep warm until required.

7 Heat the oil for frying in the wok or frying pan.

8 Drain the noodles thoroughly and pat dry with kitchen paper. Carefully lower the noodles into the hot oil and cook for 2–3 minutes or until crispy. Drain the noodles on kitchen paper.

9 Divide the noodles between 4 warm serving plates and top with the chilli beef and ginger mixture. Serve immediately.

Beef Chow Mein

Chow Mein must be the best-known and most popular noodle dish on any Chinese menu. You can use any meat or vegetables instead of beef.

NUTRITIONAL INFORMATION

Calories 341   Sugars 3g
Protein . . . . .27g   Fat 17g
Carbohydrate . . .20g   Saturates 4g

10 mins   20 mins

SERVES 4

I N G R E D I E N T S

450 g/1 lb egg noodles

4 tbsp peanut oil

450 g/1 lb lean beef steak, cut into thin
   strips

2 garlic cloves, crushed

1 tsp grated fresh root ginger

1 green pepper, thinly sliced

1 carrot, thinly sliced

2 celery sticks, sliced

8 spring onions

1 tsp dark brown sugar

1 tbsp dry cherry

2 tbsp dark soy sauce

a few drops of chilli sauce

1 Cook the noodles in a saucepan of boiling salted water for 4-5 minutes. Drain well, rinse under cold running water and drain again thoroughly.

2 Toss the noodles in 1 tablespoon of the peanut oil.

3 Heat the remaining oil in a preheated wok. Add the beef and stir-fry for 3–4 minutes, stirring constantly.

4 Add the crushed garlic and grated fresh root ginger to the wok and stir-fry for 30 seconds.

5 Add the pepper, carrot, celery and spring onions and stir-fry for about 2 minutes.

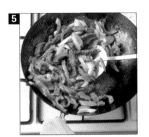

6 Add the dark brown sugar, dry sherry, dark soy sauce and chilli sauce to the mixture in the wok and cook, stirring, for 1 minute.

7 Stir in the noodles, mixing well, and cook until completely warmed through.

8 Transfer the noodles to warm serving bowls and serve immediately.

VARIATION

A variety of different vegetables may be used in this recipe for colour and flavour – try broccoli, red peppers, green beans or baby corn cobs.

Cantonese Fried Noodles

This dish is usually served as a snack or light meal. It may also be served as an accompaniment to plain meat and fish dishes.

NUTRITIONAL INFORMATION

Calories	385	Sugars	. . . . .6g
Protein	. . . . .38g	Fat	. . . . .17g
Carbohydrate	. . .21g	Saturates	. . . . . . .4g

5 mins   15 mins

SERVES 4

I N G R E D I E N T S

350 g/12 oz egg noodles

3 tbsp vegetable oil

675 g/1½ lb lean beef steak, cut into thin strips

125 g/4½ oz green cabbage, shredded

75 g/2¾ oz bamboo shoots

6 spring onions, sliced

25 g/1 oz green beans, halved

1 tbsp dark soy sauce

2 tbsp beef stock

1 tbsp dry sherry

1 tbsp light brown sugar

2 tbsp chopped parsley, to garnish

1 Cook the noodles in a saucepan of boiling water for 2–3 minutes. Drain well, rinse under cold running water and drain thoroughly again.

2 Heat 1 tablespoon of the oil in a preheated wok or frying pan, swirling it around until it is really hot

3 Add the noodles and stir-fry for 1–2 minutes. Drain the noodles and set aside until required.

4 Heat the remaining oil in the wok. Add the beef and stir-fry for 2–3 minutes. Add the cabbage, bamboo shoots, spring onions and beans to the wok and stir-fry for 1–2 minutes.

5 Add the soy sauce, beef stock, dry sherry and light brown sugar to the wok, stirring to mix well.

6 Stir the noodles into the mixture in the wok, tossing to mix well. Transfer to serving bowls, garnish with chopped parsley and serve immediately.

VARIATION

You can vary the vegetables in this dish depending on seasonal availability or whatever you have at hand – try broccoli, green pepper or spinach.

Index

A

Asparagus Parcels 183
Aubergine, Spiced 32, 174, 175

B

Bamboo
    with Peppers 165
    with Spinach 166
Beans, Stir-Fry 162, 181
Beef
    & Beans 115
    & Black Bean Sauce 110
    & Broccoli 112
    & Peanut Salad 116
    & Peppers 105
    with Baby Onions 109
    with Bamboo Shoots 108
    with Beansprouts 117
    Chilli Salad 107
    Chow Mein 252
    with Crispy Noodles 251
    Oyster Sauce 113
    Soy & Sesame 111
    Spicy 114
    with Vegetables 106
Braised Fish Fillets 121
Broccoli
    & Black Bean Sauce 186
    Gingered 163
Butternut Squash Stir-Fry 178

C

Cabbage & Almonds, Crispy 158
Cabbage & Walnut Stir-fry 187
Cantonese
    Noodles 253
    Prawns 140

Vegetables 205
Carrot, & Orange Stir-Fry 176
Cauliflower, Sweet & Sour 185
Chicken
    & Corn Sauté 68
    & Mango 60, 70
    & Rice Casserole 220
    Balls with Dip 34
    with Black Bean Sauce 72
    with Cashew Nuts 58, 61
    with Chilli & Basil 63
    Chilli Coconut 73
    Chinese Salad 66
    Chop Suey 62
    Chow Mein 221
    Coconut Curry 57
    Crispy 64
    Five-Spice with Rice 218
    Honeyed Wings 50
    Lemon 59
    Livers with Pak Choi 49
    Noodle Soup 28, 29
    Noodles 243, 245
    Spicy Peanut 65
    Spicy Tortillas 69
    Stir-Fried Ginger 56
    Thai Stir-Fried 71
Chillies 15
Chinese
    Chicken Rice 219
    Chicken Salad 66
    cookery 14
    Fried Vegetables 169
    Risotto 226
    Vegetable Casserole 204
    Vegetable Rice 195
Chinese Leaves, Honey-Fried 156

Chop Suey
    Chicken 62
    Vegetable 200
Chow Mein
    Beef 252
    Chicken 221
Coconut
    & Crab Soup 23
    Chicken Curry 57
    Prawns 132
    Rice 209
Cod with Mango 120
Cooking
    implements 8–9
    techniques 14–15
Corn Balls, Chilli 177
Courgettes, Deep-fried 182
Crab
    & Sweetcorn Soup 21
    with Chinese Leaves 148
    Claws with Chilli 147
    Congee 215
    Crispy Wontons 47
    Fried Rice 216
    in Ginger Sauce 149
    Ravioli 48
Creamy Green Vegetables 159
Cucumber, Chilli 160
Curried Prawn Noodles 238

D

Duck
    with Broccoli & Peppers 77
    Fruity Stir-Fry 79
    with Leek & Cabbage 78
    with Mangoes 76
    in Spicy Sauce 75

Steamed Buns 51

E

Egg Fried Rice 210

Eight Jewel Vegetables 202

F

Fish

    & Vegetable Soup 26

    Braised Fillets 121

    Chilli Soup 24

    with Coconut & Basil 122

    Crispy 124

    Soup with Wontons 25

    Szechuan 123

Fish Cakes, Thai-Style 38

Five-Spice Salmon 129

Fruity Duck Stir-Fry 79

G

Garlic Lamb with Soy Sauce 95

Garlic Spinach 161

Gingered Broccoli 163

Gingered Monkfish 125

Green-Fried Rice 213

Green Stir-Fry 157

H

Honey Chicken Wings 50

Honey-Fried Chinese Leaves 156

Honey-Fried Spinach 184

Hot & Sour Mushroom Soup 20

Hot & Sour Noodles 230

J

Japanese Mushroom Noodles 188

Japanese Noodles with Spicy
    Vegetables 228

L

Lamb

    with Black Bean Sauce 93

    Curry 101

    with Garlic Sauce 102

    Garlic with Soy Sauce 95

    Hot 103

    with Lime Leaves 96

    Liver with Peppers 98

    Meatballs 99

    with Mushroom Sauce 100

    with Noodles 250

    with Orange 97

    Oyster Sauce 94

    with Satay Sauce 92

    Sesame Stir-Fry 104

    Twice-Cooked 249

Leeks, with Yellow Bean Sauce 179

Lemon Chicken 59

Lentils, & Mixed Vegetables 164

M

Monkfish, Gingered 125

Mushrooms

    & Noodles 248

    Hot & Sour Soup 20

    Spicy 170

Mussels

    in Black Bean Sauce 145

    with Lettuce 144

N

Noodles

    & Mango Salad 232

    with Beans & Coconut Sauce 229

    Beef with Crispy 251

    Cantonese Fried 253

    Chicken 243, 245

    with Chilli & Prawn 236

    Chilli Pork 246

    with Cod & Mango 234

    Fried Vegetable 231

    Hot & Sour 230

    Japanese 188, 228

    with Lamb 250

    Mushroom & Pork 248

    Oyster Sauce 242

    Pad Thai 247

    with Prawns 238, 239, 240, 241

    Singapore 244

    Special 237

    Sweet & Sour 235

    Yellow Bean 233

O

Omelettes

    Prawn 42, 134

    Thai-Stuffed 37

Oyster Sauce

    Beef 113

    Lamb 94

    Noodles 242

Oysters, with Tofu 146

P

Pad Thai Noodles 247

Pak Choi with Cashew Nuts 180

Pancake Rolls 53

Pans 10

Peanuts, Pan-Fry 67

Peppers with Chestnuts 198

Pork

    & Peanut Baskets 35

    Deep-Fried Fritters 89

    Fry with Vegetables 86

    with Mooli 85

    with Plums 88

    Satay Stir-Fry 80

    Spicy & Rice 81

    Spicy Balls 82

    Spicy Fried Minced 90

    Stir-Fried with Corn 91

    Sweet & Sour 83, 87

    Twice-Cooked 84

Prawns

    Cantonese 140

    with Cashews 138

    Chilli & Peanut 39

    Coconut 132

    with Ginger 136

    with Noodles 239, 240, 241

    Omelette 42, 134

    Parcels 40

Salad 41
Salt & Pepper 43
Sesame Toasts 44
Soup 22, 27
with Spicy Tomatoes 135
Sweet & Sour 45
Szechuan 133
with Vegetables 137

Q

Quorn & Vegetable Stir-Fry 190

R

Red Lamb Curry 101
Rice 12
& Chicken Casserole 220
with Beef 224
with Chicken 218, 219
Chinese Vegetable 195
Crab Fried 216
Egg Fried 210, 211
Fragrant Coconut 209
Green Fried 213
Paper Parcels 46
with Pork 223
with Sausage 225
with Seafood 217
Special Fried 214
with Spicy Beans 208
Sweet Chilli Pork 222
with Vegetables 212

S

Salmon
Five-Spice 129
with Leeks 127
with Pineapple 128
Salt & Pepper Prawns 43
Scallops
in Ginger Sauce 143
Pancakes 141
Seared 142
Seafood, Stir-Fry 153
Seafood Stew, Spicy Thai 130

Seaweed, Crispy 36
Sherry & Soy Vegetables 194
Shrimp Fu Yong 139
Singapore Noodles 244
Small Shrimp Fu Yong 139
Soy & Sesame Beef 111
Speedy Peanut Pan-Fry 67
Spicy
Beef 114
Chicken Livers 49
Chicken Noodle Soup 28
Chicken Tortillas 69
Minced Pork 90
Mushrooms 170
Peanut Chicken 65
Pork & Rice 81
Pork Balls 82
Prawn Soup 22
Sweetcorn Fritters 30
Thai Seafood Stew 130
Tofu Triangles 203
Spinach
Garlic 161
Honey-Fried 184
Spring Rolls 31, 52
Squid
with Black Bean Sauce 151
Crispy Fried 150
with Oyster Sauce 152
Sweet & Sour
Cauliflower 185
Noodles 235
Pork 83, 87
Prawns 45
Tofu 192
Sweetcorn, Spicy Fritters 30
Szechuan Prawns 133
Szechuan White Fish 123

T

Thai
cookery 12
Stir-Fried Chicken 71
Stuffed Omelette 37

Thai-style Fish Cakes 38
Tofu
Casserole 191
with Mushrooms & Peas 193
with Peanut Sauce 33
with Peppers 189
Spicy Triangles 203
Sweet & Sour 192
with Vegetables 171
Trout with Pineapple 126
Tuna & Vegetable Stir-Fry 131
Turkey with Cranberry 74

V

Vegetables 14
Cantonese Garden 205
Chinese Casserole 204
Chinese Fried 169
Chop Suey 200
Creamy Green 159
Dim Sum 168
Eight Jewel 202
Fried Rice 212
with Hoisin 196
Noodles 231
Sherry & Soy 194
Spring Rolls 31
Stir-Fry 197, 199, 201, 190
with Yellow Bean Sauce 167

W

Wontons, Crispy Crab 47

Y

Yellow Bean Noodles 233